Presidents & Promises

Presidents & Promises

From campaign pledge to presidential performance

Jeff Fishel
American University

A division of Congressional Quarterly Inc.
1414 22nd Street N.W., Washington, D.C. 20037

Printed in the United States of America

Library of Congress Cataloging in Publication Data

Fishel, Jeff.
    Presidents & promises.

    Includes index.
    1. Presidents—United States. 2. United States—Politics and government—1945- . 3. Political parties—United States—Platforms. I. Title. II. Title: Presidents and promises.
JK518.F57   1985   353.03'1   84-23782
ISBN 0-87187-336-2 (pbk.)
ISBN 0-87187-344-3

In Memory of my Father and Brother

Paul Edward Fishel and Kenneth Paul Fishel

who redeemed the most important promise we can make,

> *The heart is all, and the name*
> *Nothing but clamor and smoke*
> *Clouding the glow of the sky.*
>
> —Faust

Contents

Tables

Preface

This modest-length book has an immodestly long history. It has evolved as yet another example of the Iron Law of Slow Scholarly Output: all projects, no matter how large or small, take a minimum of seven years to complete. The research and writing has taken that much time, indeed a bit more, and probably would have kept burbling along for a lifetime had not my editors at CQ Press finally said, "Now or never!"

A first version was nearly completed in the fall of 1980 when I decided to step back and consider the possibilities of a Reagan presidency, possibilities that might fundamentally challenge my thesis and many of the generalizations derived from the original time frame of the study, 1960 to 1980. The "Reagan Revolution" turned out to be a formidable challenge—to American political life, to students of the presidency, and to some of my assumptions about electoral accountability and presidential behavior. After four years, however, it should be clear that his rhetoric is more "counterrevolutionary" (in James Reston's sense of a clock going tock, tick, tock, tick) than most of his actions. It is also clear that the Reagan administration, like its predecessors, must contend with a political system far more complex and multivalued than it seems from the perspective of his upbeat version of old-fashioned American conservatism. Counterrevolutionary the Reagan administration is not, but it has affected, and affected considerably, the current and future public agenda of the United States. My decision to suspend writing in 1980, take a short break, and then resume field work did sharpen and clarify some problems in my own thinking and in the analysis. I hope the final product will do the same for the reader.

Focus and method

Decisions about how to research a topic as vast as presidential promise and presidential performance are necessarily decisions that limit, constrain, and order. The first limiting factor of this book is scope. Although foreign policy, generally "high policy," is considered from time to time, domestic concerns are emphasized. Issues of foreign policy frequently help determine election outcomes; ironically, many of these "issues" are symbolic, involving highly subjective estimates of leadership style, and, as such, they are only marginally useful in predicting what candidates might do once in office. Some scholars seem to approve of this; others, including myself, lament it.

In both foreign and domestic policy, incumbents stand on seemingly clear records. Voters can reject and have rejected incumbent administrations for foreign policy disasters (for example, the Democrats in 1952 and—although less clear cut—in 1968 and 1980). But accountability in foreign policy, much more than domestic policy, provides us with a half-loaf: we can penalize or reward incumbents after the fact, knowing the future will be as ambiguous as the past is clear. In any event, a thorough examination of presidential accountability in foreign policy would require far more space than is possible here.

Successful presidential candidates have two general methods of redeeming their campaign promises. They can advance and champion substantive proposals through legislation or executive orders, and they can promote their policy goals by the appointment of loyal and ideologically compatible managers and federal court judges. Groups in a winning electoral coalition have as much at stake in the "who" of policy as they do in the "what" because the who helps determine the what. On the whole, however, my analysis focuses on substance, on presidentially advanced legislation and executive orders, leaving the systematic examination of presidential appointments to others.[1]

Another limiting factor of my analysis is the historical period being considered. I selected 1960 as a starting point for several reasons. First, John F. Kennedy's presidential campaign and presidency mark a significant shift in the relative importance of mass media and party organization. Kennedy was the first presidential candidate to use television as a major form of communication—an important change in the style of presenting issues.

Second, the end of the Eisenhower years constituted an end to the practical utility of a limited presidency. To be sure, Roosevelt revolutionized the office, establishing the contours of the modern institution, but I agree with those who argue that the *office* of the presidency will be activist, no matter what the personal orientation of the incumbent.

Last, like many of my generation, my political involvement, intellectual and personal, begins with the Kennedy presidency, and, depending on the reader's values, my political orientation moves either forward or backward from that date. Emphasis on the Carter and Reagan years stems from a variety of factors. I had greater access to individuals and documents for their administrations, devoted more time to "poking and soaking" in and around their campaigns and presidencies, and felt my contribution would be more original and well grounded by concentrating on these two presidents. So I am using data from the pre-Carter years to provide historical perspective only.

The book also rests on a commitment to methodological pluralism. I conducted interviews with 136 people, selecting individuals from each administration, although a majority were connected with Carter's and Reagan's. All the interviews were structured but open-ended. I used a modified "snowball" interviewing technique and make no claim about its scientific representativeness, although I sought as diverse a group as possible: insiders and outsiders, journalists and participants, top-level as well as middle-level officials.

The interviews ranged from 12 minutes to 3 hours, averaging 45 minutes to 1 hour. I am well aware of the deficiencies of this type of data. The responses are not tabulated, correlated, or regressed. Evidence from interviews is always problematic, but I believe it is useful. As C. Wright Mills observed years ago, such evidence must be weighed, not counted. Others may weigh it differently. All quotes from the interviews are unattributed to protect confidentiality. I do not believe anything published here is particularly controversial, but confidentiality seems necessary to ensure the access of other scholars.

The second data source stems from a quantitive content analysis of presidential campaign speeches, position papers, and platform presentations, building on and borrowing from the pioneering work of other scholars, particularly Gerald Pomper and Fred Grogan.[2] Similar coding and analysis were used for all presidential legislative proposals and executive orders, which I matched with campaign commitments. This was a massive undertaking, as the reader may appreciate, particularly if he or she has ever done content analysis. Some of the burden was carried by research assistants.

Third, I combed through presidential libraries, Republican and Democratic national committee files, private files, throw-aways, handouts, and give-me-backs-or-I'll-be-ruined. Access is always a critical problem; after all, political scientists and historians, unlike journalists, have little to offer in return for cooperation. Yet most of those I contacted (or cornered) were exceedingly cooperative.

Acknowledgments

Scholars who write books under their own name engage in a deception. All research and writing reflect cooperative and collective effort, even if xiv *Preface*

one name happens to end up on the book's cover. My debts to others are considerable, and their contributions to my thinking and work have challenged, nourished, and sustained me for a long time.

Stephen J. Wayne, close friend and crosstown colleague, helped this project and me in more ways than can be conveyed in a preface. Paul C. Light and Bert A. Rockman read the final manuscript and assisted me in matters large and small with their honest, meticulous, extensive, and constructive commentary.

Of the many friends, colleagues, fellow president watchers, political staffers, and presidential campaign junkies who discussed, read, criticized, and encouraged me over the years, I also want to implicate the following: Lynn Andretta, Michael E. Baroody, Richard Bianchini, Dom Bonafede, Ellen Boneparth, David S. Broder, Ernest A. Chaples, Robert E. Cleary, Thomas E. Cronin, Isaac Fischer, A. Lee Fritschler, David George, Ralph M. Goldman, Edward S. Greenberg, William Greider, Paul Halpern, Susan Webb Hammond, Robert Harmel, John Hart, Jack Hession, Francis Hoole, Charles S. Hyneman, Paul H. Jensen, William R. Keech, John H. Kessel, Peter Löesche, Burdett A. Loomis, Ian McNett, John J. Martin, Bernard S. Morris, James A. Nathan, David J. Olson, Benjamin I. Page, David L. Paletz, Marian Lief Palley, Edward P. Papin, Sandra S. Powell, Leroy N. Rieselbach, Michael Rogin, Walter A. Rosenbaum, Bernard Ross, Susan Rouder, James A. Sandberg, Edward Schneier, Morley Segal, Margaret Shannon, Gloria Steinem, John G. Stewart, Whitney Stewart, Richard E. Stryker, A. David Stutz, Elaine Thompson, Timothy Tilton, and James A. Thurber.

Four hardworking research assistants, first at Indiana University, then at American, rescued me in various ways, and I am greatly appreciative. They are Linda Cohn, Thomas O'Hara, Orlando Pacheco, and Cheryl Rau.

Small but critical grants from the Indiana University Graduate Faculty Council and the Lyndon Baines Johnson and Ford foundations were essential in providing necessary support. A senior fellowship at the Woodrow Wilson International Center for Scholars allowed me to concentrate on assessing the Carter administration in an intellectually luxurious environment that included novelists, literary critics, and foreign ambassadors as well as social scientists. Since the community of political science is my natural habitat, this opportunity was especially welcome. A senior Fulbright scholarship to Australia in 1983-1984 again reminded me how important comparative perspectives are in thinking about the usual preoccupations of a "Americanist." I want to thank my hosts and colleagues at the University of Sydney.

Jean Woy, the first director of CQ Press, gave me considerable encouragement at the beginning of the project and persuaded me that the press was the best outlet for my work. Joanne Daniels, her successor, continued that support. Carolyn Goldinger served as manuscript editor and is unquestionably the toughest and most accomplished editor with whom I have ever worked.

Washington, D. C., of course, is a community dominated by government and politics. Happily, it has grown in other ways since I first arrived, retreated, then returned. I owe a large debt to my nonacademic, largely apolitical family of choice, the Washington Pathwork. They rekindled in me the belief that a "New Age" vision and community is a very ancient need, particularly for someone who is a cranky, skeptical, overly empirical political scientist, but who has engaged in a life-long romance with the transcendentalists. Walt Whitman and his twentieth century New Age descendants are an essential corrective to the vocation of political science.

Finally, my nuclear family, Ellen and Joshua, has helped restore the gift of love in my life, a gift whose abundance is inexhaustible if one is willing to take the risk of giving and receiving it.

Notes

1. See G. Calvin Mackenzie, *The Politics of Presidential Appointments* (New York: Free Press, 1981); and Hugh Heclo, *A Government of Strangers* (Washington, D.C.: Brookings Institution, 1977). An excellent case study of appointments in one presidency is Richard L. Schott and Dagmar S. Hamilton, *People, Positions and Power: The Political Appointments of Lyndon Johnson* (Chicago: University of Chicago Press, 1983).
2. Gerald Pomper, with Susan S. Lederman, *Elections in America*, 2d ed. (New York: Longman, 1980); and Fred Grogan, "Candidate Promise and Presidential Performance: 1964-1972" (Paper delivered at the 1977 annual meeting of the Midwest Political Science Association). Other important quantitative studies include Benjamin I. Page, *Choices and Echoes in Presidential Elections* (Chicago: University of Chicago Press, 1978); Benjamin Ginsberg, "Elections and Public Policy," *American Political Science Review* 70 (March 1976): 41-49; Paul T. David, "Party Platforms as National Plans," *Public Administration Review* 31 (May 1971): 303-315; John H. Kessel, "The Seasons of Presidential Politics," *Social Science Quarterly* 58 (December 1977): 418-435; and Michael G. Krukones, "Presidential Campaigns as Predictors of Performance in Office: 1912-1972" (Paper delivered at the 1978 annual meeting of the Midwest Political Science Association).

Presidential elections and public policy

1

> *It's certainly unwise to admit any sort of*
> *responsibility for our actions, whose consequences*
> *we are never able to foresee.*
>
> —Joseph Conrad

Of what consequence are presidential elections in the formation of public policy? "The choice of a president," James David Barber observes, "is the most important single act in American politics [and] it is the most thoroughly studied process in American political science." [1]

Ironically, given the quadrennial scholarly and popular hoopla, it is unclear whether it makes much difference who becomes president; unclear, that is, because the final choice so often seems unrelated to the policies and programs actually pursued by the people who are skillful, lucky, or energetic enough to win office.

To be sure, elections usually have screened out dangerous neurotics and ideological fanatics. These consequences should not be dismissed as unimportant or trivial. Many observers, with sophisticated theoretical flourishes, see these two features as *the* premier contributions of a viable presidential selection and election process. [2] If we could be sure elections prevented the ascendancy to power of errant personality or ideological types, and they accomplished little else, voting would be a sensible and essential attribute of modern democratic politics.

But on matters of public policy, on the fundamental issue of establishing clear and coherent national agendas through the electoral process, does it matter whether a Democrat or Republican is elected president? In the 1980s, indifference mounts, cynicism abounds.

How justified is this cynicism? Ronald Reagan, for example, was consistently accused of "sliding toward the center," of "making more reversals than any Republican of recent memory." Likewise Jimmy Carter was damned for "failing to adhere to the basic tenets of the Democratic party's platform on which he ran in 1976," of "promising more and doing less than any president in modern history." Richard M. Nixon spent a lifetime building a political career by denouncing the "Red Menace," but then opened a bridge to Communist China and orchestrated a policy of détente with the Soviet Union. Lyndon B. Johnson promised over and over again in the 1964 election that "we don't want our American boys to do the fighting for Asian boys [and] we don't want to get tied down to a land war in Asia," then promptly escalated America's role in Vietnam, sending more than 500,000 soldiers into that tragic war. John F. Kennedy promised to abolish racial discrimination in federally aided housing "by a stroke of the presidential pen," then took 18 months in office to issue a timid executive order covering very little of the country's housing. Even Franklin D. Roosevelt, who presided over the most sweeping changes in public policy of this century, ran in 1932 on a platform promising a balanced budget and unremitting efforts to remove government from "America's free enterprise system."

Can this list of candidate promise and presidential (mis) behavior be multiplied endlessly? Surprisingly, the answer is no; *well*, mainly no, with a variety of "maybes" scattered here and there—enough to keep the question and findings lively, subject to continuing dispute and debate. The main contours of presidential and candidate activity under examination here, from Kennedy through Reagan in a period reflecting vast changes in the political environment, lead to a conclusion different from the conventional wisdom of cynics and other nonbelievers.

How can anyone doubt it? For better or worse, Reagan and the coalition he led moved forcefully during their first years in office (with a backstep here, a sidestep there) on a significant part of their campaign agenda. His most famous promises—to increase defense capabilities, reduce taxes, and balance the budget—were contradictory unless the administration was truly prepared to dismantle discretionary social/economic programs. Short of this Draconian option—one that neither moderate Republicans nor Democrats in Congress were willing to permit, had the administration attempted it—presidential success in this pursuit could be accomplished only as John B. Anderson suggested in one of the early 1980 debates:

> How do you balance the budget, cut taxes, and increase defense spending at the same time? It's very simple. You do it with mirrors.[3]

Contradictory or not, Reagan's economic agenda came directly from his campaign. The first authentic conservative to win the presidency since Herbert Hoover, he made fewer concrete and specific promises (economic or otherwise) than any successful nonincumbent candidate since 1960. Many of his initiatives were reflections, however, of the campaign pledges he did make. Of course, he hedged and reversed himself on important issues and "deferred" action on the social agenda after its more important components were defeated or stalled in Congress.

Understanding why both sides of this presidential coin are true—the willingness of presidents to act on portions of their campaign agenda and abandon or defer the rest—is the topic of this book. Holding this double, seemingly contradictory, vision about what presidents do in office, leaves one with a slightly different, more complex picture about the relationship of presidential elections and presidential performance. The belief that elections are merely exercises in issue ambiguity, involving only questions of personal character and leadership style and conducted in such manner as to evade, scramble, or mislead voters about what candidates might do in office, is dissected, reexamined, and finally rejected.

Of course, every election *is* a contest involving judgments about leadership style, candidate personality, party loyalty, and media diversions; they are also struggles over policy alternatives, past and future program development, over a loose but identifiable national policy agenda. Presidential elections are more than battles over who will govern; they also provide serviceable, if crude, guidelines about *what* presidents will do on *most* domestic policy issues, *most* of the time. But the fit between campaign past and presidential future is far, *very* far, from perfect.

One important reason why skeptics find a large gap between pledge and performance is that they confuse two essentially different measures of follow-through. Assessments of performance should distinguish between presidential *effort* (legislation proposed, executive orders signed) and presidential *achievement* (legislation passed, executive orders implemented). With the exception of Lyndon B. Johnson, every president examined in this study has been much higher in effort than achievement, suggesting that electoral accountability is, of necessity, indirect and incomplete, but not irrelevant when holding presidents responsible for their actions.

Political responsibility
and the voter

Voters do *not*, as Joseph Conrad's character implies, simply hire and fire
their leaders, leaving to chance, because of the unforeseen consequences
of their actions, the political responsibility of presidents for their
decisions. The protagonist in Conrad's novel *Chance* is shrewd about
many things, political and otherwise. He is wrong, in the judgment of
the novelist, about not accepting responsibility for his actions. Even
though the future is open-ended and uncertain, even though decisions
have unpredictable consequences, presidents should be held accountable for the most important promises they make. If other leaders and
citizens ignore or are misled into believing they do not bear some
responsibility for making presidents accountable for what they promise
as candidates, then elections are truly meaningless as institutions for the
representation of policy alternatives.

One political scientist has observed that many people complained
bitterly that Carter did not live up to his party's platform and "at the
same time, actively hoped Reagan wouldn't live up to his ... what is
seen as a vice in Carter is rendered a virtue in Reagan."[4]

Can we have it both ways? Of course! As in *Alice in Wonderland* and
only if we are willing to give up policy accountability in presidential
elections. Certainly liberals and other opponents of Reagan's programs
hoped he would not seek to implement objectionable parts of his
campaign agenda and the Republican platform; they worked actively in
Congress and other institutions to prevent him from doing so, praised
the president for "coming to his senses" when he compromised, and so
forth. Organized and sophisticated opposition, using every nonviolent
tool available in democratic politics, is as essential to policy accountability as presidential follow-through. All this is desirable and need
not lead to the potentially destructive belief that, when one is opposed to an administration, it is desirable that it function in a manner
that runs completely contrary to what the president promised in the
campaign.

The key problem is how much difference should there be between
party candidates on major issues to satisfy a norm of *accountability within
a shared policy consensus.* This is an old and honorable question in
democratic theory. If elections reward candidates with extreme differences on policy, losing coalitions, as in many societies, will feel so
threatened by having lost that they will seek violent alternatives for
redressing their grievances. With severe polarization between parties,
no form of democratic accountability is possible.

Alternatively, presidential candidates and presidents can so converge on policy options that cynicism and indifference among voters becomes legion, undermining the legitimacy of the electoral process because real cleavages, authentic problems, and viable alternative solutions are ignored or finessed. American presidential elections have more frequently suffered from this type of miasma rather than from problems caused by irreconcilable differences. It is a matter of perspective, however, and political specialists disagree about which deficiency, too much consensus or too much cleavage, characterizes recent presidential politics.

Since the New Deal, both major American parties have nominated presidential candidates who have reflected a broad consensus on certain policies that are considered sacrosanct. They can and do differ vigorously on others. Whatever his earlier rhetoric, Reagan would have been defeated had he run for office advocating an end to Social Security or unemployment compensation, or junking the civil rights laws of the 1960s and 1970s, or urging that women be returned to their 19th century prisons. Enormous latitude is possible within this usual consensus in American politics. Presidential accountability is undermined if those campaign promises, offered as different solutions within a spirit of shared values, are systematically broken or ignored.

This is *not* to suggest that one can mechanically add up a president's promises, tick off the number of programs proposed or enacted, and vote or judge accordingly. Incumbent presidents face new issues, new problems, new contingencies that cannot be anticipated from the campaign. They must be willing to change, to compromise, to be flexible about some of their campaign promises; if they are unwilling to alter their course and unable to persuade voters that it is essential to do so, they will down their party and themselves at the next election. This is a sticky problem, an inherent trade-off in any conception of presidential accountability. Evaluating an incumbent president or party seeking reelection involves retrospective and prospective judgments, as well as some ordering principle, no matter how rough, that permits observers to separate the important from the inconsequential, the old from the new, the controllable from the uncontrollable.

'Textbook' elections and the 'textbook' presidency

Many Americans seem to alternate between a belief that presidential elections are ordained in heaven as the earthly instrument of democratic salvation and a conviction that they are frauds, dominated by a self-serving elite, designed to hoodwink even a nation of Aristotles. Heroic and demonic expectations about the electoral process lead straight to the same impasse: a classic double bind.

It is argued frequently that the direct, national election of a president is the only (heavenly?) way of selecting a leader consistent with democratic principles. In fact, some election enthusiasts are so convinced of this that they would like to spread the wealth around, suggesting we also need a national primary. Whether a national primary is urged or not, it is then noted that the individuals actually selected, who have survived the real world process of building supporting coalitions in a complex society of more than 200 million people, or even in one of the major parties, might not feel entirely comfortable or accepted at a gathering of the Democratic Socialist Organizing Committee or the Committee for the Survival of a Free Congress.

"Why," someone always then will ask, "doesn't our system produce 'statesmen' rather than 'politicians'?" The search for a candidate who has found the Holy Grail is on. Exaggerated? Only slightly. The presidency and the selection system that churns leaders into it are frequently interpreted *as if* they were parts of a Wagnerian saga or, more recently, an old cowboy movie, complete with mythical qualities of individual struggle against the Inevitable Forces of Fate.

Clever but misbegotten movies (*The Candidate*), misleading best sellers (*Advise and Consent*), television news (any network, any time), presidents themselves (selection left up to the reader), all newspapers (even that old worthy, the *New York Times*), sophisticated and unsophisticated dinner conversation (everybody's)—all stress aspects of public life that are elusive, highly personal, and superficial. If you have doubts about the universality of this (and are old enough), try to remember the number of times you engaged in conversations on the topic, "Who is Jimmy Carter?" Or, more recently, "Is Ronald Reagan as simplistic a person as his rhetoric suggests?"

For as long as the United States has had presidents, one of the major preoccupations of those for whom politics is a day-to-day business has been presidential personality and style. Naturally, therefore, the usual response of those with a more casual interest in politics will be the same. Evaluating presidents as good or bad, tough or weak, bold or timid, smart or dim-witted, cagey or clumsy, even "active/positive" or "active/negative" is a game played with relish by everyone who cares about politics. Unfortunately, with the exception of the less vulgar psychological studies of leadership,[5] it is also a game that diverts attention from other more important concerns.

The habit of assuming that presidential elections are concerned primarily with selecting the candidate whose personality and character are best suited for the position, and not equally a struggle over a public policy agenda, is deeply ingrained in both popular and scholarly literature, as well as among those who are most active in the political arena. Unsurprisingly, the same attitude—emphasizing the personal attributes associated with policy making rather than the substance of policy proposals—carries over into, and dominates, assessments of performance in the presidency. Two quotations, widely separated in time, illustrate this problem. One is concerned with electoral behavior and the other with behavior in office. The first is from Theodore White's pioneering study of the 1960 presidential campaign, the second from a series of highly publicized *Atlantic* articles by Carter's first chief speech writer, James Fallows.[6]

From White the following:

> In the hard life of politics it is well known that no ... program advanced by either party has any purpose beyond expressing emotion. Platforms are a ritual with a history of their own and, after being written, they are useful chiefly to scholars who dissect them as archeological political remains ... in actual fact, all platforms are meaningless; the program of either party is what lies in the vision and conscience of the candidate the party chooses to lead it.

Nineteen years later, Fallows wrote:

> These clues told me part of the answer, but there was one part missing, the most fundamental of them all. Carter's willful ignorance, his blissful *tabula rasa*, could—to me—be explained, only by a combination of arrogance, complacency, and—dread thought—insecurity at the core of his mind and soul. For a while, I thought the arrogance was the unfortunate by-product of life in a small town ... it [big-city life] would not have left him satisfied, as the real Jimmy Carter too often is, with what burbles up in the usual bureaucratic fashion with the people who happen to come to hand.

Thus, John Kennedy's famous telephone call to Coretta King, indicating his concern over her husband's jailing, is treated as the "real" measure of his promise, not his somewhat belated support of the most comprehensive civil rights platform plank of the post-Civil War period. Thus, Carter's methodical attention to paperwork is disproportionately emphasized, while what he was putting on paper was ignored. Thus, Reagan's exceptional talent as a "communicator" is trundled out with predictable monotony or, if the observer is of a more critical bent, his numerous verbal mistakes, misstatements, inaccuracies are chronicled as if these Reaganisms are the most important feature of his presidency. This is not to suggest that the leadership style of Kennedy, Carter, or Reagan is unimportant in assessing their performances; the very opposite is obviously the case so far as popular support, electoral victory, and political survival are concerned. Presidents, for better or worse, *are* symbolic and political as well as programmatic leaders.

Successfully utilizing the skills of symbolic leadership can influence presidential success in policy. Fallows, White, and others who emphasize stylistic and personal attributes are taken seriously because what they have to say is usually informed and serious, and their observations can have serious consequences—for those inside and outside the presidency. What journalists and other opinion leaders believe and write *will* affect the substance of what presidents achieve. Such perspectives clarify, but they also distort.

The distortion associated with the emphasis on leadership style has reached epidemic proportions in terms of assessing individual presidents, all the more so because it is resurrecting what political scientists thought Thomas E. Cronin properly buried a number of years ago: the "textbook" presidency.[7] Cronin summarized the attributes of this mystique as follows:

> 1. The president is *the* strategic catalyst for progress in the American political system and the central figure in the international system as well.
> 2. Only the president can be the genuine architect of United States public policy, and only he, by attacking problems frontally and aggressively and by interpreting his power expansively, can slay the dragons of crisis and be the genuine engine of change to move this nation forward.
> 3. The president must be the nation's personal and moral leader; by symbolizing the past and future greatness of America and radiating inspirational confidence, a president can pull the nation together while directing its people toward fulfillment of the American Dream.
> 4. If, and only if, the right person is placed in the White House, all will be well; and, somehow, whoever is in the White House is the best person for the job—at least for a year or so.[8]

Cronin goes on:

> The significance of the textbook presidency is that the whole is greater than the sum of the parts. It presents a cumulative presidential image, a legacy of past glories and impressive performances . . . which endows the White House with a singular mystique and almost magical qualities. According to this image . . . only men [!] of the caliber of Lincoln, the Roosevelts, or Wilson can seize the chalice of opportunity, create the vision, and rally the American public around that vision.[9]

Moreover, even discussions of presidential power less gross and misleading than the textbook variety frequently overlook or minimize the independent and powerful role of Congress or of state and local political institutions, ignore the reality of corporate and noncorporate centers of established power, underestimate structural restraints on

presidential decision making, and fuel a continuing cycle of overprom-
ise and underdelivery by presidents themselves. The inevitable result, as
Cronin suggests, is to embellish the myth of presidential omniscience:
either they are celebrated as Olympian heroes or damned as incompetent bunglers. Less dramatic but more directly related to the concern of
this study, stylistic appraisals obscure the distinction between what
presidents realistically can and cannot accomplish in all but the most
turbulent, crisis-dominated historical periods.

Abraham Lincoln and Franklin D. Roosevelt faced domestic crises
without parallel in contemporary history. To assess recent administrations from the viewpoint, implicit or explicit, of what Lincoln or
Roosevelt accomplished or how they accomplished it, is to mislead
observers about the possibilities inherent in a radically different social,
economic, and political structure. Lincoln and Roosevelt were also
extraordinarily gifted symbolic leaders. Political genius like this is rare
in every society and in every century; our assessments of contemporary
presidential performance will not be improved by comparing recent
incumbents to the legends, real and romanticized, of a Roosevelt or
Lincoln presidency.

Presidential rhetoric
and presidential agendas

The rhetoric of presidential candidates themselves further dims the
hope of gaining agreement about more precise standards of evaluation,
let alone forging mechanisms of stricter accountability through the
electoral system. Later in the book, a quantitative content analysis of
promises made, programs sought, and policies enacted is presented. In
developing this scheme, borrowed heavily from other scholars, I have
not considered candidate claims whose fulfillment would require celes-
tial intervention, or at least control over so many variables that no
honest human being, no matter how noble or sincere his intentions,
could ever hope to achieve them. Yet seemingly intelligent, politically
sophisticated, and well-intentioned presidential candidates continue to
make inflated rhetorical claims about what they can or do accomplish.
Equally important, many citizens seem to take them at face value, accept
these claims as if they were achievable, then damn presidents when it is
clear they cannot be fulfilled or praise them as if presidents truly
redeemed their most outlandish promises.

Take two examples from an infinitely large number: Reagan campaigned throughout 1980 to "get the federal government off the backs of
the people." And Carter frequently stumped the country saying that

"my major goal is to help restore the confidence of our people in this nation's governing institutions." These are noble, even useful, sentiments
given what had been practiced in the Oval Office by some of their
recent predecessors. Consider, however, the impossibility of actually
assessing their administrations as if these were viable promises.

The promises are functionally meaningless. Was there ever a Democratic
presidential candidate who promised to crush our collective spinal cords
with "big government"? Nor can I recall Ronald Reagan or Gerald R.
Ford running on a promise of "eroding" the confidence of people in
their government. American presidential campaigns, campaigns the
world over, generate tons of such statements. One can appreciate the
value of well-crafted emotive rhetoric without accepting it as appropriate language for evaluating the performance of public leaders. "The
French don't care what they do so long as they say it properly," a
whimsical line from *My Fair Lady,* is a beguiling sentiment when
applied to presidents.

The promises are programmatically meaningless. If agreement were
possible on precisely what actions or programs would actually get
government "off our backs," or even if "government," rather than what
government actually does, were the real issue, then campaigns and
elections would be pointless. Or useful for other purposes. But clearly
large groups of people disagree—liberals and conservatives, farmers and
urban dwellers, easterners and westerners, feminists and nonfeminists,
blacks and whites, business owners and consumers, Christians and non-
Christians, environmentalists and developers, hawks and doves—and
virtually every combination one can conjure reinforces the wisdom of an
alternative conception about the utility of the electoral process.

If elections are mechanisms for temporarily resolving conflict over
which groups and which programs, more or less, will be favored as
experimental means to ends most citizens desire, then we need to focus
more attention on the specifics of what presidents promise and how
those promises match performance. If a large majority of citizens
actually knew which experiments would work, if we had agreement on
means as well as ends, then nobody would worry about promises and
performance. We could simply elevate any capable manager in the
society and get on with other concerns. Elections are useful precisely
because people disagree over means, over solutions to national problems. Elections provide an interim group of leaders *and* policies—
nothing more, nothing less.

Strategically, however, "meaningless" rhetorical promises can have
powerful political consequences. Code words and symbolic phrases
frequently provide the glue of stable coalitions, or they help to dissolve
them. In understanding how presidential coalitions are built, main-

tained, and transformed, it is important to examine the use of rhetoric, even when that rhetoric is empty of precise policy commitment.[10] When one is assessing presidential campaign-to-office behavior, however, it is imperative that evaluations move beyond the indirect clues provided in rhetoric to considering more specific language and proposals. Otherwise we will continue to wander in a limbo of linguistic ambiguity, unable to separate the concrete from the elusive. We may wander in that limbo anyway, but at least we will have better tools for poking around in presidential verbiage if we focus more attention on campaign promises that convey more detail than the usual rhetoric.

Another complicating factor in dissecting the meaningfulness of campaign promises stems from the fact that most voters focus on outcomes rather than means, results rather than process. If the economy is doing well, unemployment and inflation both within tolerable margins, voters will reflect less concern about *why* this is true, or *how* it got that way, than they will be concerned with sustaining the "good times." Conversely, economic downturns will find voters less knowledgeable about what specific policies might solve these problems and more willing to rely on what they perceive, experience, and understand about the current reality in the context of their past experiences. This is particularly true on matters of "high policy"—those involving governmental management of the economy or U.S. conduct in world affairs where that conduct involves war or coming close to war.

Candidates sometimes promise outcomes that are comparatively specific no matter how contradictory—lowering inflation, unemployment, interest rates, and federal deficits—with means (supply-side economics, for example) that most voters do not understand. Once the promise makers are in office, however, voters may come to believe that implementation of the candidate's programs are associated with unacceptable consequences, such as recessions, generous tax rebates to the well-off making them comparatively more well-off, and so on. Should presidents be held accountable when the promised results of their programs go astray? Or should they benefit when outcomes are positive but only tangentially related to proposed means?

On questions of the economy and war, voters certainly believe they should, and many behave consistently with these beliefs in rendering retrospective judgments on presidential performance by "throwing the rascals out" or renewing their lease for another four years.[11] But most voters ignore more precise questions about the actual degree of presidential responsibility, about the relative role (relative to other institutions, private and public) of presidential policies in shaping economic or international outcomes. So, when judging presidents about promised outcomes, rather than proposed means, it is imperative that any analysis embrace both those factors presidents truly can control and those that clearly are beyond their capacity to affect.

Questions about the promise and performance of political leaders are as ancient as the history of government. From the perspective of world history, the American presidency is a young institution, as indeed democracy, American-style, is a young experiment. Modern presidential campaigns, with their emphasis on television, sophisticated technology, and complex rules and procedures, are younger still. Nevertheless, the comparatively brief time period covered in this study, from 1960 to the present, has witnessed staggering changes in the policy and political landscape of American life. The questions I seek to examine are deceptively simple. Predictably, attempting to answer them moves one farther away from that simplicity. The book now turns to a consideration of some of these problems in assessing agenda building in campaigns and follow-through in office.

Notes

1. James David Barber, ed., *Choosing the President* (Englewood Cliffs, N.J.: Prentice-Hall, 1974).
2. Among the many, see Nelson Polsby and Aaron Wildavsky, *Presidential Elections: Strategies of American Electoral Politics*, 6th ed. (New York: Scribners, 1984). Further elaborations are found in Robert A. Dahl, *Polyarchy: Participation and Opposition* (New Haven: Yale University Press, 1971); and Gerald M. Pomper, with Susan S. Lederman, *Elections in America*, 2d ed. (New York: Longman, 1980).
3. Quoted in *The Pursuit of the Presidency 1980*, ed. Richard Harwood (New York: Putnam, 1980), 214.
4. Thomas E. Cronin, "Why Carter?" *Washington Star*, Nov. 1, 1980, E4.
5. Good examples of sophisticated work include James David Barber, *The Presidential Character: Predicting Performance in the White House* (Englewood Cliffs, N.J.: Prentice-Hall, 1977); Bruce Buchanan, *The Presidential Experience* (Englewood Cliffs, N.J.: Prentice-Hall, 1978); Betty Glad, *Jimmy Carter: In Search of the Great White House* (New York: Norton, 1980); Doris Kearns, *Lyndon Johnson and the American Dream* (New York: Harper & Row, 1976); and Alexander L. George and Juliette L. George, *Woodrow Wilson and Colonel House: A Personality Study* (New York: Dover, 1956). A synthesis of psychological and historical perspectives can be found in James MacGregor Burns, *Leadership* (New York: Harper & Row, 1978). The most comprehensive and compelling recent study of presidential leadership, combining historical, structural, and strategic factors, is Bert A. Rockman, *The Leadership Question: The Presidency and the American System* (New York: Praeger, 1984).

6. Theodore White, *The Making of the President* (New York: Atheneum, 1961), 193; James Fallows, "The Passionless Presidency," *Atlantic,* May 1979, 33-46.
7. Cronin first circulated an unpublished paper on this theme in 1970. The ideas are more fully developed in his *The State of the Presidency,* 2d ed. (Boston: Little, Brown, 1980).
8. Cronin, *The State of the Presidency,* 84.
9. Ibid.
10. In this, as in most aspects concerning the political use of language, the work of Murray Edelman is instructive. See *The Symbolic Uses of Politics* (Urbana: University of Illinois Press, 1964); "The Politics of Persuasion," in *Choosing the President,* ed. James David Barber (Englewood Cliffs, N.J.: Prentice-Hall, 1974), 149-174; and *Political Language: Words That Succeed and Policies That Fail* (New York: Academic Press, 1977). Creative recent work on campaign rhetoric will be found in Darrell M. West, "Rhetoric and Agenda-Setting in the 1980 Presidential Campaign," *Congress and the Presidency* 9 (Autumn 1982): 1-21; and his longer study, *Making Campaigns Count* (Westport, Conn.: Greenwood Press, 1984). Other consequences of presidential rhetoric are being studied by a group of scholars originally centered at the University of Virginia. For an initial report, see James W. Ceaser et al., "The Rise of the Rhetorical Presidency," *Presidential Studies Quarterly* (Spring 1981): 158-171.
11. Retrospective accountability was at the core of V. O. Key's concept of party responsibility in the United States. See V. O. Key, with the assistance of Milton C. Cummings, Jr., *The Responsible Electorate* (Cambridge, Mass.: Harvard University Press, 1965). The concept is updated, modified, and refined by Morris Fiorina, *Retrospective Voting in American National Elections* (New Haven, Conn.: Yale University Press, 1981).

Presidential campaigns and presidents in office ═══ 2

> *A man came to Bayazid and said that he had fasted and prayed for thirty years, and yet had not come near to an understanding of God. Bayazid replied: "Even a hundred years will not be enough. Expect nothing!"*
>
> —A Sufi tale

Question presidential specialists about the problem of issue development in elections, and many will respond with an appropriate retort of Anthony Downs: candidates formulate programs to win elections, not win elections to formulate programs.

Does it make any difference which emphasis is correct if we have comparatively little analysis of *how* such programs are formulated, *what* these programs are likely to entail, *whether* they are ever implemented, or what the *consequences* might be on important values in American society? [1]

Like the man who came to the Sufi teacher Bayazid, most citizens are still praying and fasting when it comes to expecting serious issues to be articulated and debated in presidential campaigns. Everyone "knows" these struggles are merely exercises in issue ambiguity or, more cynically, outright treachery. [2] Why examine them as if they have any serious meaning from the viewpoint of public policy?

15

In time-honored fashion, various media commentators compete in ridiculing the idea that presidential campaigns might have substantial policy content or fundamental policy consequences. Thus Howard K. Smith's observation about the Ford-Carter campaign:

> Every election contains portions of fluff and nonsense, but this is the first presidential one since Al Smith was beaten for allegedly aiming to put the Pope in the White House that has been almost entirely fluff.[3]

John Chancellor, speaking to a group of editors about the same campaign, complained that in 20 years of covering national politics, he had never seen "a pettier campaign, an emptier campaign, a campaign so lacking in a discussion of the real issues than this one." [4] Neither of these condemnations exactly broke new ground; they are a perennial complaint about all elections, even those before Al and Howard K. Smith.

Much like the "textbook" presidency, there is also "textbook" campaign commentary. The latter, unlike the former, contains a powerful half-truth—there *is* a lot of fluff in every presidential election. Of course, there is considerable nonfluff, too, so we need more precise ways of considering the tensions between clear agenda development and obvious issue displacement in the electoral process.[5]

When one moves from commentary on campaigns to analysis of the agendas presidents actually pursue in office, cynicism deepens further. Do presidents attempt to follow through on the promises of their campaigns or party platforms? "Only a political scientist," observed one of my Washington acquaintances, "would think of formulating that as a question!"

Linking campaign promise to presidential performance is a complex task that has received little attention. What is missing in most popular commentary is precisely what political science ought to provide: a perspective guided by recent historical and comparative example, quantitative and systematic where possible, and connected to larger questions of party and presidential acountability and performance.

The quantitative performance data examined later in this chapter may surprise readers. Since 1960, from the presidency of John F. Kennedy through that of Ronald Reagan, American presidents have made a considerable number of remarkably precise campaign promises, and, just as important, *attempted* to follow through on a majority of these commitments. Every president also has deferred, avoided, or abandoned important promises, and some (Jimmy Carter, Lyndon Johnson) have paid a substantial price because those reversals resulted in damaging primary challenges to their renominations.

Comparing campaign behavior to performance in office makes the assumption that American presidential campaigns provide policy cues about what party coalitions will do when they win. The analysis initially is devoted to examining this assumption—first, by developing a framework for thinking about policy development in elections and, second, by sketching some aspects of presidential campaigns that keep candidates from making very precise commitments. Nevertheless, all candidates do in fact make important promises, and I will be examining how and under what conditions presidents fulfill these pledges. Statistical comparisons are made for the Kennedy, Johnson, Nixon, Carter, and Reagan presidencies. Of necessity, my measures of fulfillment are suggestive rather than definitive. Detailed case studies of the Carter and Reagan presidencies are presented in later chapters, supplementing these broad quantitative indicators with extended analysis of the past two presidents.

Agenda development in presidential campaigns

Popular stereotypes about campaigns have led to a seemingly indestructible hypothesis: elections are irrelevant for predicting what candidates might do once they are in office. It is indestructible precisely because there are so many reasons, personal and institutional, *not* to frame concrete and detailed future proposals of action during campaigns. What are some of these reasons and how do candidates, party activists, issue-oriented staff, interest group leaders, and media personnel cope with them?

'The art of ambiguity'

First, the most familiar and powerful constraint on clear issue positioning in presidential campaigns, a necessary but not sufficient condition of agenda formation,[6] stems from the nature of the electorate and the electoral system. Policy ambiguity is not only required, some observers suggest, but it is positively functional for the political system.[7] According to this argument, elections provide a choice between leaders and only incidentally between policies; policy, therefore, is decided by bargaining among elites *after* the election has been won:

> A candidate and a set of policies, however loosely joined, must be found that can blend disparate party elements for the purpose of securing electoral victory . . . thus the temptation for political parties to avoid specific policy commitments is very great. The American population is so extraordinarily varied . . . that it is exceedingly difficult to guess at the total distribution of policy preferences in the population at any one time . . . the self-interest of parties and candidates . . . might

best be served by vague, ambiguous, or contradictory policy statements which will be least likely to offend anyone. The advantages of vagueness about policy are strengthened by the fact that the vast majority of citizens are not interested in policy, or are narrowly focused on a few things.[8]

Countervailing pressures, it is noted, stem from the specific demands of interest groups who are part of the party coalition (organized labor and the Democratic party, for example), from the policy commitments of party activists, and from the historic identification of parties with broad orientation to enduring questions of public policy.[9] During the 1984 primaries Walter Mondale was condemned for promising "too much" to "special interests" in the Democratic coalition. Absent the policy demands of groups like labor unions, environmentalists, civil and women's rights organizations, and others, Democratic candidates would have little incentive to make any concrete policy commitments. They could just increase the amount of campaign rhetoric "least likely to offend anyone" or virtually replace concrete policy discussion with an even greater concentration on candidate style and nonspecific "thematic" presentations.

The important question is not whether candidates promise too much, but rather what groups in the candidate's coalition are the most important and potentially helpful. Gary Hart's early appeals for leadership by a "New Generation" emphasized agenda items that were somewhat different from those associated with traditional, New Deal groups. Nevertheless, his future, or that of any candidate like him, depends on his capacity to weld the old and the new together, and understanding the policy agenda of a Hart-like candidate will depend on assessing the relative power of traditional as well as new groups within the Democratic party. *Thus, agenda development in presidential campaigns is a trade-off between the electoral incentives to fudge and the coalition incentives to deliver.*

Benjamin I. Page, in a sophisticated elaboration of this theme, suggests that Democratic and Republican presidential candidates differ most clearly on domestic social/economic issues, least clearly on others.[10] Page divides theories of policy competition (spatial theories that pose a classic division of left to right) into two varieties: "public opinion" theories, in which candidates from both parties converge in the middle because most voters' preferences are bunched around the ideological center, and "party cleavage" theories, in which candidates diverge from the center and accommodate, through choice or necessity, the preferences of their own most active party identifiers, who are more liberal or conservative than the average voter. He then suggests that even on those (social/economic) issues where presidential candidates differ most, they communicate their stands by using the "art of ambiguity."

The policy commitments of presidential candidates, Page argues, are always ambiguous. True clarity would require the following: a precise statement of intentions (what they plan to do); a specification of direction and timing (commitments about exactly when); and a statement about the magnitude of action their policies will require (how much will be spent, for example). "In each of these respects, and especially magnitude, even the candidates' most specific proposals fell far short of clarity." [11]

Campaign agendas do not require the same specificity expected of legislative agendas, of course, but Page's research supports the earlier argument about the attractiveness of ambiguity. He diverges from it most forcefully, however, in assessing the normative consequences of vagueness: if the positions of candidates are vague and obscure, then voter nonperception, misperception, and projection are significantly enhanced. Page concludes:

> Vagueness reduces the amount of real difference between candidates, and obscurity (being specific where it won't be amplified) hides whatever differences may exist. In both ways it robs voters of the opportunity to choose between candidates on policy grounds. . . . Without question, candidate vagueness greatly obstructs the process of democratic control.[12]

Agenda development is a trade-off between the coalitional incentives to deliver and the unwillingness or inability of presidential candidates to specify the magnitude of how much will be delivered.

Another line of inquiry, most commonly associated with the work of Murray Edelman, treats ambiguity as a device for shoring up the legitimacy of a political system since elections are largely symbolic and expressive in function involving "mass audiences emotionally in politics while rendering them acquiescent to policy shifts through that very involvement." [13] He does not assert, as some critics have alleged, that symbolic and expressive activities are uniformly to be condemned or that the symbols associated with "policy" are *always* a cover for oligarchical manipulations. Rather he suggests that ambiguity in campaigns is primarily a device for mobilizing mass support of future or past leadership behavior, independent of whatever policy choices presidents make. Voters, therefore, have little control over the *specific* policy choices presidents make. *Agenda development is a trade-off between the coalitional incentives to deliver and the practice of mobilizing mass support, through symbolic appeals, for past or future presidential behavior.*

Given all these attributes, it should be clear why presidential campaigns provide considerable opportunity for displacing, rather than developing, policy agendas: they ignore many controversial issues and shift attention to nonpolicy objects like candidate style, personal qualities, or issueless sloganeering. Ambiguity is a fundamental barrier to examining the linkage of campaign promises to behavior in office.

Bias in the development of agendas

"Nondecision making" and "nonissues" are concepts that have spawned a contentious intellectual conflict in recent political science debate. One useful formulation is the concept, "mobilization of bias," first popularized by E. E. Schattschneider, who used it to stress the selective qualities of all political organizations. He wrote: "Organization is the mobilization of bias. Some issues are organized into politics while others are organized out." [14] Peter Bachrach and Morton Baratz, among others, picked up this strain in Schattschneider's analysis and expanded it as part of a comprehensive criticism of pluralism, designating bias as "a set of predominant values, beliefs, rituals, and institutional procedures (the 'rules of the game') that operate systematically to the benefit of certain persons and groups at the expense of others." [15]

Concurrently, a group of neo-Marxist scholars, dissatisfied with the simplifications of "vulgar" Marxism, have argued that the political process of advanced capitalist systems provides several mechanisms for filtering out various alternatives. They suggest that "ideological norms" and the "bias of rules" factor out all "interests" other than those that are severely restricted but nevertheless beneficial, leading to marginal but minimally necessary economic benefits for the working class.

Scholars of this persuasion go on to argue that government leaders are primarily concerned with crisis management and the avoidance of long-term destabilizing forces in society. Leaders must, therefore, be responsive to the limited material interests of the "masses," even when these conflict with the power and prerequisites of the economic elite. [16]

Political parties and their leaders can reward, indeed *must* reward, those low in resources from time to time, the neo-Marxist argument goes, but these rewards will be limited, never more than enough to sustain the legitimacy of governing elites. Symbolic rhetoric about "threats to American security," or the "erosion of the American family," or the "ebbing productivity of American workers" blames the victim and replaces open and comprehensive discussion of fundamental and alternative policies. Some of these alternatives are a normal part of the electoral choices in other democratic societies like Sweden. Certainly, much of this is true.

But no observer has ever argued that American presidential campaigns do not filter out some alternatives. Indeed, defenders of the

American political system frequently argue the reverse. The "genius of American politics," to paraphrase historian Daniel Boorstin, is precisely that elections have rewarded moderate and centrist leaders and policies, excluding radical alternatives and thus avoiding extreme social and political polarization in the electoral process.

The politics of moderation, as even its proponents concede, has costs, sometimes very large ones. Blacks paid an enormous price in repression, poverty, and powerlessness for the conditions that held the Democratic coalition together until the 1948 convention; the needs of poor people are frequently discussed, programs of assistance advanced, and some progress made, but poverty still exists in the United States; tragic military interventions, as in Vietnam, are legitimized because "politics" stopped, until 1968, "at the water's edge"; women were treated until recently as "necessary" appendages to an unacknowledged patriarchy in both parties; the environment, domestic and global, has been periodically savaged in the name of progress; and individual and group dependency sometimes is fostered by public and private programs that are justified by the "helping" professions as "compensatory" policies.

Moreover, democratic radicals and other progressives, as well as those conservatives who preach the old-time gospel of unregulated capitalism, will always find the parameters of choice constricted. No major party coalition, not even that of the early New Deal period or the one led by populist William Jennings Bryan in 1896, has ever proposed fundamental alteration of the economic or political structure of the United States. For better or worse, post-New Deal presidential elections, and the subsequent behavior of presidential coalitions in office, have functioned to reinforce and/or expand the "Positive State," a political system that combines policies, which protect sometimes socially responsible corporate power, with the gradual diffusion of social welfare and other reform programs.[17]

The important question about agenda formation stemming from those themes is how senior campaign staff and candidates conceptualize the values, beliefs, and ideological norms that exclude some alternatives and include others, while keeping within the broad contours of a general acceptance of the Positive State.

Classifying presidential agendas as moderate or centrist is not much help when one deals with specific policy dimensions over time. What was considered extreme and politically objectionable in civil rights during the 1956 and 1960 campaigns had become established policy by the 1980 election. So an important addition to the propositions formulated under ambiguity is: *Agenda development is a trade-off between what campaign decision makers consider politically acceptable and the influence of group leaders who are interested in expanding or limiting the range of acceptability.*

The mobilization of bias describes that range of values resting outside the trade-offs suggested here. It can be seemingly permanent and systemic ("socialism"), or painfully long but temporary (civil rights for women, blacks, other minorities).[18]

Environmental uncertainty and issue complexity

A serious problem faced by participants in American presidential campaigns is deciding how to react to sudden and unanticipated major crises. Planning to reduce uncertainty, a preoccupation of systems analysts in all organizations, is particularly difficult and risky in the campaign environment. A police "riot" at the 1968 Democratic convention (confidently predicted as impossible by Attorney General Ramsey Clark two weeks earlier), the sudden disclosure of a hidden $25,000 campaign "slush-fund" for Richard Nixon in 1952, the assassination of Robert F. Kennedy in 1968, the unfolding of the Eagleton affair in 1972, the 1976 *Playboy* brouhaha, the seizure of Americans in Iran in 1980—all were sudden eruptions that forced candidates and their organizations to alter their approaches and resources to meet the demands of unanticipated events. All diluted the control candidates had over setting their campaign priorities.

Organizational theorists are fond of citing some early work by Herbert Simon, Albert Ando, and Franklin Fisher on the effects of complexity on increasing organizational error. The incremental model of decision making—mixing ends and means, simplification, postponement, serial evaluation, coordination through adjustment, so characteristic of many campaign organizations—can be highly error prone under certain conditions. Daniel Metlay adopted the Simon-Ando-Fisher framework, simulated the conditions of increasing complexity, and found that error rates increase *exponentially* if organizations rely on incremental assumptions for making decisions.[19] Whether it is policy or organizational units, incremental adjustments on the assumption that problems are divisible and independent (simplification), rather than related and interdependent (complex), can increase, not reduce, error.

Since 1968 the United States has witnessed the emergence of large interdependent problems—in energy, the environment, the economy, population and food supply, world order and arms control, and centralized bureaucracy—for which the "adjustments" of New Deal liberalism and classic American conservatism no longer seem adequate or politically as compelling. Many observers have called for a fundamental redirection in the assumptions and positions of the standard political ideologies of the United States (see Mark Satin's *New Age Politics* for a provocative example). To them, the older solutions associated with American liberalism and conservatism seem increasingly irrelevant for many contemporary issues.

Yet large factions in both parties must be accommodated by candidates who articulate the traditional ideological visions. Innovative policy agendas are rare in presidential campaigns precisely because candidates cannot afford to antagonize group leaders or group followers who have provided the core of each party's traditional electoral strength. Despite the vast changes in American life since the New Deal, party differences in the 1980s are still rooted in many of the same cleavages spawned by the eruptions of the 1930s. Each party has sought to accommodate post-New Deal breakthroughs, but that accommodation has occurred slowly, incrementally, grafting on newer demands and groups to the constellations formed 50 years ago. *The content of the Democratic party agenda is a trade-off among environmental uncertainty, issue complexity, and the policy and electoral claims of the New Deal coalition and its residual elements. The content of the Republican party agenda is a trade-off among environmental uncertainty, issue complexity, and the policy and electoral claims of the anti-New Deal coalition and its residual elements.*

In-party and out-party variations

Control of the presidency is a potent electoral resource. This is true despite the increasing number of challenges experienced by incumbents bent on reelection. Eugene McCarthy and Robert F. Kennedy, who challenged Lyndon B. Johnson in protest over Johnson's Vietnam policies, reopened creative possibilities in agenda development through the electoral process. The classic posture of the in-party leader, the president, had been that presidents were beyond serious challenge to renomination from within the party. The in-party's job was to defend its record, mobilize its troops, promise a "continuation of the progress we've just begun," utilize the considerable media and patronage advantages inherent in control of the White House, watch the out-party cut itself up in a struggle to name its candidate, and focus its energy on the upcoming general election.

The problem with the classic strategy is that it has become the exception, despite the Reagan administration's brilliant use of it. Perhaps it was always too orderly. Complexities intrude. The incumbent decides to withdraw (Johnson) or is prohibited from running again (Eisenhower). Both Richard Nixon in 1960 and Hubert Humphrey in 1968 found belonging to the in-party problematic. Each had to defend his party's past record while creating substantial distance, in policy and political matters, from his predecessors. Their parties' records and the loyalty of their own partisans were questionable. Humphrey, particularly, faced a severe problem in defending the administration's Vietnam policies and simultaneously carving out new directions that would mollify antiwar McCarthy-Kennedy partisans.[20]

Or consider two of the most recent incumbents, Ford and Carter. Both faced exceptionally powerful challenges from coalitions deeply unhappy about the policy and political direction of their parties. Only the renomination of Nixon in 1972 and Reagan in 1984 fit the classic mold. *When the incumbent is faced with intense competition for renomination, agenda development is a trade-off between the electoral incentives to continue existing policies and the coalitional incentives to shift toward the preferences of the challenging faction.*

The issue here is not whether incumbents or front-runners have a policy agenda. The in-party *always* has an agenda, given the nature of incumbency; rather, it involves the direction, the potentially changing content, of that agenda. The Democrats were unable to resolve this tension in a major part of their program in 1968, first supporting Johnson's war policies at the convention in a vote on a platform plank, then straddling the issue throughout the general election. And again in 1980, Democrats were bitterly divided over whether to continue supporting the incumbent's agenda.

There are few incentives to change policy direction when competition for the nomination is absent. Whatever the negative effects, a primary challenge is the major intraparty instrument for changing the in-party's policy direction—perhaps the only viable option if a faction feels particularly alienated. So far as the election is concerned, the "past is prologue" when considering what the in-party, if returned without a primary challenge, might do.

One important exception is notable. Unanticipated events during the incumbent's term—rampaging inflation, or an international event like the invasion of Afghanistan by the Soviets at the midpoint of Carter's presidency, or ballooning deficits in the Reagan administration—can fundamentally shift what the in-party is capable or desirous of doing in its second term. *Change in the in-party's agenda is a trade-off between the impact of unanticipated crises and the coalitional incentives to sustain traditional policy commitments.*

One other observation should be made about in-party policy behavior. There is substantial, although not conclusive, evidence suggesting that post-World War II presidents, excluding Eisenhower and Carter, have intentionally stimulated economic booms to assure their own reelection.[21] The Nixon administration, in this as in most things, was by far the most aggressive in manipulating the economy. For the presidents under consideration here, the incentives to engineer short-run economic gains, creating an electoral-economic cycle of boom and bust, are considerable. After all, the president's success at the polls depends on the illusion of sustained economic prosperity. Some American presidents seem to follow a variation on ex-Naderite Mark Green's golden rule: he who spends the most gold before election day, rules.

The Reagan administration was fortunate in emerging from a severe recession as the 1984 campaign began, although there is no evidence that this was a matter of intentional planning by the White House. Quite the contrary: supply-side economics predicted that both the booms and busts would be avoided if Reagan were elected in 1980. The 1984 boom, however, emerged only after the United States had experienced, during Reagan's first two years in office, the most severe recession of the post-World War II era.

The constitutional restriction of two terms dramatically reduces the political incentives to remain accountable to one's party or to any other electoral coalition. Accordingly, it *may* also restrain attempts at economic manipulation in the White House and simultaneously diminish the willingness of presidents to be responsive to the economic fortunes of those from the middle and working classes.[22] This is a cruel paradox, seemingly built into the American political economy. The two-term restriction leaves us with only two constraints on presidential performance during a second term: how presidents perceive their "ultimate place in history," usually obscured by rhetoric about "serving the public interest" in some uncharted stratosphere "above politics," and their own consciences, beliefs, values, and goals. Whatever the original intent of the amendment, one effect is to diminish electoral accountability in the American presidency.

To the out-party has always fallen the task of suggesting the desirability of program change, sometimes policy innovation. For obvious reasons, the struggle to regain the White House provokes more agenda activity. The incentives are clear and powerful. One problem, however, is that it is possible to score major political gains by attacking the in-party without proposing coherent program alternatives. Policy accountability is not served by this behavior, even if it is strategically appealing and predictable.

Attacks on an incumbent's "misguided leadership" are standard and irresistible. Criticism of this type reinforces the stylistic dimension in presidential evaluation and is hardly conducive to issue development or policy accountability. The greater the emphasis on program alternatives, the greater the possibility of policy accountability in the electoral process when the opposition unseats the incumbent.

The 'seasons' of presidential politics and party platforms

John H. Kessel suggests that one can distinguish three basic "seasons" in presidential behavior: nomination, general election, and governing. After conducting an extensive content analysis of documents from the 1972 national election, he found that candidates tend to be more concerned with distinctive and specific policies in the nomination period, followed by an emphasis on stylistic questions and group rhetoric in the general election, moving back to specific policies in the governing phase.[23]

The reasons individuals and their coalitions shift behavior over time may be obvious—the political environment changes dramatically, from scrounging for votes and support in New Hampshire, to uniting the party at the national convention, to competing for the presidency in the fall. Inevitably, the goals, tasks, and resources of presidential coalitions change.

Analytically, it is important to add another season to Kessel's three, relabeling them primary, *convention*, general election, and governing. The coalitions necessary to function in each grow organically, moving outward from a core of supporters in the primary stage, through the larger party at the convention, to the general electorate, and finally to the complexities of governing from the White House.[24] Rarely is the core displaced; the circle expands, although that very expansion is a major source of competition, tension, conflict, cleavage. How could it be otherwise? From the standpoint of issue information, two of these periods require greater specificity about public policy—the convention phase, when a platform, no matter how ambiguous, must be written, and the governing period, when a legislative and executive agenda must be advanced and supported.

Presidential candidates have the option of being specific in the other two seasons (for example, Reagan's detailed "alternative national budget" in the 1976 primaries and McGovern's family assistance plan in 1972), but they also have the choice of being quite ambiguous, emphasizing stylistic concerns (Carter's focus on "integrity" and "honesty" in the 1976 primaries and general election) or fudging in other ways on policy commitment.

Rational choice theorists have been working for a number of years on "optimal" policy strategies for presidential contenders, in which assumptions vary about the sequence of primaries, number of competitors, size and preference of the primary electorate, and spatial dimensions of policy disagreement.[25] My concern, however, is with the "seasonal correlates" of presidential campaigns, so I will concentrate here on the one campaign season, the national convention, where policy concerns are likely to be the greatest.

Party platforms, somebody once observed, are one part apology, one part evasion, and large part bunkum. More empirically oriented students of these documents might agree but would want to add two additional and contrary parts: first, from 1948 to 1976, slightly better than one-fourth of each party's platform consisted of fairly specific and testable policy pledges. Second, the record of fulfillment was surprisingly higher than one might expect. When testable pledges are allocated among policy areas, the proportion fulfilled by the party controlling the presidency ranged from a high of 91 percent in agriculture and defense to a low of 54 percent in labor.[26] Paul David places these findings in appropriate perspective:

> [T]he platforms involve a remarkable paradox of perception. [Many people] have made it their business to denigrate the platforms as campaign trivia—ephemera to be forgotten as soon as the campaign is over. On the other hand, it is not possible to watch the amount of struggle that goes into any platform, the thousands of hours of toil, sweat, and strain that are devoted by people who value their time highly, without concluding that the platforms must be important to some people, for some purposes.[27]

One consistent argument is that the importance of platforms is residual and indirect. Platform building permits different factions to agree on the main programmatic conditions under which they will support and work for the presidential nominee. Platforms provide a reasonably precise reflection of the trade-off between what the probable nominee's organization considers politically acceptable and the influence of group leaders who are interested in expanding or restricting the range of acceptability. This becomes more complex when no frontrunner for the nomination exists.

Moreover, platforms have grown larger since 1948, now covering an astonishing number of policy areas. A glance at Table 2-1 easily confirms the expansion in length; a comparative reading of the 1948 and 1984 party platforms will just as easily confirm the assertion about policy variety. Platforms reflect the general growth in governmental activity since the New Deal and the growth and variety of interest groups whose goals and needs must be accommodated through bargaining by the parties and the presidential nominees. For those who want issue information, modern platforms are far superior now, covering more topics and covering them in greater detail than they did even during the 1950s. Unfortunately, they are examined seriously by a minuscule number of the adult voting population. ("Thank God!" said one pro who helped write a number of them.)

Table 2-1   The parties have become wordier: growth in the length of
national party platforms, 1948-1984

	Platform length (in words)[a]	
Year	Democrats	Republicans
1948	2,800	2,000
1952	7,200	5,500
1956	10,000	8,000
1960	20,000	9,000
1964	5,500[b]	7,000
1968	14,000	11,200
1972	24,000	30,000
1976	20,200	23,700
1980	33,000	29,600
1984	47,800	28,000

[a] Platform length is rounded to the nearest 100th word.
[b] The Democrats produced a two-part platform in 1964, one of the regular variety, which was distributed by the DNC as "the" platform, and a lengthy appendix called "The Record," summarizing achievements since 1960. If one includes the second part, total length was 18,500 words.

The relationship between what platforms promise and what presidents *attempt* to do in the governing season is remarkably high. This holds for every president considered—Kennedy, Johnson, Nixon, Carter, and Reagan. *Agenda development is a trade-off between how intensely presidential coalitions feel bound to individual platform planks and the electoral incentives to ignore/avoid/transform them.*

Communication imperatives and the mass media

Agenda items not communicated are agenda items displaced. But communicated to whom, how, and with what effects are classic problems faced by campaign staffs. Presidential campaigns live or die on the basis of mass media coverage. Enormous resources are devoted to "getting the story across," assiduously courting national and local media persons, reacting to bad or good press. Media events, those curious appendages of the television age, have become as common to campaigns as have elaborate organizing devices geared primarily to meeting the daily schedules and sociology of press routine.

Impressive evidence has accumulated recently, as in the work of Doris Graber and Thomas Patterson,[28] that documents what cynics have believed for a long time: the media, even newspapers like the *New York*

Times, devote a very small proportion of total campaign coverage (ranging from 4 to 10 percent) to discussion of "issue and candidate philosophy." Arguments over the explanation for this have taken on a chicken-and-egg aspect with journalists blaming candidates and candidates blaming journalists. Properly sorting this out is a problem I leave to others.[29]

More important than who is at fault is the fact that presidential campaigns and the mass media exist in a symbiotic relationship. It is clear that issues *must* be cast either in a broad and partially ambiguous way or in a very specific but truncated and simplistic fashion if candidates are to get any mass media coverage about policy. Moreover, reporters who are unable to write stories with dramatic punch and flair (or short "straight" descriptions of the day's main events in the notorious "he said/someone else said" variety) soon find themselves reassigned to the obituary page. These pressures are increased drastically for television reporters, who must cover campaigns in greatly reduced time and space, with the added mandate of preventing visual monotony at all costs.

The mass media, whether through journalistic coverage or candidate-controlled advertising, comprise only one means, albeit the most pervasive, of communicating information about issues. Campaigns produce thousands of messages that are devoted to servicing special groups and that provide far more expansive and specific issue information. All candidates target appeals to special audiences in highly predictable and resourceful ways. Ghost-written articles, interviews, special "messages to the membership," position papers, as well as direct and surrogate speeches are developed as instruments for supplementing mass media coverage. *Agenda development is a trade-off between the communication requirements of the "front channel" (mass media) and the communication requirements of the "back channel" (specialized media and personal contact).*

In the front channel, the emphasis is on the drama of campaigns, with greatest attention devoted to the usual horse-race aspects, together with summaries of broad themes of potential policy agendas. The front channel is especially well suited for "thematic" rather than "issue" communication. In the back channel, however, specific items about the current agenda and any future agenda are much more likely to be developed and amplified.

Potential conflict between messages communicated in the back channel and information conveyed in the front channel is quite probable. The main reason is not outright candidate inconsistency, but that candidates are communicating in a different format. Also, because highly active coalitional partners (or potential partners) are usually plugged into both channels, indeed aggressively use them for sending messages back and forth in attempting to confirm the accuracy of their own perceptions, the main sources of reducing conflict are mutual trust and a clear understanding about what can and cannot be communicated through these different media. Some of a president's main coalitional problems, in their campaigns and in office, have stemmed from failures to overcome the inherent tensions of this difficult communication trade-off.

Given the obvious disincentives for candidates to make concrete promises, issue development in the electoral process closely resembles Dr. Johnson's description of a dog walking on its hind legs: it's not done very well, but you are surprised to see it done at all. Presidential candidates must surmount considerable barriers in making promises that can plausibly become part of their agenda in office. What is the nature of those promises? How many have recent candidates made? And, most important, what is the record of follow-through for those candidates who have gained office since 1960? The next section examines these questions, emphasizing the records of Carter and Reagan in comparison with the performance of their predecessors.

Do presidents redeem their promises? A quantitative assessment

In his first year in office, President Reagan moved forcefully and skillfully to redeem a substantial part of his campaign agenda on economic policy, including a large 3-year tax cut and the imposition of dramatic reductions in government spending for social services. In his second year in office, Reagan "reluctantly" supported a tax "reform" bill that increased taxes in many sectors, seeking to recover about 25 percent of the revenue lost in the 3-year package supported in the first year.

In his first year in office, President Carter issued an executive order granting pardons to all Vietnam War draft resisters and establishing procedures for case-by-case review of deserters. In a direct, visible, and unambiguous way, he redeemed a campaign pledge on one of the most bitterly disputed issues in the aftermath of the war. In early 1979 the Carter administration submitted legislation as part of its second National Energy Plan that would totally deregulate the price of crude oil, thereby reversing a frequently stated campaign promise to oppose the deregulation of prices for "old" crude oil.

Is this about all one can expect—that presidents will act consistently in some areas and inconsistently in others, in predictably unpredictable fashion? Or do each of these presidential responses to reasonably specific campaign promises represent a pattern of follow-through and/or reversal that might be anticipated from what has been noted about presidential campaigns in general? Answering this question requires a short detour. First it is necessary that one further examine claims about the lack of detailed campaign promises made by candidates.

Types of campaign promises

Using a modified version of the content analysis strategy developed by Gerald Pomper in his examination of party platforms, I evaluated a vast array of candidate position papers, speeches, and background materials, relying on both published and unpublished sources. Rhetorical evaluations of past government policy, leadership style, or programmatically meaningless commitments were eliminated. *Example of a meaningless commitment:* "I will bring together leaders of American business, labor, government, and the academic world to develop a new American strategy of competitiveness," Reagan said in 1980. The emphasis in my scheme is on more specific statements about future policy, in increasing order of specificity, using four of Pomper's six categories.[30]

1. *Pledges of continuity.* A pledge to maintain present government policy, but without specification of its character or with reference only to the general nature of the program.[31]

Example: "Ensure that any reform of Social Security will have one overriding goal—that the benefits of those now receiving—or looking forward to receiving—Social Security must be protected." Reagan—1980.

2. *Expressions of goals and concerns.* Stated intentions to meet a specific problem or to achieve a particular goal, but without specification of the means to be employed or without complete commitment to the goal.[32]

Example: "There are many ways to extend health coverage to those persons who are inadequately insured without forcing all Americans into a compulsory system . . . and we should explore these alternatives." Reagan—1980.

3. *Pledges of action.* Definite promises about the direction of policy, as well as the problems to be considered, although detailed provisions are not included. Pledges in this category dealing with government finances or other quantitatively measurable policies indicate the direction, but not the amount, of intended changes.[33]

Example: "I will put top priority on getting a simplified, accelerated capital cost recovery policy to replace the overcomplicated present regulations, with such programs like these: 1) providing for immediate passage of accelerated depreciation allowances; and 2) adjusting depreciation procedures to account for true costs of replacement." Reagan—1980.

> 4. *Detailed pledges.* The character of the action pledged, as well as its direction, is stated. A specific bill or executive order may be mentioned or its context explicated. Pledges to continue specific past policies or to exact quantitatively defined policies are included as well. Even in this category, however, the statement will contain considerably less specificity than an actual public law.[34]

Example: "I strongly oppose universal service, which rests on the assumption that people belong to the state ... moreover, I oppose military draft in peace-time ... finally, I oppose the establishment of a stand-by registration system." Reagan—1980.

Like party platforms, future policy pledges that fall within the above categories constitute only 25 percent of those questions upon which candidates focus their energies. Most of what presidential candidates talk and write about has little specific policy relevance. This conceded, some questions remain. How many promises about future policy do candidates make? Did the number and specificity of Reagan and Carter campaign promises differ substantially from those of Kennedy, Johnson, or Nixon? Data on the latter question are presented in Table 2-2 using the above classifications.

Insofar as presidential campaign material meets standards of reasonable specificity, the data suggest an intriguing finding about Reagan and Carter. First, and most surprising, Reagan made far fewer promises in the domestic arena (108) than Carter (186), who in turn outdistanced Kennedy (133), Johnson (49, domestic policy only), and Nixon (117, domestic policy). These pledges do not meet Benjamin Page's more elaborate criteria of specificity because Pomper's standards are less demanding. In this respect, Reagan, Carter, and all the earlier candidates framed proposals that were remiss. Still, the amount of specific information provided in the pledges reported here is surprising given the normal tendency to dismiss most campaign issue information as mere rhetoric. More important, the data in Table 2-2 make it clear that Carter was more ambitious than any of the earlier candidates in drafting program commitments that were fairly specific and that Reagan, whose promises were more far-reaching in their impact, was much less ambitious in the number made.

The importance of the promises made by Carter and Reagan also is reflected in some unprecedented developments in tracking presidential commitments. The national committees of both parties are now keeping and publishing comprehensive policy score cards of the opposite party incumbent's record. The Carter transition staff took the first step when it prepared and released in February 1977 a 121-page book entitled *White*

Table 2-2 Number and specificity of presidential campaign promises, Kennedy to Reagan[a]

Type of promise	Kennedy (1960)	N	Johnson[b] (1964)	N	Nixon[b] (1968)	N	Carter (1976)	N	Reagan (1980)	N
Pledges of continuity	10%	(11)	10%	(6)	4%	(6)	3%	(5)	20%	(22)
Expression of goals and concerns	26	(34)	30	(19)	32	(49)	30	(56)	44	(47)
Pledges of action	43	(59)	44	(28)	44	(68)	41	(76)	25	(27)
Detailed pledges	21	(29)	16	(10)	20	(30)	26	(49)	11	(12)
Totals	100%	(133)	100%	(63)	100%	(153)	100%	(186)	100%	(108)

[a] For obvious reasons Ford was omitted and Nixon's second term was considered atypical. Data are from the general election period but reflect what is carried over in position papers from the primaries. Coding followed those categories used in Gerald Pomper, *Elections in America* (New York: Dodd, Mead, 1968). The material for Johnson and Nixon is taken from Fred I. Grogan, "Candidate Promise and Presidential Performance, 1964-1972" (Paper presented at the 1977 meeting of the Midwest Political Science Association). Data for Kennedy, Carter, and Reagan are the author's and reflect their *domestic policy commitments only.*

[b] Grogan includes foreign policy promises in his data for Johnson and Nixon. It proved impossible to eliminate these foreign policy promises and retain the coding categories for purposes of comparing his data and mine. Of Johnson's 63 promises, 14 involved foreign policy, giving him a total of 49 domestic policy commitments; of Nixon's 153 promises, 36 were in foreign policy, leaving him with a total of 117 in the domestic arena.

House Promises that contained virtually all of the most important campaign pledges.[35] Some Carter aides later regretted doing this, but it would have made no difference anyway. The Republicans, fueled by their own naturally partisan bias, prepared a similar study on Carter; his record would have been assembled even if his staff had never published its own book.

The Republican National Committee, under the leadership of the Research Division's director Michael Baroody, developed a comprehensive assessment, listing 660 promises and commenting on their fulfillment or lack thereof. The data in this book, entitled *Promises, Promises—A Republican Accountability Project*, were placed in computerized format, updated throughout the Carter years, and gave the RNC a large, flexible, and efficient system of monitoring the president's campaign and record.[36] Naturally, the RNC's analysis of fulfillment is highly partisan (as it ought to be), but the comprehensive nature of the effort was impressive. The Democrats, using the research capability of the Democratic Congressional Campaign Committee, followed suit in 1981 and published an assessment of the Reagan years entitled, *The 1980 Campaign Promises of Ronald Reagan*.

The significantly larger number of promises listed in both party books is due to the differences in categorizing "true" campaign pledges. Promising "to rebuild public confidence in government," a recurrent campaign theme, is treated in my analysis as rhetorical and untestable because no candidate has ever run promising *to erode* confidence in government. Both books include substantial material that is meaningless in terms of assessing concrete programs. My categories require achievement in a way that minimizes the usual campaign rhetoric.[37] The Carter and Reagan campaigns, like each of its four predecessors, did construct a policy-relevant domestic agenda against which to assess performance in office.

Comparative presidential performance

What constitutes presidential fulfillment of campaign promises is a deceptively simple question.

Carter, for example, frequently promised during the campaign that he would "substantially increase" the number of women appointees in major governmental positions. On October 2, 1976, he addressed the National Women's Agenda Conference, saying:

> I will insist on hiring policies that will bring far more women into top grades and throughout the entire government. This administration [Ford's] has only paid lip service to women's rights and it has been argued—always by men—that qualified women do not exist. They do

exist and I intend to find them and put them to work. We are now working ... to find several hundred, perhaps thousands, of women all over the country, qualified women to serve in different positions in government.[38]

As of the end of 1980, 21 percent of Carter's executive political appointments had gone to women (436 of 2,110). This was a larger percentage than any previous administration (Ford appointed 13 percent), and there were impressive "first women to" appointments:

—only 6 women had ever served as Cabinet secretaries; 3 of these were appointed by Carter;

—only 4 women had ever served as undersecretaries; 2 were appointed by Carter;

—only 34 women had ever served as assistant secretaries; 14 were appointed by Carter;

—only 11 had ever served as heads of agencies or independent regulatory commissions; 5 were Carter appointments;

—of the 32 women who were federal judges in 1980, 28 were appointed by Carter.[39]

And so forth. Do these efforts constitute fulfillment on this one promise about women? They did not satisfy Eleanor Smeal, who was the president of the National Organization for Women. Her group publicly repudiated the Democratic president in 1979. Smeal's objections are understandable if one remembers an important *political* consideration leaders of such organizations face. They are always under pressure to define fulfillment in a way that is consistent with their need to retain influence within the group and with their organization's agenda, in this case, having female appointments approximate the distribution of women in the population or at least in the professional pool from which appointments are drawn. If group leaders appear to backslide, they risk censure from their members and a potential diminution of their own power base.

These tensions are not, as some observers suggest, a unique feature of single-issue politics. Why the Chamber of Commerce, who presumably represents business interests, is considered a multi-issue organization, and NOW is not, is not easily understood. Nor is it a matter of professional versus amateur outlooks in politics: George Meany, long-time president of the AFL-CIO and hardly an amateur, was as stern and uncompromising in his denunciation of the Carter administration as any feminist. Rather it stems from 1) the imperatives of group leadership and representation, particularly if the group is low in power resources, like women's groups, and 2) from the very different roles and outlooks associated with holding and exercising some influence in government and attempting to shape the administration's agenda from outside, as

NOW and other women's rights organizations do. NOW, incidentally, reassessed its strategy in light of the Reagan administration's policies and endorsed Walter Mondale in late 1983. But even Mondale's selection of New York representative Geraldine Ferraro as his running mate would not make him immune to future criticism from women's groups.

As this one example makes clear, presidential fulfillment is an intensely political question, subject to enormous variation, depending on the relative position of group leaders in the campaign and governing coalitions. Obviously, scholars' judgments, too, depend on their own political definition of what constitutes fulfillment.

Or ponder another part of the question of presidential fulfillment: what are the administration's true priorities? The Reagan administration publicly backed the abolition of the departments of Education and Energy throughout its first two years in power. Early in the 1980 campaign, Reagan had committed himself to these and other "anti-bureaucratic" measures designed to reduce the scope of the federal government. Despite his rhetoric, the administration was unable to agree on a concrete piece of reorganizing legislation to submit to Congress.

Discussions with staff in the Reagan White House, Congress, and among lobbying groups documented that these reorganization commitments were of very low presidential priority—and rightfully so. The GOP congressional leadership, which felt lukewarm about abolishing the agencies in the first place, would not make such legislation high priority. Why, then, should the White House risk losing legislative support on other critical issues by forcing a major struggle over abolishing two departments? A large problem in assessing presidential performance stems from the difference between what is proposed by any administration (drafting legislation, publicly supporting it, and so forth) and committing the necessary political resources to wage battle for congressional and/or other forms of approval.

A third aspect of the question is the shift in the president's agenda priorities over time. Sometimes, as in the Carter administration's dramatic reversal in economic goals from reducing unemployment to reducing inflation, this is related to an unanticipated event. In Carter's case, the unanticipated event was the 13 percent inflation rate during 1979 and 1980. At other points, the shift represents a calculated projection about how the new initiative, inconsistent with the president's original campaign promises as it might be, will affect the incumbent's reelection campaign. Nixon's expansionary economic policies during 1971-1972 are an example. Each president has done a turnabout or deferred action on critical commitments, usually after the midpoint of his first term in office.

Measuring presidential performance

These factors—the inevitable political and personal definition of fulfillment, the flexible range of possible presidential responses, and the shift in priorities as reelection activity mounts—impinge on any effort to assess performance. Such problems notwithstanding, I have developed some broad and crude performance measures for each president since Kennedy, relying heavily on Fred Grogan's categories and research.[40] Naturally, these categories involve considerable subjectivity in their application. The first, for example, is a measure of presidential office activity—executive orders and *proposed* legislation. I compare each campaign pledge that met the criteria of specificity with legislative proposals and executive orders, providing a rough measure of presidential *effort*, not achievement. The following categories were used:

1. *Fully comparable.* The president's proposal met the requirements of the pledge in a complete and comprehensive manner; examples are the Reagan administration's 1981 3-year tax reduction measures and the Carter administration's first welfare reform bill.
2. *Partially comparable.* The president's proposal did not meet the full requirements of the pledge, but still contained large and similar components or represented action that was similar in purpose; examples are the Reagan administration's legislative package on tuition tax credits for private schools and Carter's first set of amendments to the tax code in 1978.
3. *Token action.* The president's proposal represents a gesture, and little more, to the pledge; examples are the Reagan administration's halfhearted support of a constitutional amendment mandating a balanced budget and the Carter administration's final support of the version of Humphrey-Hawkins that provided national economic planning measures, but no specific unemployment remedies.
4. *Contradictory action.* The president's proposal represented the opposite of what was suggested by the pledge; examples are the Reagan administration's support for continuing draft registration and the Carter administration's initial opposition to the deregulation of natural gas.
5. *No action.* Neither legislation nor executive orders could be found that were consistent with the pledge.
6. *Mixed action.* The president's proposal simultaneously met some requirements of the pledge, but went in opposite directions on other parts; examples are the Reagan administration's "deregulation" package for natural gas and aspects of the Carter administration's National Energy Plan.

7. *Indeterminate.* The nature of the pledge or proposal did not permit any classification.

The quantitative results of this classification, applied to the administrations of Kennedy, Johnson, Nixon, Carter, and Reagan are presented in Table 2-3.

It is important to reemphasize the very crude nature of the content analysis and to point out that this is not a comprehensive accounting of each president's policy record. Each president submitted more legislative proposals and issued more executive orders than is represented by the data. The proposals considered here are only those that relate to campaign pledges. The ratio of total presidential activity to proposals stemming from campaign pledges is about 3½ to 1. The Kennedy administration, for example, submitted more than 800 legislative proposals in the two plus years of his presidency, but only 133 campaign pledge-to-presidential proposals are shown in the table.

What conclusions can be drawn from scanning these data? Without question, each president has in fact submitted legislation or signed executive orders that are broadly consistent with about two-thirds of their campaign pledges (the sum of Fully comparable and Partially comparable). The Carter administration led all the others in developing a larger ratio of proposals to pledges. Adding proposals from the first two categories, Fully comparable and Partially comparable, gives a total of 123 proposals from Carter in four years. By comparison, Kennedy took reasonably positive action on 91, Johnson on 40, Nixon on 91, and Reagan on 57. A large part of the difference stems from the point made earlier: Carter promised more of a specific nature during his 1976 campaign than the other four. His record of follow-through is thus higher in terms of aggregate performance. While all these presidents abandoned or deferred some of their campaign pledges once they were in office, most framed legislation or attempted to impose their preferences through executive orders before letting items slip to the bottom of their agendas. Only Nixon reflects a significant tendency to skip any presidential activity whatsoever: 27 percent of his campaign promises were classified "No action" compared with 6 percent for Kennedy, 10 percent for Carter and 9 percent for Reagan.

Ironically, Lyndon Johnson, the president with the most far-reaching innovations in domestic policy during this period, conducted one of the most "promiseless" campaigns of the four. Perhaps this should not be so surprising. James L. Sundquist skillfully traces the origin and planning of the Great Society to the Kennedy administration and before.[41] Johnson's major contribution was in helping to galvanize a large majority into action on what had developed as policy consensus in

Table 2-3 Presidential proposals in relation to campaign promises, Kennedy to Reagan[a]

Type of proposal	Kennedy (1961-1963)	N	Johnson (1965-1968)	N	Nixon (1969-1972)	N	Carter (1977-1980)	N	Reagan[b] (1981-1984)	N
Fully comparable	36%	(49)	41%	(26)	34%	(52)	45%	(84)	35%	(38)
Partially comparable	31	(42)	22	(14)	26	(39)	20	(39)	18	(19)
Token action	6	(8)	8	(5)	5	(7)	11	(19)	9	(10)
Contradictory action	5	(6)	4	(3)	2	(3)	8	(15)	7	(7)
No action	6	(8)	5	(2)	27	(42)	10	(18)	9	(10)
Mixed action	12	(15)	13	(8)	4	(6)	2	(4)	11	(12)
Indeterminate	4	(5)	8	(5)	3	(4)	4	(7)	11	(12)
Totals	100%	(133)	100%	(63)	100%	(153)	100%	(186)	100%	(108)

[a] Data are from the general election period but reflect what is carried over in position papers from the primaries. Coding followed those categories used in Gerald Pomper, *Elections in America* (New York: Dodd, Mead, 1968). The material for Johnson and Nixon is taken from Fred I. Grogan, "Candidate Promise and Presidential Performance, 1964-1972" (Paper presented at the 1977 meeting of the Midwest Political Science Association). Data for Kennedy, Carter, and Reagan are the author's and reflect their *domestic policy commitments only*.

[b] The Reagan data is complete through February 1984.

the Democratic party. This was a major achievement, but one that was accomplished absent a large number of specific campaign proposals.

Moreover, in 1964 Johnson, like Nixon in 1972, Carter in 1980, and Reagan in 1984, was an incumbent. The in-party does not have the incentives to develop the same type of comprehensive campaign agenda for the future that is characteristic of out-party candidates. Neither Nixon nor Carter came close to matching their earlier number of specific promises in their bids for reelection (data not shown).

Incumbents stand or fall on their records and on the hope or fear that four more years will bring more of the same. Reagan's second campaign followed the precedent set by earlier incumbents. Because Johnson was the only president during this period to stand as an incumbent and to complete a term after so standing, it is impossible to know whether his substantial achievements would have been matched by any of the others. Certainly there is little in the multiple-term presidencies of most twentieth century presidents, including Woodrow Wilson, Franklin Roosevelt, and Eisenhower, to suggest they accomplish more, particularly from the viewpoint of campaign pledges. Indeed, a second term, under nonsuccessorship assumptions, frees presidents from paying *much* attention to the coalitions that put them in office, thus further weakening electoral accountability. The policy consequences of this "freedom" have been a very mixed bag. Witness Eisenhower's indifference to the harsh recession of 1958 and Wilson's catastrophe with the League of Nations. Johnson's legendary commitment to passing civil rights legislation and the Great Society programs of the mid-1960s was at least as much a response to his fierce desire to be elected in 1964, after serving out the remainder of Kennedy's term, and, before he withdrew, in 1968, as it was to his own sense of historical mission.

Given the general cynicism about presidential campaigns, the important finding here is what proportion of the campaign agenda presidents are likely to act on. Paul Light argues that this conversion rate is not exceptional: "[while] the president can be expected to convert roughly three out of five campaign promises into policy proposals, the prediction rate is only slightly higher than the toss of a coin, leaving room for considerable presidential discretion." [42]

Of course, his observation is true. Presidents do have substantial discretion in the issues they select to include, emphasize, exclude, or defer in the construction of their agendas. However, his flip-of-the-coin analogy, while statistically accurate, is irrelevant and misleading. It is misleading because the pool of issues from which presidents select their agendas is directly related to what they have emphasized and promised in their campaigns—at least during the early years of their presidencies. Their agendas may not be shaped exclusively by campaigns (to say the least!), but the structure and power of their electoral coalitions, insofar as these groups are reflected in Congress, the executive branch, and among lobbying organizations, impose on presidents and their staffs a policy menu that is far from random, and hence far from what flipping a coin might imply.[43]

A predictable chasm always exists between presidential proposal and actual policy achievements, as every president since the turn of the century has learned. The growing complications and challenge to the Reagan presidency by Congress were hardly unique. His stunning early successes inevitably were followed by major setbacks, a fate shared by every president no matter how skillful they have seemed. A mythology about the congressional relations of Johnson, and even Kennedy, has developed that ignores the very real and significant defeats suffered by these presidents.[44] Yet it is fair to assess the extent to which presidents have redeemed their campaign promises by also looking at their comparative legislative records. Despite the growth of executive power in the twentieth century, most of the specific commitments presidential candidates make are dependent on congressional approval. Clearly, the president is not responsible for Congress, even when both institutions are controlled by the same party, but, because presidential achievement is so dependent on the national legislature, it is necessary to examine aspects of their interaction, particularly as this bears on follow-through. Two broad performance measures are presented in Table 2-4 and Table 2-5.

The first is an assessment of presidential achievement relative to how many of their pledges are dependent on congressional approval, a measure borrowed and adapted from Grogan. The second is Congressional Quarterly's "Presidential Support" voting study, which measures the number of times a member of Congress voted in agreement with the president's stated position. It should be pointed out, however, that CQ's data reflect only those issues that reach the floor for a roll-call vote.

The findings in Table 2-4 quickly underscore the obvious: many of the agenda failures of the last two presidents were a reflection of how their proposals fared in Congress. First, consider Carter. More of his promises were dependent on congressional action (labeled "P/CD"or Presidential/Congressional dependent) than any of his predecessors', and his administration was considerably less successful than those of Kennedy or Johnson, but somewhat more successful than Reagan's, in obtaining favorable action. His record of legislative success is better than Nixon's, who faced a Congress controlled by the opposition party, or Reagan's, who had a divided legislature. Of P/CD proposed legislation that was submitted and that represented full or partial action on their proposals, Kennedy was successful in 81 percent of his requests, Johnson

Table 2-4 From presidential promise to legislation, Kennedy to Reagan

Legislative flow	Kennedy (1961-1963)	Johnson (1965-1968)	Nixon (1969-1972)	Carter (1977-1980)	Reagan (1981-1984)
P/CD promises[a]	59/91=61%	28/40=70%	64/115=56%	90/158=56%	45/70=64%
P/CD proposed legislation passed[b]	48/59=81%	25/28=89%	39/64=61%	64/90=71%	31/45=68%
P/CD promises passed[c]	48/91=53%	25/40=62%	39/115=34%	64/158=41%	31/70=44%

Sources: For coding conventions and Johnson and Nixon data: Fred I. Grogan, "Candidate Promise and Presidential Performance, 1964-1972" (Paper presented at the 1977 meeting of the Midwest Political Science Association). For Kennedy, Carter, and Reagan: author's data.

[a] Presidential/Congressional dependent. For example, the figures here mean that the Carter administration submitted or reported 90 pieces of legislation that met the criteria of "full" or "partial" action on promises made. The figure of 158 represents all promises requiring congressional action; in other words, it excludes executive orders and the "indeterminate" category.

[b] Percentage passed of that submitted.

[c] Percentage passed of *total* requiring congressional action.

Table 2-5   Presidential support in Congress, Kennedy to Reagan

Kennedy		Nixon-Ford	
1961	81%	1974	59%
1962	85%		
1963	87%	Ford	
Kennedy-Johnson		1975	61%
1964	88%	1976	54%
Johnson			
1965	93%	Carter	
1966	79%	1977	75%
1967	79%	1978	78%
1968	75%	1979	77%
Nixon		1980	78%
1969	74%		
1970	77%	Reagan	
1971	75%	1981	82%
1972	66%	1982	72%
1973	51%	1983	67%

Source: *Congressional Quarterly Weekly Report*, Dec. 31, 1983, 2782.

89 percent, Carter 71 percent, Reagan 68 percent, Nixon 61 percent. The differences are further underscored if the reader examines the last line of the table, P/CD promises passed (the ratio of successful legislative struggles to total promises dependent on congressional approval). Here Carter's record (41 percent) is slightly higher than Nixon's (34 percent), considerably less successful than either Johnson's (62 percent) or Kennedy's (53 percent), and slightly lower than Reagan's (44 percent).

Kennedy's legislative success, measured either by my index or CQ's Presidential Support voting study, is a mild surprise. Many of his most important proposals were cleared posthumously—in the last session of the 88th Congress (1964) or during the first year of Johnson's full term (1965). Part of the reason for his high success rate stems from the statistical measures, which include secondary as well as major presidential proposals. Because CQ's Presidential Support score is restricted to those measures reaching the floor for a roll-call vote, the data do not show that many of Kennedy's most important proposals never got that far. Thus, his high support score conceals numerous disappointments at the committee level. Kennedy, nevertheless, was able to score some victories on important bills. Some revisionist scholars have concluded that he was a legislative failure because of his *mixed* record of achievement;[45] others that his record was far better than these revisionists suggest, though not exceptional.[46]

One of Kennedy's most important contributions in dealing with Congress did not involve policy. His Office of Congressional Relations (OCR) was the first that worked exclusively on legislative affairs and, by all accounts, it was one of the best of all the administrations under consideration.[47] While Kennedy's legislative record is not dramatically better or worse than Carter's, the difference between Lawrence O'Brien, Kennedy's legislative liaison chief, and Frank Moore, Carter's congressional assistant, perhaps reflecting a fundamental difference in the political wisdom and skills of Kennedy and Carter, *is* dramatic. Carter's OCR operation improved after 1977, but the damage of numerous initial mistakes dogged it for the remainder of his administration. One of Reagan's great assets was the consistently high quality of his legislative liaison, at least through 1983.

The Carter administration's legislative record looks better if one uses CQ's support score (Table 2-5), although it is still problematic when compared with those of the two earlier Democratic presidents. The contrast is due to the fact that CQ counts most bills on which the president took a position and my count represents only those bills related to campaign pledges. Carter was unable to deliver on many (not all, of course) of those promises made in 1976, even though he framed thoughtful proposals and placed them before Congress. The *perception* that he actually had reneged on most of his promises was widespread, and largely erroneous. This is particularly ironic because, measured against their interest in making good on much of the 1976 campaign, the record of the Carter White House was every bit as strong as that of Kennedy or Johnson. Of course, Carter also reversed direction on the broad contours of his economic and defense policies after 1978, and this fueled the belief that he reneged in a wholesale manner on the promises of 1976.

The Reagan administration, on the other hand, was remarkably successful in its first year—reaching a CQ Presidential Support score that matches Kennedy's and is close to Johnson's even though it faced a Congress that was divided in party control. After the impressive first year, however, Reagan's team began to lose on a growing number of its legislative struggles. The mid-term election of 1982 further weakened the Reagan presidency in Congress; Democrats made a net gain of 26 seats in the House, and moderate Republicans in the Senate, chastened by a number of near defeats, were openly challenging Reagan's agenda in economic, social, and defense policy. Reagan dropped 15 percentage points on the Presidential Support index between 1981 and the end of 1983, falling below Carter's worst year (1977, 75 percent success rate) in 1983 when the Reagan administration prevailed on 67 percent of the roll-call votes. Reagan's congressional performance properly can be characterized as high and focused achievement in 1981-1982, sporadic effort and lower achievement thereafter. The House of Representatives, controlled by Democrats, was particularly consistent in defeating many White House initiatives, and, by 1983, opposed the president on 52 percent of the floor votes. By comparison, the GOP majority in the Senate gave the president a support score of 86 percent.

Selective reversals in campaign agendas

Pressures to modify or fundamentally alter their earlier campaign-related agendas grew substantially in both the Carter and Reagan administrations as they neared, then came out of, the midterm elections. Why? Many of the tensions inherent in the trade-offs of presidential campaign politics are directly transferable to presidential governing politics. But some are not. Other critical aspects of agenda development, unique to governing and absent in campaigning, provide additional clues.

Every president during this period reversed himself or deferred action on major domestic policy commitments stemming from his first campaign, partly in response to unanticipated events, partly because of the different political demands of governing rather than campaigning, and partly as a response to the upcoming reelection struggle. These reversals introduce a major element of uncertainty into the president's agenda.

Agenda unpredictability

Consider the earlier observation about tensions in Democratic party *campaign* agendas: ever since the Roosevelt administration, trade-offs among environmental uncertainty, issue complexity, and the economic claims of the New Deal coalition have been resolved in favor of "New Deal" or comparable solutions. Until recently, Democratic presidential campaigns have encouraged policy commitments of relatively high federal spending, low interest rates, and bountiful money supplies. Recession, not inflation, has been the major economic problem faced by Democratic presidents.

Both Kennedy and Johnson, at least until the economic squeeze of the Vietnam War shifted Johnson's priorities, carried this emphasis into office. The Carter administration moved in precisely the same direction during its first 18 months and then altered course in a dramatic fashion. What caused this change, obviously, was the uncertainty associated with a 7 percent annual inflation rate that then climbed to 13 percent. No Democratic president in recent history had faced such rapidly rising inflation.

Little consensus exists among economists typically associated with the Democrats or liberal members of Congress about appropriate remedies, remedies that are economically and politically feasible. Edward Kennedy's support of wage and price controls during the 1980 primaries, and Carter's opposition to them frequently were portrayed as reflective of a liberal/conservative conflict. In fact, most liberal economists opposed mandatory controls, too, and thus support or opposition to them cannot be used as a useful predictor of liberalism or conservatism within the Democratic party. This leads to the conclusion that unpredictability in Democratic presidential agendas increases dramatically when uncertainty about causes and effects (in this case involving inflation) undercut the legitimacy of New Deal-style solutions. William R. Keech has made an astute observation: Jimmy Carter was sandbagged by the irresponsible economic policies of Lyndon Johnson and Richard Nixon, particularly Nixon. The Nixon administration intentionally overstimulated the economy in 1971 and 1972, seeking to reverse negative voter reactions to its early monetary and fiscal policies. The results of this manipulation affected the economy adversely in both the Ford and Carter presidencies.

The problem of unpredictability in agenda action becomes more intense when a general consensus fails to materialize among the elements of the "old" Democratic party coalition. Energy politics and environmental regulation, as in the struggle over deregulation or clean air standards, are good examples. Liberals, moderates, and conservatives are likely to be identified with each solution, rather than divided along predictable ideological lines.

Further, Norman Furniss and Timothy Tilton have argued persuasively that every Democratic president since and including FDR has encouraged or been forced to conduct a war, sometimes "hot," sometimes "cold," and that the consequences have been devastating for further innovation in their domestic agendas.[48]

A pattern of early attempts to redeem much in the campaign agenda, followed by *selective* reversals, drift, or deferrals, also was characteristic of other administrations. While deferring many commitments, Kennedy avoided major reversals because the agenda he was championing, later incorporated into the "Great Society," was perceived by Kennedy staffers as politically viable, in fact central to his reelection. Reagan, too, deferred important parts of his 1980 campaign agenda but skillfully kept his options open for reiterating his support of them when it was politically advantageous to do so.

Unpredictability in Reagan's agenda

Historically, Republican presidents have had to worry about their commitment to "sound" money and low inflation leading to recession. Supply-side economics attempted to overcome these fears by promising prosperity through heightened investment in private sector economic growth. The extravagant claims made about the beneficial consequences of Reagan's first-year budget policies were confronted shortly thereafter by the harsh reality of a severe recession and its consequences: 1) the highest unemployment rates in the past 30 years; 2) the failure of business investment and savings to increase in the way predicted by supply-side economics; 3) an increase in both the number and rate of business bankruptcies; and 4) a mushrooming federal deficit for fiscal years 1983, 1984, and 1985, deficits that were economically and politically unacceptable to many leaders in both parties. Moreover, the substantial increases in defense spending sought and won by the administration were clearly boomeranging by late 1982; even conservative Republicans and Democrats were looking for ways to alter the administration's defense increases and proposed budget cutbacks in domestic social and economic programs. One White House staffer put it bluntly: "Everyone around here knew our [FY 1984] budget would be dead in the water before it got to Congress." Another, reflecting on the costs and benefits of their early strategy, said:

> I am proud of the way we moved in the first year. We knew it was a high-risk strategy, that we called in a lot of chips, to get those votes for the president's program. Well, some think it failed, others believe that we need more time. Who knows? But I know you won't be surprised when I say that, of course, we're changing some aspects of our program, and of our strategy. 1982 could have been worse [more Republicans could have been defeated] but we don't intend to repeat those errors. Don't underestimate this president. He is flexible!

Because the Reagan White House was extremely sensitive to the political costs of appearing to abandon their 1980 promises ("Look what happened to Carter!" said one staffer) they opted to gamble on emphasizing an upbeat interpretation of some, such as low inflation and the fourth year recovery, while ignoring or finessing others, such as the recession and the deficit. In addition, the legislative components of the president's social agenda, all of which were defeated in Congress during 1981-1984, were still there to be reemphasized or downplayed during the 1984 campaign, depending on political circumstance and coalitional needs.

Selective reversal usually occurs around the midterm elections, when incumbent presidents and their advisers come to believe that the *trade-offs between pursuing the policy commitments of the last campaign and winning the next one substantially favor a shift in the priorities and direction of the old agenda.*

Other barriers to presidential follow-through

Three additional and perhaps obvious factors need mentioning in assessing presidential follow-through and its absence in the presidency. The first can be summarized briefly: pluralism and its discontents.

Presidential campaigns are constituted in such fashion that disparate elements of a party can be absorbed to some extent by verbal concessions on one or two vitally important issues to these groups *and* by appeals for solidarity based on party loyalty and the hope of power.

Governing in the U.S. political system, on the other hand, is constituted in such fashion that leaders and their factions, particularly in Congress, can exact much more than verbal concessions if they are strategically well located and have the power resources and are willing to use them. Thus Sen. Russell Long, D-La., and the interests he represents were much more formidable in shaping Carter's presidential agenda than they were in the campaign process. One Carter staffer put it nicely:

> Long was a good man to have on board during the campaign and he didn't bother us much. Here he's driving us nuts! He's everywhere, on taxes, on trade, on welfare, on health, on Panama—you name it and he's bartering for it. We need him and *he* knows how to use that.

The "textbook" presidency and the expectation it generates consistently depreciate or ignore the independent role of Congress and its influential members in shaping national policy. Hence, *agenda action in the presidency is a trade-off between the degree of policy consensus in the majority party in Congress and the strategic location and resources of potential blocking factions.* Needless to say, blocking factions with considerable resources also exist outside of Congress, in the American economic and cultural structures and in state and governmental units dispersed throughout the society.

The second point is even more basic: uncertainty in the environments presidents face undermines accountability to commitments made during the *last* campaign because all presidents face many unanticipated policy questions. It isn't only American foreign policy that is affected by unpredictable events.

Finally, there is an analysis emerging among party and voting specialists that holds that the decline of party influence has made both electoral and governing coalitions more unstable by increasing the discrepancy between what it takes to win the nomination and what it takes to govern.[49] Despite major changes in delegate selection and nomination rules, particularly those that have led to the dominant position of primaries in the nomination process, it is not certain that these rule changes are responsible for whatever coalitional instability now exists. The rise of candidate-centered coalitions in the primary process has made an important difference, but one would have to look back considerably before Kennedy, perhaps to Roosevelt, to locate the source of an eroding party system and its impact on the stability of governing coalitions. Whatever the specific causes, the decline of party and, with it, the decline of trust and loyalty as important ingredients for encouraging cooperation between Congress and the presidency, has increased the uncertainty of presidential follow-through.

Conclusion

Casual and many not so casual observers of presidential campaigns have been too quick in dismissing these "American melodramas" as little more than the personal competition for power, rather than contests over the establishment of a national agenda. Nor will repeated assertions that elections merely confirm the viability (or bankruptcy) of the "center" move us any closer to understanding the agenda-building functions of campaigns. Candidates often take positions that are truly different. For example, candidate Gerald Ford was prepared to permit Vietnam War resisters to remain in exile as permanent outcasts from this society, while Jimmy Carter went before a national VFW convention and was loudly booed for gently but firmly committing himself to a pardon. Neither position could be explained by the axiom that where "the distribution of opinion conforms to a multivariate normal distribution, the dominant strategy is to take the mean position on each issue."[50] Convergence theories, theories that predict candidates will take similar positions on important issues, simultaneously explain too much and too little.

Platforms and candidate issue papers, ambiguous as they frequently are, provide useful information about the broad contours of future presidential initiatives—even if they are ignored by a vast majority of the voting population. Presidential promises are not ignored, however, by the press, political activists, or by potential rivals for leadership of the party. Although their fates differed, Johnson, Ford, and Carter all learned that reversing directions in their agendas, or, as in Ford's case, not paying sufficient attention to the aspirations of conservative Republicans, can have devastating consequences for their desire to be re-elected. Each paid the price—in primary challenges to his incumbency—for failing to sustain the unity of the party coalitions that put them in power. Again, Ford's case is different, but he, too, failed because the task of party leadership also involves policy leadership in a manner that is broadly acceptable to dominant elements in the party coalitions.

The seasons of presidential politics, from the primaries to the process of governing, reflect different opportunities for agenda development and leadership. Powerful factors in the political and social system reduce the incentives for candidates to advance unambiguous promises about future policy, particularly during the primary and general election seasons. Countervailing pressures, stemming from the coalitional incentives to deliver to important groups, reemerge more strongly at the national conventions. Platforms are not "trivial" or "irrelevant" precisely because public policy, issue stands, and more specific commitments are an important currency in negotiating party unity. Back-channel communication through position papers and targeted group appeals provide reinforcement for wavering supporters as well as more detailed clues about future presidential agendas. All candidates, however, seek to keep their options open, to use symbolic appeals as a substitute for specific policy commitments, to hedge and evade because elections are partly a device for legitimating past or future presidential behavior, independent of which policy choices are selected.

In light of the enormous advantages of remaining ambiguous or contradictory during elections, it is remarkable that candidates *do* make a substantial number of reasonably precise promises. It is even more remarkable that, once elected, every president, from Kennedy through Reagan, has demonstrated considerable good faith, seeking through legislation or executive order to follow through on a majority of his campaign pledges. Each president also has reversed direction or deferred action while in office, sometimes, as in the case of Vietnam policy, with consequences that have reverberated far beyond the geographical confines of the United States.

The quantitative evidence surveyed here challenges conventional assertions about wholesale presidential irresponsibility. Of course these measures are crude, very broad indicators of presidential activity that do not and cannot fully address the complexities of candidate pledge or presidential fulfillment. More detail and analysis is needed to assess these issues properly. The next four chapters, focusing on the Carter and Reagan years, seek to amplify and refine the implications of my agenda-building framework and the quantitative overview presented in this chapter.

Notes _____

1. For good and sensible reasons, most work on presidential selection has focused primarily on other questions. See Robert E. DiClerico and Eric M. Uslaner, *Few Are Chosen: Problems in Presidential Selection* (New York: McGraw-Hill, 1984); Stephen J. Wayne, *The Road to the White House*, 2d ed. (New York: St. Martin's Press, 1984); Nelson Polsby and Aaron Wildavsky, *Presidential Elections*, 6th ed. (New York: Scribner's, 1984); James David Barber, *The Pulse of Politics: The Rhythm of Presidential Elections in the Twentieth Century* (New York: Norton, 1980); John J. Aldrich, *Before the Convention: Strategies and Choices in Presidential Nomination Campaigns* (Chicago: University of Chicago Press, 1980); John H. Kessel, *Presidential Campaign Politics: Coalition Strategies and Citizen Response* (Homewood, Ill.: Dorsey Press, 1980); Herbert Asher, *Presidential Elections and American Politics: Voters, Candidates, and Campaigns Since 1952* (Homewood, Ill.: Dorsey Press, 1980); Stephen J. Brams, *The Presidential Election Game* (New Haven, Conn.: Yale University Press, 1978); James W. Ceaser, *Presidential Selection: Theory and Development* (Princeton: N.J.: Princeton University Press, 1979); Stephen Hess, *The Presidential Campaign* (Washington, D.C.: Brookings Institution, 1978); William R. Keech and Donald R. Matthews, *The Party's Choice* (Washington, D.C.: Brookings Institution, 1977); Donald R. Matthews, ed. *Perspective on Presidential Selection* (Washington, D.C.: Brookings Institution, 1973); and the classic by Paul T. David et al., *The Politics of National Party Conventions* (Washington, D.C.: Brookings Institution, 1960).

2. As in fact they sometimes appear to be. Lyndon B. Johnson campaigned in ways that suggested the opposite of what he and his advisers were planning—military intervention. See James A. Nathan and James Oliver, *United States Foreign Policy and World Order*, 2d ed. (Boston: Little, Brown, 1981), 327-329; New York Times, *The Pentagon Papers* (New York: Bantam Books, 1971), especially 274-287; and Daniel Ellsberg, *Papers on the War* (New York: Simon & Schuster, 1972).

3. ABC News, Oct. 11, 1976.

4. Reported by Charles Seib in *Washington Post*, Oct. 22, 1976.

5. Throughout the book, I use the terms "agenda," "issue," "program," and "policy" interchangeably. Following Roger W. Cobb and Charles D. Elder, the concept "agenda" is used to mean "a general set of political controversies that will be viewed at any point in time as falling within the range of legitimate concerns meriting the attention of the polity." Cobb and Elder further distinguish between "systemic" and "institutional" agendas. The former refers to problems and solutions that are much more abstract and general and that may or may not correspond to the items of an institutional agenda. The latter is more concrete, usually represented by a formal specification of problems and solutions in legislative calendars, court dockets, presidential messages, platforms, and so forth. Campaign agendas seem to be a mix of systemic and institutional phenomena. Much of their work is concerned with broad and comparative system-level generalizations, far beyond the more narrow focus here. See Cobb and Elder, *Participation in American Politics: The Dynamics of Agenda-Building* (Boston: Allyn & Bacon, 1972); Cobb et al., "Agenda-Building as a Comparative Political Process," *American Political Science Review* 70 (March 1976): 126-138. For an application of agenda-setting theory as it applies to circumstances involving the

"required" and "discretionary" agendas in the Senate, see Jack L. Walker, "Setting Agendas in the U.S. Senate: A Theory of Problem Selection," *British Journal of Political Science* 7 (October 1977): 423-445. The notion of "required" used by Walker for the Senate (annual cycles in the budget, for example) is quite different from what one might specify for the "organized anarchies" of presidential campaigns, although, as I attempt to show, the coalitional incentives anchored in historic differences between the parties provide a rough equivalent. I am using the dictionary definition of "displacement"—"to supplant, ignore, take the place of"—rather than in the psychological sense of shifting attention from an appropriate to an inappropriate object, as in the early work of Harold Lasswell or later studies.

6. Conversations with Hugh Bone of the University of Washington helped me with a variety of problems on this question. If both parties provide identical solutions to problems, then it is true that the potential for agenda formation still exists, although a voter's choice is irrelevant. If neither party takes clear positions on any issue, then one cannot assert the elections are necessary for agenda setting.

7. Polsby and Wildavsky, *Presidential Elections*, 270-284.

8. Ibid., 26-27.

9. Ibid.

10. Benjamin I. Page, *Choices and Echoes in Presidential Elections* (Chicago: University of Chicago Press, 1978). Also useful in this respect are John H. Kessel, "The Seasons of Presidential Politics," *Social Science Quarterly* 58 (December 1977): 418-435; his earlier *The Goldwater Coalition* (Indianapolis: Bobbs-Merrill, 1968); and Hess, *The Presidential Campaign*, 53-66.

11. Page, *Choices and Echoes*, 161.

12. Ibid.

13. Murray Edelman, *The Symbolic Uses of Politics* (Urbana: University of Illinois Press), 15.

14. E. E. Schattschneider, *The Semisovereign People* (Hinsdale, Ill.: Dryden Press, 1960; reissued 1975).

15. Peter Bachrach and Morton S. Baratz, *Power and Poverty: Theory and Practice* (New York: Oxford University Press, 1970), 43.

16. I am indebted to one of my former graduate students, Eric S. Moskowitz, for forcefully (through the persuasiveness of his work) getting me to reconsider my own "mobilization of bias." Although I am still a nonbeliever, see Clauss Offe, "Political Authority and Class Structures—An Analysis of Late Capitalist Societies," *International Journal of Sociology* 2 (Spring 1972): 73-108. Two general texts on American government using aspects of this perspective are Edward S. Greenberg, *American Government: A Radical Approach* (Boston: Little, Brown, 1982) and Ira Katznelson and Mark Kesselman, *The Politics of Power* (New York: Harcourt Brace Jovanovich, 1975).

17. Norman Furniss and Timothy Tilton, *The Case for the Welfare State: From Social Security to Social Equality* (Bloomington: Indiana University Press, 1977). Furniss and Tilton formulate and analyze a series of important distinctions between the "Positive State" (the United States), the "Social Security State" (Great Britain) and the "Social Welfare State" (Sweden).

18. This contention depends on how one defines "socialism." Some socialists, like Michael Harrington or Irving Howe, move in and out of this range, depending on time, place, and circumstance. Whether the results of the "Second Reconstruction" in civil rights are permanent or temporary is

unanswerable, although it's hard to see how certain aspects, such as the legal attributes of civil rights, could be reversed unless extraordinary transformations occur in the future. On this see Freeman Pollard, "The Transformation of Political Culture in Alabama" (Ph.D. diss., Indiana University, 1981).

19. Daniel Metlay, "On Studying the Future Behavior of Complex Systems," in *Organized Social Complexity: Challenge to Politics and Policy*, ed. Todd R. LaPorte (Princeton, N.J.: Princeton University Press, 1975), 220-255.

20. The poignancy of this tension is illustrated in Hubert Humphrey's autobiography, *The Education of a Public Man: My Life and Politics* (Garden City, N.J.: Doubleday, 1976).

21. Edward R. Tufte, *Political Control of the Economy* (Princeton, N.J.: Princeton University Press, 1978). Tufte's assertions are challenged by Richard Winters et al., "Political Behavior and Public Policy," in *The Handbook of Political Behavior*, vol. 5, ed. Samuel Long (New York: Plenum Press, 1981), 39-111.

22. Henry W. Chappell, Jr., and William R. Keech, "Welfare Consequences of the Six-year Term Evaluated in the Context of a Model of the U.S. Economy," *American Political Science Review* 77 (March 1983): 75-96.

23. Kessel, "The Seasons of Presidential Politics."

24. These phrases receive meticulous elaboration in Kessel, *Presidential Campaign Politics*.

25. Reviews and findings are provided by Aldrich, *Before the Convention*; Page, *Choices and Echoes in Presidential Elections*; and Brams, *The Presidential Election Game*.

26. Gerald M. Pomper, with Susan S. Lederman, *Elections in America*, 2d ed. (New York: Longman, 1980); Benjamin Ginsberg, "Elections and Public Policy," *American Political Science Review* 70 (March 1976): 41-49; Paul T. David, "Party Platforms as National Plans," *Public Administration Review* 31 (May 1971): 303-315; and a rarely cited but first-class development study by John P. Bradley, "Party Platforms and Party Performance Concerning Social Security," *Polity* 1 (Spring 1969): 337-358.

27. David, "Party Platforms," 303-304.

28. Doris A. Graber, "Press Coverage Patterns of Campaign News: The 1968 Presidential Race," *Journalism Quarterly* 48 (Fall 1971): 502-512; Doris A. Graber, "Personal Qualities in Presidential Images: The Contribution of the Press," *Midwest Journal of Political Science* 16 (February 1972): 46-76; and Thomas Patterson, *The Mass Media Election* (New York: Praeger, 1980).

29. On these themes, see David L. Paletz, "Candidates and the Mass Media in the 1976 Presidential Elections," in *Parties and Elections in an Anti-Party Age: American Politics and the Crisis of Confidence*, ed. Jeff Fishel (Bloomington: Indiana University Press, 1978), 256-261; Michael J. Robinson and Margaret A. Sheehan, *Over the Wire and On T.V.* (New York: Russell Sage Foundation, 1983); David L. Paletz and Robert M. Entman, *Mass Media Power Politics* (New York: Free Press, 1981); Michael B. Grossman and Martha J. Kumar, *Portraying the President: The White House and the News Media* (Baltimore: Johns Hopkins University Press, 1981); Richard Rubin, *Press, Party, and Presidency* (New York: Norton, 1981); Thomas E. Patterson, *The Mass Media Election: How Americans Choose Their President* (New York: Praeger, 1980); Stephen Hess, *The Washington Reporters* (Washington, D.C.: Brookings Institution, 1981); Doris Graber, *Mass Media and American Politics*, 2d ed. (Washington, D.C.: CQ Press, 1984); William C. Adams, ed., *Television Coverage of the 1980 Campaign* (Washington, D.C.: Ablex Publications, 1982); James David Barber, *Race for*

the Presidency: The Media and the Nominating Process (New York: Prentice-Hall, 1978); Thomas E. Patterson and Robert D. McClure, *The Unseeing Eye* (New York: G. P. Putnam's Sons, 1976); Timothy Crouse, *The Boys on the Bus* (New York: Random House, 1973); and the classic study by Kurt Lang and Gladys Engel Lang, *Politics and Television* (Chicago: Quadrangle Books, 1968).

30. Pomper, *Elections in America*, 236-237. Of Pomper's six types of future pledges, I retained the four requiring the most specificity, eliminating his categories, "Rhetorical" and "General pledges." See n. 40 for additional details about sources and methodology.

31. Ibid.

32. Ibid.

33. Ibid.

34. Ibid.

35. Stu Eizenstat and David Rubenstein, "Memorandum to President-Elect Carter: Campaign Promises" (Washington, D.C.: Carter Transition Planning Group, Memorandum, dated Nov. 30, 1976; released Feb. 17, 1977.

36. Republican National Committee, Division of Public Affairs, *Promises, Promises—An RNC Republican Accountability Project* (Washington, D.C.: Republican National Committee, 1978, 1979, 1980). The Democrats published a comparable volume in 1984, assessing President Reagan's record: Democratic Congressional Campaign Committee, *The 1980 Campaign Promises of Ronald Reagan* (Washington, D.C.: Democratic Congressional Campaign Committee, 1984).

37. See n. 40 for further details.

38. U.S. House of Representatives, Committee on House Administration, 95th Cong., 2d sess., *The Presidential Campaign 1976: Jimmy Carter*, vol. 1, parts 1 and 2 (Washington, D.C.: U.S. Government Printing Office, 1978), 879.

39. Data from *The Record of President Jimmy Carter on Women's Issues* (Washington, D.C.: Carter/Mondale Presidential Committee, 1980).

40. Fred Grogan, "Candidate Promise and Presidential Performance: 1964-1972" (Paper delivered at the 1977 annual meeting of the Midwest Political Science Association). Treating my findings for Kennedy, Carter, and Reagan as comparable to his for Johnson and Nixon poses some methodological problems. First, Grogan included foreign policy pledges for his two presidents: 14 of Johnson's 63 promises and 36 of Nixon's 153 were classified as foreign policy. This reduces their domestic policy totals to 49 and 117 respectively. His brief analysis of fulfillment distinguishes between foreign policy and domestic areas, and the percentage he lists as "kept and not kept" is virtually identical for the two areas, suggesting that in *statistical* terms the same *general* pattern holds for domestic and foreign policy. However, there is no way the researcher can be certain, so more than the usual caution is required. Second, no tests of intercoder reliability were possible between us and we may, therefore, be using different standards. More important, the written record of the Reagan, Carter, and Kennedy general election campaigns, particularly issue-relevant information, may be more complete. The findings reported in Table 2-3 may understate the number of promises made by Nixon and Johnson.

   For Kennedy, the source was two volumes published by the U.S. Senate, Committee on Commerce, Subcommittee on Freedom of Communication, 87th Cong., 1st sess., *The Campaign Speeches of John F. Kennedy* (Washington, D.C: U.S. Government Printing Office, 1961); for Carter, the source was the author's collection of issue papers and campaign speeches, plus U.S. House of Representatives, Committee on House Administration, 95th Cong., 2d sess., *The Presidential Campaign 1976: Jimmy Carter,* vol. 1, parts 1 and 2 (Washington, D.C.: U.S. Government Printing Office, 1978). The Carter organization released a total of 184 issue papers from December 1975 to November 1976. These ranged in length from a three-paragraph statement on abortion to a 14-page document on the economy. Of the total, 94 issue papers were released before the convention, 90 after. Many of the latter were rewrites of the former. The House Administration Committee also prepared volumes on Gerald Ford's 1976 campaign and sponsored their publication in 1979.

Despite the active interest of committee staff in repeating the process in 1980, the House Administration Committee decided against doing it. To my knowledge, therefore, no official policy-relevant record of Reagan's 1980 campaign exists. A record of Carter's major speeches can be found in *Weekly Compilation of Presidential Documents,* and *Public Papers of the Presidents of the United States.* I lobbied friends in Congress to keep the committee's 1976 effort going but with no luck. Warren Miller, then of Michigan's ICPR, and John Kessel of Ohio State University also worked to persuade relevant people in Congress of the historical and scholarly importance of such information. Perhaps others can bring some weight to bear in the future; it seems an eminently worthwhile activity for Congress or another institution to sponsor. The major source for Reagan is the author's collection of issue press releases, organized under the "Reagan for President" imprimatur, and kindly made available by Michael Baroody, who was the public affairs director at the RNC, and Reagan's major speeches and secondary reports in *Congressional Quarterly Weekly Report.* The Reagan campaign organization distributed 91 issue press releases from January 1 through November 1980, most of which were prepared during the primaries.

41. James L. Sundquist, *Politics and Policy* (Washington, D.C.: Brookings Institution, 1968).

42. Paul Light, *The President's Agenda* (Baltimore: Johns Hopkins University Press, 1983), 96.

43. Light's interview data suggest that campaigns and platforms are less important as sources of ideas (20 percent of his White House respondents mentioned them) than are Congress (51 percent), events and crises (51 percent), executive branch (46 percent), or public opinion (27 percent). The problem with his assessment is that the *broad* policy concerns of the president's associates in Congress and the executive branch are also likely to be reflected in the platform and his campaign promises, even if specific legislative details are not. Much of the platform is a reflection, not a determinant, of policy that is percolating in other institutions. Light's other contention, that presidents and their staffs spend much of their time reacting to events, mini-crises, other "external" sources, is certainly true. Indeed the reactive nature of presidential agenda formation grows as presidents spend more time in office. See his analysis, *The President's Agenda,* 81-103.

44. For a more balanced view on this issue, see John F. Manley, "Presidential Power and White House Lobbying," *Political Science Quarterly* 93 (Summer 1978): 255-275; George Edwards III, *Presidential Influence in Congress* (San Francisco: Freeman, 1980).

45. Revisionist positions will be found in the work of Gary Wills, *The Kennedy*

Imprisonment (New York: Simon & Schuster, 1982); Henry Fairlie, *The Kennedy Promise* (New York: Doubleday, 1973); Louis J. Paper, *The Promise and the Performance: The Leadership of John F. Kennedy* (New York: Crown, 1975); and the work of Bruce Miroff, a political scientist who questions the moral and strategic assumptions of "pragmatic" liberalism in the presidency: *Pragmatic Illusions: The Presidential Politics of John F. Kennedy* (New York: McKay, 1976).

46. John Hart, "Assessing Presidential Leadership," *Political Studies* (December 1980): 567-578; John Hart, "Kennedy, Congress, and Civil Rights," *American Studies* (1979): 165-178. Randall Ripley provides a good statistical and analytic overview of Kennedy's record in *Kennedy and Congress* (Morristown, N.J.: General Learning Press, 1972). Another scholar, James L. Sundquist, rejects the contention that Kennedy was a failure and details the gradual progress the administration was making through late 1963. See *Politics and Policy: The Eisenhower, Kennedy and Johnson Years* (Washington, D.C.: Brookings Institution, 1968), particularly pp. 471-506.

47. A point stressed in Hart, "Assessing Presidential Leadership," and his more recent, "Staffing the Presidency: Kennedy and the Office of Congressional Relations," *Presidential Studies Quarterly* (Winter 1983): 101-110.

48. Furniss and Tilton, *The Case for the Welfare State.*

49. Lester G. Seligman, "Electoral and Governing Coalitions in the Presidency," *Congress and the Presidency* (Autumn 1983): 125-147; Nelson Polsby, *Consequences of Party Reform* (New York: Oxford University Press, 1983); and the essays by Anthony King, Austin Ranney, and Jeane J. Kirkpatrick in *The New American Political System*, Anthony King, ed. (Washington, D.C.: American Enterprise Institute, 1978).

50. Benjamin Page undertakes a compelling and comprehensive critique of formal spatial theories in his *Choices and Echoes in Presidential Elections.*

Presidential campaigns from the outside, southern style: the promises of Jimmy Carter

3

Contact is the appreciation of differences.

—Fritz Perls

Republicans hedge against the future; Democrats confound it.

Leading students of the party system had been predicting ominous consequences for the Democrats in 1976 because of the previous eight years of severe political polarization, extensive rule changes in the nomination process, and the accelerating decline of the old party system.

From the perspective of the 1980s, after a crippled Carter administration was defeated by Republicans, one may need to be reminded of an important fact about the 1976 Democratic convention: despite all the predictions to the contrary, the first nomination of James Earl Carter was a love-in, supported by every major element in the Democratic coalition, liberal and conservative. And, as is the case with many marriages between near strangers—Carter was a comparatively unknown ex-governor of Georgia when he stunned the Democratic establishment with his first victory in New Hampshire—the disillusionment that followed was traumatic.

Think back, if you can, to the scene on that warm New York night in July at the 1976 convention and hear Martin Luther King, Sr., say of this leader of a mostly white, southern political faction: "Surely, the Lord sent Jimmy Carter to come on out and bring America back where she belongs." The nomination of a southerner in 1976, even one as moderate on race issues as Carter, was a moving symbol of how powerful is the unpredictable in American politics.

Despite these surprises, the agenda-building processes of the 1976 Carter campaign were highly consistent with many of the propositions stated in the previous chapter. He did *not* "waffle" on the issues any more than other presidential candidates of recent memory; he was *not* a southern conservative masquerading as a northern moderate or liberal; he was *not* a born-again Baptist running to impose his special religious vision on the rest of the country; he was *not* an incessantly smiling con man, hiding a Nixonesque character flaw. A shrewd commentator pegs this ex-president accurately: "Carter the Conscientious spoke the language of moral revival,"[1] a rhetorical style he shared with earlier candidates like Woodrow Wilson, Wendell Wilkie, and Barry Goldwater, even if his accent and ideology were different.

Underneath this style, one that unnerved reporters and others preoccupied with the "Character Question," the Carter organization was forging a policy agenda that was vintage New Deal/Fair Deal/Great Society. With a few Carter twists, of course. Carter emphasized a concern for fiscal austerity and a contempt for the "pork-barrel" projects cherished by many old-line Democrats, and these emphases were later to prove an important destabilizing factor in the Democratic coalition. But, in content and specificity, most of his major campaign proposals were similar to all Democratic nominees since 1960.

The intent of this chapter is to explore this assertion and its implications by tracing the Carter campaign through the electoral seasons of presidential politics in 1976.

Southerners as outsiders in presidential politics _____

For candidates of the out-party, winning, or at least not losing, the most important primaries has been a necessary if not sufficient condition for successful nomination since John F. Kennedy demolished the party regulars in 1960. Indeed, the most important recent institutional change has been the growth in the number of primaries. The number of states using primaries to select Democratic delegates almost doubled from 16 in 1968 to 31 in 1980, then declined in 1984 to 25. National conventions serve increasingly to ratify nomination decisions made in the primaries. This is not an iron-clad rule, however, and there are some notable exceptions like the 1976 Ford-Reagan tussle.[2]

Accordingly, winning presidential strategies now depend on clever media use, the development of skilled field and operations staff, careful planning, access to and intelligent use of money, exploitation of some important issues, and superhuman qualities of physical endurance. All of these, as numerous commentators have argued, increase the importance of candidate-based organizations and diminish the classic role of political parties, opening the process to ambitious and skillful outsiders.

"Outsider" in what sense? Frequently the term is synonymous with anyone not formally or informally endorsed by the Washington and national political party establishment. Or sometimes a candidate not intimately known by the national press corps and the top layers of Washington politicians is labeled an outsider. Democratic senator Gary Hart is the most obvious recent example. George McGovern was mistakenly considered an outsider on the second criteria—ideologically speaking—even if he was, or should have been, a known quantity in Washington. Ronald Reagan, too, was considered an outsider, although he had been a visible and powerful force in Republican politics since 1968. The concept of the outsider is elusive and ambiguous. Yet candidates, their staffs, and the media act as if it carries fairly specific campaign imperatives.

From the first planning documents, written by Gerald Rafshoon and Hamilton Jordan in 1972, four years before the primaries were to begin, the Carter organization was guided by a classic outsider strategy. Its first thrust was to increase his visibility as "presidential material," another notoriously elusive concept, in the national news media and among the small number of activists who constitute an informal screening elite—"The Great Mentioners," as Russell Baker once called them. Key individuals from the media and elsewhere were carefully selected and invited to Georgia for backgrounders. A small and energetic staff, under Tim Kraft, conducted early organizational forays into Iowa and Florida, all because of those states' media, *not* delegate, value. This part of the Carter story is well known and need not be retold here. The other part, more important from the viewpoint of presidential agenda building and less understood because less glamorous, involves issue development.

Carter was perceived as an outsider, not only politically and geographically, but also ideologically. Like any southerner, even a moderate, he needed to prove that he fit northern expectations on the major issues with which the Democratic party had been identified since the New Deal. Thus, the second part of Carter's strategy, one that was to haunt him throughout his presidency, consciously focused on overcoming stereotypes about white southern conservatism.

Carter's positioning in the 1973-1975 preprimary period and in the first wave of primaries (through Pennsylvania) was geared to the pitch that he was "a national Democrat in the tradition of FDR, Harry Truman, John Kennedy, and Lyndon Baines Johnson." One staff member, who joined the campaign in late 1975, put it this way:

> Jimmy [virtually all Carter's staff, from paperpushers to heavyweights called him "Jimmy," "the candidate," or "the governor"] may refer to himself as a "fiscal conservative," but he's just as progressive as Udall, Humphrey, or Jackson on major economic and social issues. When he says "fiscal conservative" he means he believes in tough performance standards for spending, unlike a lot of liberals in Congress. He was on record very early in support of a national health care system, welfare reform, increased aid to cities, and for public works projects and public service jobs in much greater abundance than we've seen ... this thing about "fuzziness" is a cheap shot, usually made by reporters who won't read what we give them or supporters of the other candidates who are trying to make him seem like a southern reactionary. It just isn't true.

Another staffer tied Carter's main social and economic ideology to many "tough-minded and thoughtful liberals" in Congress and to the work of the DNC's Democratic Policy Council, which later became the Advisory Council of Elected Public Officials. Both these groups were the source of countless economic and social task forces:

> Carter did more than use his position on the Democratic Campaign Committee to make contacts around the country. He made sure that people in Congress and around the country knew that he was a progressive just like them ... and that he also understood, having run in a state like Georgia, the difficulty of running when the opposition keeps accusing you of being a wild spender. ... Further, he went out of his way to make sure that others knew he was supportive of many ... not all, of course ... of the goals and recommendations of the Joint Economic Committee in Congress and the advisory policy council.

The Carter campaign released 13 "issue statements" between the day he formally announced, December 12, 1975, and the New Hampshire primary, which took place in February. The statements were devoted to clearing up any doubts about his commitment to conventional Democratic social/economic programs, although they also insisted on "comprehensive, rational, business-like management evaluation" for existing and new programs. His frequent use of stump rhetoric, which emphasized conservative approaches to social/economic programs, and the simultaneous use of informal contact and issue papers, which endorsed traditional liberal approaches, was bound to generate doubt and suspicion. Without question, the Carter administration was plagued by the same tension.

Once these ambiguities had become apparent, Carter himself, of course, did much during the campaign to sustain them. One study of his positions noted that Carter frequently would say: "I'm a fiscal conservative" and then go on to explain that "the essence of conservatism is an orderly, logical, and planned approach to problems and the allocation of public funds. . . . [Meanwhile,] prominent members of his staff would be telling reporters that 'Jimmy is a Keynesian on the budget.' " [3] Needless to say, these contradictions drove many reporters up the wall. And the contradictions were clearly linked to an early primary strategy. One member on the field operations side of the campaign said:

> Let me tell you what we faced. We had to make sure that everyone got the message that Jimmy was not antilabor, antiliberal on economic issues. Labor, however, was in the hip pocket of Jackson, and liberals were all over the map, with Harris, Bayh, Udall, and Shriver. There was no center among Democrats, and I mean *among* Democrats, not between Republicans and Democrats, which is another thing. So, we figured we had to carve out the Democratic center, while not completely alienating labor or the liberals, who we figured would come to us later. Jimmy was better and less belligerent than Jackson on foreign affairs, and he was more prudent and tougher than any of the so-called liberal candidates on economic issues. And as far as the voters were concerned, this was not going to be a big issue year, like it was in 1972. Democrats wanted someone who would concentrate on unemployment, keep the country out of another war like Vietnam, and who could be trusted for his honesty and integrity but who also was a good Democrat, not associated with the mess in Washington. New Hampshire was ready-made for us.

From the viewpoint of agenda development, the early primary period thus demonstrated a variation on the following coalitional strategy: hold the potential support of northern groups through back-channel issue agreement; obtain and expand the voting base by displacing as much issue concern as one could on other factors—trust and integrity, for example—through mass media front channels. This finding is quite different from what one would expect by using John Kessel's argument about the season of nomination politics. Kessel suggests that the "nomination season" reflects a larger concern with issue development.[4] As candidates move closer to the convention and become more specific on measures of most importance to party members, however, Kessel's reasoning begins to apply more forcefully to Carter.

Beginning with preparations for the Pennsylvania primary and culminating with the Democratic platform and Carter's acceptance speech, the Carter campaign systematically attempted to beef up and clarify an agenda that would be acceptable to liberals and organized labor. This was less the result of a comprehensive plan than it was a reaction to unanticipated events, the coalition incentives to deliver, and the policy and electoral claims of the New Deal coalition, all of which were geared to the strategic realities of leading a (more or less) united Democratic party in the fall of 1976.

The most widely publicized unanticipated event (other than Carter's increasing number of primary victories) of the midprimary season was the "ethnic purity" flap. Jules Witcover wrote:

> The whole business started obscurely enough in an airplane interview on April 2, the Friday before the New York and Wisconsin primaries [and three weeks before the Pennsylvania primary]. As Carter's entourage flew across upstate New York, Carter sat in the forward compartment . . . and answered questions posed by Sam Roberts, chief political correspondent for the New York *Daily News*. . . . [After saying that he was opposed to federally sponsored scatter-site housing, Carter elaborated:] "But to artificially inject another racial group in a community? I see nothing wrong with ethnic purity being maintained. I would not permit discrimination against a family moving into the neighborhood." [5]

The remark was ignored by the press until CBS directed its correspondent to ask Carter to clarify his statement, a request that wasn't fulfilled until April 6. Carter, in an Indianapolis airport interview, attempted to explain what he meant by "ethnic purity," but to no avail. The conflict rapidly escalated with the Congressional Black Caucus, including Carter's most important black adviser, Andrew Young, sending a telegram denouncing the statement. Carter finally apologized publicly two days later, and the Carter staff organized a large rally in Atlanta with numerous speeches from members of the local black community calling for support for Carter.

Meanwhile, Carter moved closer to publicly supporting an "amended" version of the Humphrey-Hawkins Full Employment Act, a decision particularly important to black leaders and toward which he had been slowly moving for months. Support of this bill was a litmus test for many liberals in the Democratic party.[6] Simultaneously, the Carter staff accelerated its search for top staff and speech writers who would provide them with added credentials in northern liberal circles. One staff member, who had been with Carter before New Hampshire, described the events of the period in this fashion:

> The ethnic purity statement and the overreaction of the press really caused a crisis around here. . . . We had just begun to beef up the issues and speech-writing section after Florida, had gotten Leonard Woodcock [president of the United Auto Workers] and some other labor coalition people on board for good, Patt Derian and Mary King were taking the lead with women activists, Andy Young and others were scoring for Jimmy with major black leaders in the north . . . and then the shit hit the fan in Indianapolis. . . . Frankly, I don't understand most of the knee-jerk liberals in Washington. Jimmy was defending a program and building support in a way they should have supported but one misphrased line and they were calling him a racist. Well, all you have to do is talk to any black people here in Georgia and you'd know what a crock that is.

Moreover, Young, who had been with Carter from the beginning, observed that "blacks were much less disturbed than white liberals by the statement," even though he reluctantly joined the Black Caucus in calling for a public apology. Black support for Carter was critical to his coalitional strategy because it legitimized his claim that he should be supported by white liberals. A comparable strategy in the 1980 renomination struggle, in which blacks again disproportionately supported Carter, was not as successful because Ted Kennedy was able to score heavily among prominent white and black progressives. In 1976, however, no other candidate matched Carter's success with black voters, a success that finally brought northern black leaders like Jesse Jackson into the Carter fold. It should be noted, too, that suspicions about Carter's progressive credentials were deeply felt among many black leaders in 1976, a fact that is often overlooked by his striking success among black *voters*. Despite Young's vigorous campaigning, most black leaders followed, rather than led, their constituencies into the Carter camp.

The larger issue, beyond civil rights, was Carter's general acceptability as a moderately progressive Democrat. Suspicions were to persist throughout the primaries (growing during his presidency) even though Carter operatives, in conjunction with others, were moving toward writing a Democratic platform that George McGovern would call "more progressive, humane, and forward-looking than that of 1972."

At the convention: platforms as symbols and commitments

The process of constructing a Democratic platform four years earlier in 1972, when reform, anti-war, McGovern Democrats were bitterly opposed by major figures in the AFL-CIO and by many party regulars like the Daley organization from Chicago, had been wild and acrimonious. The actual content of that platform was not "extremist," as some regulars had misleadingly charged. Quite the contrary: McGovern and his staff had followed normal brokerage strategies, conceding some important issues to less progressive leaders in the hope of gaining their campaign support in the fall.[7] The belief that McGovern and his organization were radicals, a belief without foundation in fact, and brilliantly used by Republicans later on, persisted throughout the campaign and into 1976.[8]

Beliefs are frequently more powerful than reality. The fact that Democrats *had* changed the platform-writing process in 1972, encouraging widespread participation by all sorts of groups even before a draft document was available, reinforced fear among Carter operatives and other Democrats that they would "lose control" again in 1976, a fear that was epidemic among professionals wishing to heal the wounds of four years earlier.

But Carter faced the ticklish problem of gaining support among those, precisely those, who had been McGovern supporters four years earlier. As previously noted, all platforms reflect a curious paradox of the nomination system: many people, including those who help draft them, dismiss the documents as "meaningless," "not the major issue," "irrelevant," and so forth. But politicians are willing to spend enormous amounts of time and energy, sometimes locked in protracted and bitter conflict, struggling over acceptable language. Why? Because neither the development nor content of party platforms is in fact meaningless; rather they reflect the trade-off between what the front-runner considers politically acceptable and the influence of constituent leaders who want to expand or restrict the scope of the candidate's future presidential agenda.

Representatives of the Carter campaign came into the first national platform hearings, held in Washington, May 17-20, 1976, concerned about meeting two goals: 1) articulating support for a program that would be acceptable to organized labor, congressional leaders, and liberals who were still holding out for Morris Udall, Frank Church, or Gov. Jerry Brown, as well as the few who still wanted Hubert Humphrey, and 2) supporting DNC head Robert Strauss in his effort to create a drafting subcommittee that would be "responsible" and "representative." [9] The fact that many issues tended to split organized labor, various liberals, and congressional leaders into antagonistic groups was handled by Carter representatives in classic fashion: simplifying and segmenting a program that might carry inherent contradiction. One Carter delegate, who was on the drafting subcommittee, put it this way:

> I see my job as communicating to others the very fine record that Governor Carter has already established in the primaries. This is the first time I've met a lot of the Udall people, and they seem a little surprised when I lay it out about his stands on environmental and conservation issues or on amnesty, civil rights, and affirmative action. . . . We're trying to keep candidate politics out of this, although of course that's probably impossible.

Asked about other groups, like labor, with which Carter was having trouble, the same delegate said:

> Same thing and much exaggerated, I might add. Jimmy's positions on jobs and the economy just haven't gotten through. We're committed to programs that will drastically lower unemployment, really get the economy moving again, doing a lot about industrial stagnation. Our labor people are not getting that message across. . . . I think the platform we're going to write is going to bring all of us together, and

there's no doubt it's going to be a progressive platform because that's what all Democratic factions want.

While Carter was clearly the front-runner by the time these initial hearings were held, three important primaries, California, New Jersey, and Ohio, were slightly more than two weeks off, and the Michigan and Maryland contests were decided in the middle of the hearings. Naturally, hallway gossip was saturated on May 19 and 20 by the "beauty contest" victory of Brown in Maryland (Carter won a majority of delegates) and the narrow Carter victory in Michigan. From the viewpoint of one Udall supporter, Udall's Michigan defeat put a virtual end to his chances. It also reinforced her desire to "hold Carter to the fire" on "basic progressive" positions:

> We still have a chance in Ohio, I guess, but I'm very depressed. We were so close. This makes what's going on here even more important. He [Carter] has just been so two-faced and the platform will be the place where his evasions and equivocations stop. Everybody I've talked to here, even some of his own people, are convinced we can nail down a strong set of commitments in the platform. We'll see.

The actual hearings produced the typically large (more than 140) parade of witnesses, from Michael Harrington speaking for "Democracy '76" (an indefatigable coalition builder, he was later much in evidence at the task force working sessions) to Hubert Humphrey, providing his usual virtuoso performance, exhorting delegates to "do their duty for those without resources in America." One unusual presentation was given by Thomas P. "Tip" O'Neill, Jr., who was the House Majority Leader. He summarized a 125-page platform report supported by the Democratic leadership in the House. The report, prepared over the previous six months under the direction of Joseph Murphy, a long-time Hill staffer, with the assistance of House committee and subcommittee chairs, was unique in the history of twentieth century Congresses. Unsurprisingly, it emphasized economic problems, mostly unemployment, providing formalized back-channel communication to Carter and his staff. While the proposals probably were anticipated by Carter issues personnel, the document was treated seriously as a set of policy and political messages from the House Democratic leadership. One Carter person later said:

> There was some tension between staff on the Platform Committee at the DNC and staff on the Speaker's Commission on the Platform, although it never got out of hand. We used some material from the report in preparing background papers and never felt their positions were much different from ours except on defense spending, where they called for a "prudent increase," or something like that, and Jimmy is on record and serious about a decrease. It was passed on to the transition team, too, and I think gave them an idea of what we could expect from Congress later on.

Carter as a mainstream Democrat

Carter's issue staff, partly to advance their goals of shoring up support among liberals and labor, partly to fend off increasing press criticism about ambiguity, and partly to integrate materials from hundreds of earlier issue papers and speeches, developed a 37-page summary of Carter's "positions" for distribution before the drafting subcommittee met. The *broad* similarities in this document, the eventual Democratic platform, and the "Campaign Promises Book," released by the White House in late February 1977, are striking. There were some significant differences, but the emphasis and orientation was vintage New Deal/Fair Deal/Great Society philosophy (or nonphilosophy, whichever the reader might prefer). The report, however, was cast in typical Carter rhetoric about "open, compassionate, responsive, efficient" government because

> the American people are tired of inflated promises which cannot be kept, of programs which do not work, of old answers to new problems ... the platform ... should set forth realistic goals and achievable, affordable policies which can and should be attained.[10]

For prominent coalition partners who had been uneasy about Carter, the basic commitments were there, even if they frequently were not very specific about timing and magnitude. For example, he promised Democrats that:

> To reach full employment we must assure:
> (a) support for the *Full Employment Act* [Humphrey-Hawkins] for 1976;
> (b) *countercyclical* assistance to cities with high unemployment;
> (c) expansionary fiscal and monetary policy for the coming year to stimulate demand, production, and jobs;
> (d) creation of meaningful and productive *public needs jobs* as a supplement to the private sector, including ... housing rehabilitation and repairing our railroad beds;
> (e) we should provide 800,000 summer youth jobs and *double the CETA program* from 300,000 to 600,000 jobs.[11]

All of these pledges are remiss in one form or another if one is seriously looking for specificity. Merely promising support for the Full Employment Act says nothing about how much, under what conditions, or with what amendments. The countercyclical assistance item fails to mention even roughly how much support might be generated, although it is exact about the timing. Even the seemingly most specific item, on CETA (Comprehensive Employment and Training Act) and Youth Employment, gives the figures but is silent on timing.

But viewed another way—as important code words for organized labor and others alarmed about unemployment—they represented a

short and powerful message: Carter was part of the Democratic mainstream. The same was true of the sections on urban problems, welfare,
health, education, environmental and conservation issues, consumer
regulation, and civil rights for women, blacks, and other minorities—all
carried important messages through the back channel to the most
interested constituencies. With few exceptions, the foreign policy component was much more ambiguous, seemingly written to strike a careful
balance between the opponents of détente with the Soviets and those
who sought a dramatic shift in the U. S. hard-line stance toward the
Soviet Union. Two of the exceptions, widely publicized, were Carter's
commitment to opposing production of the B-1 bomber ("an example of
a proposed system which should not be funded") and a statement about
Israel designed to shore up support among pro-Israeli Democrats ("negotiations can only proceed on the basis of a clear and absolute
American commitment to ensure Israel's security and survival as a
Jewish State").[12]

Conspicuous by its absence in Carter's presentation was any mention of amnesty for Vietnam resisters, although his support of pardons
rather than a general amnesty was by then well known to activists. Also
missing was any mention of abortion—he opposed a constitutional
amendment prohibiting abortion *and* federal payments for abortion
under Medicaid—gay rights, and decriminalization of marijuana. One
economic issue of particular concern to Udallites, vertical *and* horizontal
divestiture of monopolies in American industry was left out. Despite
neo-populist rhetoric on other issues, Carter was strongly opposed to
vertical divestiture.[13]

Much later in the campaign, Carter used a *Playboy* interview to
communicate an attitude of "benign neglect" and hence, latent support,
about homosexual rights. But for perhaps obvious reasons in 1976,
neither the candidate nor his staff was prepared to permit the Democratic platform or the campaign to become a vehicle for any public
discussion of the problems of gays. Said one staff person:

> The McGovern organization lost complete control on these issues and
> under no conditions are we going to permit that to happen again. So-
> called gay rights is a *private* question of sexual preference, not a public,
> and certainly not a federal issue. No way, *noooo* way, we're going to get
> caught with it, and I know most people here, no matter how they feel
> privately, feel the same.

Interestingly, the fear of a plank favoring gay rights had diminished by 1980. The Democrats, with Carter's support and without major
public conflict, added "sexual orientation" to their commitment to
abolish discrimination. This is an issue area that now appears to have
broken through the mobilization of bias. But it was clear in 1976 that

gays and their supporters were going to have to look elsewhere for public discussion.

Other major social issues were not displaced or ignored as much as folded into an acceptable formula, at least as far as Carter's campaign personnel were concerned. One month later, at the formal platform meetings, political activist Sam Brown led the opposition to Carter's position on amnesty and won a close vote in support of language that called for a "full and complete pardon" for those in "legal and financial jeopardy" because of their opposition to the Vietnam War. The statement would have included a complete pardon for deserters-of-conscience as well as resisters. Stu Eizenstat, who, along with Joseph Duffey, headed the Carter platform forces, cornered Brown and some others outside the platform committee room and won a commitment from Brown to offer an amendment for a "case-by-case review" on deserters. Brown, saying that he personally did not support this part of his own amendment but was "offering it in the spirit of unity," so moved, and it carried overwhelmingly.

Public policy regarding abortion presented a different mix in the struggle over acceptability. Carter supporters forcefully opposed any constitutional amendment prohibiting abortion but were divided over whether or how this might appear in the actual platform. Original drafts of the platform omitted any mention of the issue, as had the Carter presentation to the drafting subcommittee. Said one participant:

> Without great rancor, but with visible agitation among some members, we decided to include a statement clearly opposing the constitutional amendment option and wrapped it in language about the "justified religious and ethical concern many Americans have on the issue."

On other types of issues—the fundamental economic questions involving the distribution of wealth and concentration of corporate power in the United States, for example—Carter's campaign and the platform alternated between promising more compensatory measures and opposing any radical departure from mainstream Democratic ideology. The exceptions are difficult to evaluate. No direct mention of a balanced budget is made in the platform, although Carter long used the "balanced budget by 1981" formula in his primary and general campaign speeches. The rhetoric of the platform, however, remained largely understandable to ordinary old liberal Democrats. A "comprehensive national health insurance system, with universal and mandatory coverage," was promised as "revenues and planning permit." [14] A guaranteed annual income, as part of comprehensive welfare reform, was strongly endorsed. While hostility to "big business" permeates the language of the 1976 platform, in fact few specific proposals, other than a strong commitment to creating a consumer regulatory agency, are visible.

Vertical divestiture in the oil industry was strongly opposed by Carter and his issues staff and is clearly an example of an issue, like gay rights, that would have to seek forums other than the 1976 Carter campaign for inclusion on the agenda.

Discussion of foreign policy and defense issues, which provoked an intense controversy over defense spending and the magnitude of Soviet capability, ultimately struck the same balance in the platform as was struck in Carter's initial presentation one month earlier, with one important exception: the 1976 Democratic platform equivocated on production of the B-1 whereas Carter's position was more clearly committed to halting production. Human rights were mentioned in the platform, as they were in Carter's speeches, but there was little indication at any time during the campaign that this issue would become a major organizing theme of American foreign policy during the first year of the Carter administration.[15]

Peter Milius, an able and industrious *Washington Post* reporter who covered the platform meetings, concluded that "Jimmy Carter got exactly what he wanted from a docile Democratic platform committee on every issue but one [amnesty] ... even on the emotional pardon issue, their departure from Carter's wishes was more symbolic than real."[16] Other than to quibble over what constitutes "docility," it is difficult to disagree, except to point out that Milius omits an important additional piece of information: most of the highly active Democratic factions got *from* Jimmy Carter what they wanted, too.

How the 1976 platform compares with earlier Democratic versions

Criticism of the Carter campaign, much like criticism of his administration, has suffered from inattention to comparative and historical example. It is important to place the 1976 platform, and, in the next chapter, his campaign positions, in contemporary perspective, at least briefly. Consider, for example, the data on party platforms from 1960 to 1976 presented in Tables 3-1 and 3-2.

So far as the 1976 Democratic platform is concerned, in content, specificity, and proportion, this document is not very different from its predecessors dating back to 1960. Slightly more than one-half of the platform is concerned with future policy pledges, and 12 percent makes detailed commitments. With the exception of 1964, when an incumbent was running, these proportions have remained statistically constant. In fact, if one compares the *number* of detailed pledges, the 1976 Democratic platform was more specific than the 1960 document, but less specific than 1972's. Nor had the policy focus of the platform shifted funda-

Table 3-1   Number of general and detailed future policy pledges in party platforms, 1960-1976

Year	Democrats		Republicans		Percentage of total platform concerned with future pledges	
	N	Detailed promises (percent)	N	Detailed promises (percent)	D's	R's
1960	425	18%	289	19%	53%	56%
1964	145[a]	11	183	17	15	44
1968	461	12	396	16	56	71
1972	791	17	434	8	72	40
1976	599	12	542	10	70	56

Source: Data is from Gerald M. Pomper and Susan S. Lederman, *Elections in America*, 2d ed. (New York: Longman, 1980) 133-143.

[a] Unusually small because the Democrats produced a two-part platform, and Pomper and Lederman only coded the first part.

mentally, except in the proportional attention given to issues of health, education, and welfare after 1972—the 1976 Democratic platform focused *less* attention on these issues than did its counterparts of the mid-1960s.

The balance in a trade-off between the electoral incentives to fudge and the coalitional incentives to deliver was reached in a manner that satisfied both liberal Democrats and Carter staff during the 1976 convention period. Because most delegates believed Carter would be the candidate and because the platform was couched in broadly acceptable progressive terms, there was little danger of widespread defection from the coalition. One senior Carter operative concluded:

> What I have fought to convince people for four months is this: we are all progressives in this party now. With the exception of a few flakes from the Wallace or right-to-life groups, or from the far left, we all agree on what needs to be done. Our only disagreement is over when and how. It's better to fight that problem out when we have the White House. [Little did he appreciate how intense that fight would be.]

Then, smiling, and looking around an emptying hotel ballroom, he added: "Far as I can tell, looks like most everybody around here saw it the way I did."

Table 3-2 Issue content of future platform pledges, 1960-1976, in percent

Issue Content	1960 D's	1960 R's	1964 D's	1964 R's	1968 D's	1968 R's	1972 D's	1972 R's	1976 D's	1976 R's
Foreign policy and defense	23%	24%	21%	46%	17%	22%	16%	19%	32%	29%
Economics	15	14	13	11	18	15	9	17	11	12
Labor	5	5	11	3	4	5	6	4	6	3
Agriculture	7	9	6	7	9	6	5	3	4	3
Resources	13	8	9	5	7	7	7	8	9	7
Health/education/ welfare	18	19	24	8	25	24	26	24	17	25
Government	10	10	8	13	18	18	25	16	16	17
Civil rights	7	11	8	7	2	2	8	11	5	5

Source: Data is from Gerald M. Pomper and Susan S. Lederman, *Elections in America*, 2d ed. (New York: Longman, 1980) 138-139.

Coalition building: women's rights

"Most," however, turned out to be an important qualification. One large cluster of issues, intensely important to a growing but still small number of coalitional partners, revolved around a politically acceptable feminist agenda. The platform carried the most salient item, support for the Equal Rights Amendment, with promises of "aggressive" support by Carter. But other items, from increasing day-care facilities to stronger enforcement of equal opportunity provisions in credit, employment, education, housing, health, and for the disabled, were absorbed under a blanket platform pledge to enforce "equal treatment before the law" and the successful adoption of an amendment seeking "implementation" of Title IX of the education acts. It is important to note that Carter's initial presentation to the committee had spelled out support, item-by-item, in a broad range of policy areas, *even though the platform did not*. In this sense, Carter's personal vision was more forward looking and specific than the Democratic platform.

As is the case with many issues of public policy, the feminist challenge came not directly on the platform, but at the party's Rules Committee meeting, which took place in Washington June 19-20, four days after the preliminary platform had been adopted. Representatives of the Democratic Task Force of the National Women's Political Caucus (NWPC) proposed an amendment to a Carter-supported amendment to party rules. The Carter amendment had insisted that the national committee "promote" the selection of an equal number of men and women delegates for the 1980 convention. The NWPC amendment further specified that "the national party shall take all feasible steps to assist state parties to incorporate this goal in their delegate selection plans for the 1980 convention." Carter forces opposed the latter, agreeing with the original Rules Committee report, which held that "primary" responsibility for implementation should "rest with the States." Other feminists felt that the word "require" should replace "promote" in the Carter amendment to party rules. The original Rules Committee report had used language less forceful than "promote" as Carterites felt they had already improved the rules from the viewpoint of feminist demands. Those holding out for "require" had virtually no support, even within the NWPC, but there was considerable sentiment for beefing up the power of the national party on the question of implementation.

Obviously, these seemingly arcane rules provoked fundamental questions about the relative power of state versus national party organization—a question that involves items other than the representation of women—and neither Carter nor Strauss was prepared to support claims of national dominance. The Carter forces carried the Rules Committee, but the NWPC had more than enough votes to file a minority plank on implementation for consideration in New York. The issue quickly became a strategic question—how far and under what conditions should women's rights advocates push for a floor fight with the Carter organization?

Besides giving Georgians an opportunity to meet New Yorkers, and vice versa, the convention provided an environment for some highly useful back-channel communication. A floor fight was avoided after the women's caucus voted to accept a compromise agreed to after two days of negotiation between Carter and a group of Democratic feminist leaders. Two years later, at the 1978 midterm conference, Democrats adopted a mandatory "50-50" ratio of all future delegates at the nominating convention, a provision that passed and was implemented in 1980 with surprisingly little acrimony.[17] And, by the 1980 convention, feminists had gained enough national clout and bargaining power to win a floor fight with Carter forces (who put up a rather half-hearted "fight" because they were determined to overcome the deep chasm caused by the Kennedy/Carter primary struggle) on the issues of abortion and tactics for ratifying the Equal Rights Amendment.[18]

The actual provisions of the 1976 compromise—a slight change in the implementation language, an agreement to make the DNC Women's Division a "feminist force," and a reaffirmation to appoint "substantial" numbers of women to high posts—are less important than the coalitional implications for agenda development. Comparing Carter's response, then and during the campaign, to what had happened four years earlier, one prominent Democratic feminist said:

> We were treated like shit by senior people in McGovern's campaign; not by McGovern himself, when you could get to him, but by his staff. They were privately contemptuous of "women's issues," didn't even want to have a women's division within the campaign, and were terrified about "divisiveness." I don't trust Carter entirely either, but the attitude of his staff, at least many of them, and the candidate is very different. Of course, they aren't really feminists, some have unbelievably piggish attitudes about women. If elections mean anything, and I'm not sure they do, this one is the best chance we've had so far.

Four years had passed since women's rights activists first bid to change the party, and the perception of what was politically acceptable had responded to the different environment of 1976. Understanding the changing political environment is important in any consideration of agenda development. Feminists, like other people, respond not only to concrete policy promises but also to the realities of nomination politics and to the symbolic meaning of political transactions. The fact that feminists like Bella Abzug, Midge Costanza, Patt Derian, Elizabeth Holtzman, C. Delores Tucker, and others were strongly supportive of the compromise, and apparently of Carter the candidate, was probably more crucial to winning the support of this faction than any of the procedural issues being debated. This unanimity also delegitimized the lingering complaints of more radical feminists.

The trade-off for feminists should be clear; this kind of negotiation is universal to coalition building in all political systems. Political trust, the cement that holds coalitional partners together for longer than the short duration of a campaign, is based on the ability of organizations to deliver the tangible and intangible benefits that gaining power permits. The support of blacks, organized labor, environmentalists, and party regulars was transacted in much the same way, but with less publicity.

To the extent that the convention and the platform-writing process affected the coalitional incentives to deliver in 1976, Carter's selection of Walter Mondale as his running mate and the tone of the presidential nominee's acceptance speech furthered the perception that Democrats would attempt to implement a progressive agenda, if and when the Ford administration was displaced. David Broder neatly caught the drift: "Carter . . . thus stepped off toward the White House with his left foot. It was a small step from the middle of the road, but it was an important one."[19]

Of course, as the general election and his administration demonstrated, he was still very much in control of the *other* foot.

Carter in the general election _____

"He wavers, he wanders, he wiggles, and he waffles," proclaimed Gerald R. Ford. "He will say anything, anywhere in the United States to be President." The Republicans had an "issue" and they exploited it beautifully.[20]

In the approximately 90 days between the end of the Democratic convention and the November election, the Carter campaign opted for a classic majority party strategy: mobilize latent supporters through selective appeals to party, emphasizing long-standing group-based linkages, and attract others by articulating broad stylistic themes like personal honesty, integrity, leadership, and "getting the country moving again." The character of these appeals should not be dismissed as completely irrelevant for agenda building. The main thrust of general election strategy, however, should be to mobilize support for future presidential programs, not to discuss policy as if the general election is a kind of moot court on national issues.

An analysis of changing symbolic cues between the primary and general election supports the proposition that Carter dramatically increased his efforts to portray himself as an activist and as a dynamic leader after the convention, reemphasizing questions of personal style rather than issues.[21] This finding can be attributed either to the media's reporting, to Carter's "real" emphases, or to a combination of both. The latter explanation, stemming from a mix of campaign strategic assumptions and media biases about what constitutes "news," is the most compelling. Senior staff in the Carter organization were quite explicit about this shift:

> Issues, Issues, Issues! Can't political scientists ever think of anything else? The issues take care of themselves. Everybody who counts knows where Jimmy is, except the press who parrot back whatever some idiot Republican tells 'em. Issues are not our problem now—we've got to have good advance, good and precise targeting, good media, better polling, and a hell of a lot more on turnout. We've got one major goal between now and November: to sell Jimmy and Mondale as leaders whom voters will trust. *They* are *the* issue.

Or as a staff person in the issues division said:

> Governor Carter knows the issues. Our job is to boil down and rehash the substance of policy commitments already made. A better slant, a more precise summary, a catchier peg, a tougher focus on problems with his commitments. Every position paper or issue statement that goes out of here must have a list of five major objections to the proposed solution. A large part of what I'm doing is to anticipate what the media or Ford's organization might pounce on. Isn't that what a campaign is about? *The issues can never help you, but they can sure kill you.* [Emphasis added.]

This theme—that issues are dangerous, that they must be controlled, that the policy environment is highly risky—is pervasive in American presidential campaigns, whether in the primary or general election. As Page and others have argued, rational candidates will be risk-avoidant when uncertainty breeds a fear of antagonizing an important voting bloc. What appears to change between the pre- and postconvention period, however, is the relative mix of voting blocs and their factional power in the electoral process. Accordingly, there is greater incentive to be concerned with policy agendas during the convention stage and less during the general election. The Carter campaign moved back toward greater policy ambiguity during the period after the convention.

Organization and issue development

Ironically, the size of campaign issues staffs tends to grow at precisely the time the major strategic emphasis is directed at stylistic themes and operational matters. Of course, the number of operational personnel (media, advance, targeting, and so on) expands even faster. Consider some very crude data. The full-time, paid issues staff constituted about 11 percent of all Atlanta-based professionals in the Carter campaign; 18 percent, if one counts the transition group working under Jack Watson. The actual number of people, 26 under Stuart Eizenstat (excluding the speech writers) and 14 under Watson, is considerably higher than in earlier Democratic campaigns when the Democrats were the out-party.[22]

These 40 were primarily gatekeepers for a vastly larger number of idea people: like McGovern, Carter had 20 task forces with a total membership of approximately 350 people whose (manifest) function was to keep policy ideas and analyses rolling into Atlanta. Unlike McGovern's task forces, they were not charged with developing collective position papers, and no such reports were ever released to the press. The decision to avoid collective task force reports was intentionally made to prevent the surfacing of potentially embarrassing conflicts between the candidate's stands and those of his task forces. Former McGovern staff people had been particularly annoyed by this problem in 1972, and their messages were absorbed by the Carter organization.[23]

A look at the ratio of issues staff to operational staff (40 to 350 in 1976) is probably the best single indicator that organizational tasks are considered much more important to the success of the campaign. Does this radical disparity in staff size affect agenda development or the amount of issue discussion? Probably not. The main factors bearing on agenda development have little to do with how internal staff resources are allocated. Rather they stem from the "seasons" of politics (primary, convention, general election, control of the presidency) and from whatever balance is reached in the broad trade-offs already discussed.

Policy-oriented staff and volunteers frequently believe, however, that they are engaging in "make-work" projects, that "no one really cares about what they write," and that there is a cabal on the candidate's airplane or at headquarters that prevents them from having any impact. Unhappily for issues people, these fears are frequently true. Nor does there appear to be much that can be done to prevent disillusionment from surfacing, although it can be controlled. These tensions were even more notable four years earlier in the so-called "issue-oriented" presidential campaign of George McGovern.

Xandra Kayden has skillfully identified a number of factors that contributed to the massive decline of morale in the McGovern general election campaign, particularly in the issues division.[24] Some were unique to the McGovern organization, some endemic to all presidential campaigns. One significant difference between the McGovern and Carter campaigns was the way Ted Van Dyke, McGovern's issues director, and Eizenstat, the counterpart in Carter's organization, felt about their positions. Various commentators have indicated that Van Dyke believed that he had lost influence by being "confined" to issues and to Washington during the campaign. Apparently, he never had consistent and effective access to McGovern, and this, combined with his attitudes about the position, trickled down to the staff.

On the other hand, Eizenstat came to the Carter operation with much less political experience and only a minimal Washington reputation. Said one staffer who served on both campaigns:

> Ted was a heavy in Democratic circles in Washington before the McGovern campaign, and he resented the treatment he received during the election. Stu, on the other hand, came out of a completely different ball park, without Van Dyke's hang-ups about power or his super-aggressive style, and it made a difference in how Stu was treated, how he behaved, and how we felt.

One problem for issues staffs in both campaigns might be called "The Fear of Not Flying." The psychology of "the plane" is ubiquitous; more accurately, there is extraordinary staff anxiety over whether you're on it, or your friends are on it, or anyone you trust and who has access to the candidate is on it. This problem demoralized top issues people in the McGovern operation, and, while not as intense in the Carter campaign, came to be seen as the main reason that many ideas and positions developed by the issues staff were going astray.

> We had great communication *to* the plane and terrible communication *from* the plane. Not until Stu went on [during the last three weeks of

the campaign] did this change.... Part of the problem was that Jody [Powell] didn't like ___, and it was reciprocated, but this hurt the issues staff in terms of having any effect on what was going on. Jody was *the* main gatekeeper, and of course you've got to have someone like that, but the conflict between him and ___ wasn't doing *us* any good. When Stu joined the plane group, he lobbied hard for what he felt were our priorities and it paid off.

While it might have little effect in changing the broad commitments agreed to before the general election phase begins, there is an obvious advantage to having a major issues person on the plane who is also considered an insider. This seems to be an idiosyncratic function of the power relations established between the candidate and senior staff, and among the senior staff, rather than anything that can be mandated. Another individual commented:

Hell, we could have had 40 of our people on the plane and it wouldn't have made one bit of difference. ___ was on the whole time, and ___ was on during the final stages, but to this day I don't know what either of them did, and they were supposed to be our main input. Not until Stu went on did it make a difference. Without him, you might just as well have closed down our entire operation.

There were other organizational tensions in the Carter campaign—the growing conflict of Jordan and the issues staff, who were on one side, with Watson and the transition group, who were on the other, about future personnel in a Carter presidency. The transition group was working separately from the main campaign organization, and this aroused considerable suspicion that they might try to outflank Jordan/Powell/Eizenstat in securing appointments for their preferred candidates. Something like this did emerge in the administration's early days, but Jordan reasserted his authority and overrode Watson. Because control over future personnel appointments is critical in shaping future policy, issues and operational staff have a legitimate interest in maintaining control over transition planning groups.

A predictable response to the coalitional bargains that were struck and highlighted during the convention and platform phase was an increased concern about their liberal flavor. Jordan and Powell had both begun to worry publicly immediately after the convention about "Jimmy being seen as too liberal, too far out on some of the issues." Bob Dole's later crack, "He's just Southern-fried McGovern," remained undeveloped in the *Ford* campaign, but was of prime concern inside the Carter organization. While no evidence could be found that Carter ever reneged on any of the commitments made before the general election, or that he was intentionally inconsistent from audience to audience, the *tone* of his discussion clearly reemphasized "conservative" values as a condition and result of achieving "liberal" goals.[25]

With the exception of voluminous and targeted back-channel communications, Carter's main campaign themes reverted to those of the early primary period. He either dwelt on matters of style or couched his program discussion in the conventional symbols of the American Dream. It must be acknowledged that the honesty and integrity of presidential candidates *was* an important "issue" in 1976—for obvious reasons, given Nixon's exit from office in 1974—and that I do not mean to denigrate this "stylistic" emphasis as inevitably less important than "substance." Still, presidential campaigns should and do have important functions, beyond the basic one of screening out individuals of questionable integrity.

The role of mass media in agenda development

The communication imperative of the mass media, particularly television, during the general election, also has an effect on agenda development. The *Playboy* interview in which Carter, attempting to show that he was not a Sunday school goody-two-shoes, admitted to having "lusted in his heart" after various women, was certainly a great boon to the newspapers, including the so-called elite press. And they played it that way—day after day. It was, nevertheless, a massive nonissue in terms of future agendas or personal character. Such unanticipated events, like the ethnic slur gaffe discussed earlier, can literally swamp a campaign organization. Carter's was no exception. From September 20 until mid-October, Carter's issues people worked frantically to overcome the negative effects of coverage of *Playboy*. One person on the staff concluded:

> The period from September 20th on we called Three Weeks to the Bottom. No matter what we or Jimmy did, the press kept piling up stories on "lust" and "immorality." Some of the best stuff we did during the campaign was in this period, but do you think we got any coverage? Absolutely not! I began to really hate reporters, many of whom I've known for some time, but I guess it's not their fault. It's the desk people and editors back home. And then there was the first debate, which everybody thought had gone badly. This place [the issues division] was never very loose under any conditions, the people around were too young and not very experienced and savvy about campaigns, but *Playboy* just sunk us all further. You can't believe how grim it was until John Stewart and Ted Van Dyke came down from Washington to help on the debate briefing books. They had been through the swamps before, with Humphrey and McGovern, and their presence made a hell of a difference. But it was altogether a very grim period.

The debates were probably the single most important front-channel device for communicating anything about agendas during the general election. Content analysis of earlier presidential debates has shown they improved the *style* of issue discussion even if they are remembered for other things.[26] Of the three held in 1976, the first debate saw candidates making their most detailed exposition of policy items. Predictably, Carter was roundly condemned for being "boring," for using "too many statistics," and injecting "too much detail in his answers." David L. Paletz seems persuasive in evaluating these charges:

> Most commentators blamed the candidates.... I am inclined to blame the media. Obviously newsmen raised untoward expectations about the debates. More important, the debates were boring mainly in comparison with the dramatic and entertainment quality of regular television fare. They offered static visuals, ninety minutes of words, no commercial interruptions, no dramatic structure with conflict and resolution, and no witty one-liners. One need only compare them to Kojak.[27]

The general election moved into early November with a growing and monotonous media chorus echoing the cynical and discordant sentiments of Howard K. Smith about the saturation of campaign fluff. If, in fact, Smith was correct about 1976 being "fluffier" than any campaign since 1928, at least part of the reason was bluntly stated by Carter in the other, and largely unreported, part of the *Playboy* interview: "The media have absolutely no interest in issues." The candidates and the media must each assume part of the responsibility for this, and the rest lies with the other attributes of the seasons of presidential politics. And those seasons, rain and all, affect equally the willing and unwilling.

Conclusion

Walter Dean Burnham called the first nomination of Jimmy Carter the "ultimate bankruptcy of liberalism."[28] Many liberals who supported Carter in 1976 agreed with Burnham three years later, arguing, however, that Carter, and not liberalism, was bankrupt. In 1976 the only evidence of liberal bankruptcy I discovered involved that old, humdrum, and honorable profession of being defeated in the primaries: Carter demolished an army of more conventional liberal contenders, as well as George Wallace, who symbolized throughout the late 1960s and early 1970s a racist and backward-looking American South.

Of course, Carter was not Hubert Humphrey, Morris Udall, Fred Harris, Birch Bayh, or any of the others who attracted early and visible "liberal" support. But his 1976 campaign agenda, first developed and then displaced in the usual messy, partially contradictory, incremental way that has characterized all Democratic candidates since the New Deal should not be entirely unrecognizable—even to liberal Democrats.

Obviously, the proposed solutions to various problems that typified approaches of earlier Democratic administrations underwent significant change in the Carter administration. By 1979 the administration had shifted so far on economic and defense issues that Democratic progressives dropped out of the Carter camp by the droves, joining Edward Kennedy in his failing bid to wrest the nomination away from the incumbent. Solutions to policy complexity, as in the tensions between reducing unemployment and pushing up inflation, were sloughed off during the 1976 campaign in favor of the political demands of the old (mainly liberal) Democratic coalition.

Agenda development in the 1976 campaign reflected many of the propositions developed earlier, emerging as a trade-off between the strategic advantages of remaining ambiguous and the necessity of building a winning coalition among dominant Democratic factions. Carter's efforts to place himself in the mainstream of Democratic party ideology by promising policies that were congruent with that ideology paid off. He used voluminous back-channel communication—through issue papers and direct negotiations—to consolidate support among liberal/labor groups in the North, Midwest, and West without losing the broader voting constituency of a winning primary campaign. Negotiations on the 1976 platform were the most important component of this strategy, and that platform and Carter's support of it assisted in reducing the political cleavages that were opened by his unanticipated and dramatic victories in the early primaries.

As was pointed out in the last chapter, the Carter organization made more concrete promises than any of its predecessors, and *most* of its commitments were consistent with the preferences of the Democratic party's liberal/labor wing. Carter frequently cloaked these promises in moderately conservative rhetoric and thus developed a reputation for being contradictory (particularly on macroeconomic policy) even when his position papers were forthright and consistent about future policy options. Three areas in which he pledged government action—national health insurance, welfare reform, and a comprehensive national energy plan—were potentially as far-reaching as any of Lyndon Johnson's Great Society programs. Johnson, however, was able to redeem a larger proportion of his campaign promises than Carter. History is kinder to presidential achievement than presidential effort, a reality that plagued Carter's reputation from the midpoint of his presidency to the present day.

Reporters and campaign analysts miss much of substance in presidential campaigns because candidates, the media, and the public are concerned with aspects of electoral politics that are unrelated to or only indirectly concerned with future public policy. Carter's 1976 campaign was no exception. Thoughtful position papers were prepared and circulated, important policy commitments established, competing policy claims reconciled (temporarily!) in the agenda-building process of Carter's bid for the presidency.

On the other hand, nothing in my research can provide solace for those who take seriously the classic model of democratic control. Carter and Ford *were* evasive and ambiguous on numerous major issues, in the primaries, at the conventions, and in the general election. Even if voters devoted extraordinary attention to both back and front channels of information, the tasks of sorting out where Carter actually stood on many questions of central importance or how he might respond to the complexities of decision making once in power were herculean tasks—indeed, impossible. Moreover, the range of political acceptability, the subjective parameters of the mobilization of bias, fixed the options in a powerful if reasonably predictable manner. The Michael Harringtons of this system, no matter how pragmatic their radicalism, will always be more visible at platform gatherings than in actual positions of power.

Jimmy Carter and Fritz Perls, the Gestalt pyschologist whose epigraph started this chapter, shared an important insight: the appreciation of differences, and the comprehension that there were many unpublicized similarities on major issues, did increase the contact between Carter and the most important factions of the Democratic party. Unhappily for this one-term president, the struggle to resolve those differences by alternating between two different economic agendas once in office—one roughly liberal, the other conservative—led to splintering the coalition that helped bring him to the presidency in the first place.

Notes

1. James David Barber, *The Pulse of Politics: The Rhythm of Presidential Elections in the Twentieth Century* (New York: Norton, 1980), 210.
2. Ronald Reagan almost defeated incumbent Gerald R. Ford at the 1976 Republican convention, losing by a hair, 1,187 to 1,070. By contrast, there was never any doubt that Carter had sufficient delegate votes before the 1980 convention convened, despite the so-called "open-convention" movement. Carter forces defeated Kennedy supporters on a key procedural move by more than 500 votes, and Kennedy, therefore, did not have his name placed in nomination. For the 1976 election, see William R. Keech and Donald R. Matthews, "Patterns in the Presidential Nominating Process, 1936-1976," in *Parties and Elections in an Anti-Party Age: American Politics and*

the Crisis of Confidence, ed. Jeff Fishel (Bloomington: Indiana University Press, 1978), 203-216.

3. Phil Stanford, "Carter—The Citizen's Guide to the 1976 Presidential Candidates" (Washington, D.C.: Capitol Hill News Service for Public Citizen, 1976).

4. Kessel does not differentiate between the primary and convention seasons for operational reasons, although my analysis suggests very strongly that the two present quite different strategic environments for presidential aspirants. See John Kessel, "The Seasons of Presidential Politics," *Social Science Quarterly* (December 1977): 418-435.

5. Jules Witcover, *Marathon: The Pursuit of the Presidency 1972-1976* (New York: Viking Press, 1977), 302.

6. Witcover treats this as a "bald attempt to silence liberal and black discontent." Perhaps it was. On the other hand, Carter clearly was edging toward an endorsement of some of the major provisions *before* the ethnic purity statement. For example, on April 1, 1976, one day before the ethnic purity statement, his press office released a statement "supporting many of the aspirations and aims" of the Humphrey-Hawkins proposal. This was a sharp break with earlier statements by Carter.

7. The best study of the 1972 Democratic platform is Benjamin I. Page's contribution in Denis G. Sullivan et al., *The Politics of Representation: the Democratic Convention 1972* (New York: St. Martin's Press, 1974).

8. One person's "extremist" is another's "moderate." The fact that George McGovern was perceived by some voters as "too liberal" did not, in fact, make him too liberal, let alone an extremist. With the exception of his longstanding opposition to the Vietnam War, there were few substantive issues on which he and Hubert Humphrey, the choice of party regulars, differed. In my estimation, both were articulate advocates of a liberalism long associated with the upper Midwest. McGovern attracted supporters whom many Democrats considered extreme, but that is a different question.

9. One Democrat provided a definition of "responsible" that is not unusual in American party politics: "We don't want any crazies running around, like [has] happened before."

10. Jimmy Carter, "For America's Third Century, Why Not the Best?" (Carter's presentation to the 1976 Democratic Platform Committee, undated), 1-2.

11. The language is verbatim from the Carter's presentation to the 1976 Platform Committee.

12. Carter, "For America's Third Century," 34.

13. Stanford, "Carter—The Citizen's Guide," 7.

14. The revenue section is from a Carter press release; the comprehensive health promise is from his presentation to the Platform Committee.

15. An insightful account of this curious anomaly will be found in Elizabeth Drew, *American Journal: The Events of 1976* (New York: Random House, 1977).

16. *Washington Post*, June 16, 1976.

17. Efforts to restructure the delegate selection procedures, adding approximately 500 mostly male officeholders as uncommitted delegates and adopted in early 1982 by the Democratic National Committee, did not function to dilute the hard-won influence of women at the 1984 national convention. The equal division rule remains in effect for all other delegates.

18. Two of the 14 minority reports adopted at the convention (of a total of 23 submitted) involved women's issues. First, the 1980 platform, as amended,

called for the Democratic party (presumably the DNC and other national party committees) to "withhold financial support and technical campaign assistance from candidates who do not support the ERA." Second, it went against Carter's position on federal funding of abortions for poor women, saying that the Democratic party "opposes restrictions on funding for health services for the poor that deny poor women especially the right to exercise a constitutionally guaranteed right to privacy (abortion)."

19. David Broder, "Carter Commits Himself to Democrats' Liberalism," *Washington Post*, July 16, 1976, A19.
20. Good descriptive accounts of the 1976 general election can be found in William L. Miller, *Yankee from Georgia* (New York: Times Books, 1978); Jules Witcover, *Marathon: The Pursuit of the Presidency 1972-1976;* Gerald M. Pomper et al., *The Election of 1976: Reports and Interpretations* (New York: David McKay Co., 1977); Martin Schram, *Running for President in 1976: The Carter Campaign* (New York: Stein & Day, 1977); and Drew, *The American Journal: The Events of 1976.*
21. Darrell M. West, "Rhetoric in the 1976 Campaign" (Seminar paper, Indiana University).
22. For example, John F. Kennedy had one full-time person who was responsible for *all* questions involving health, education, and welfare; Carter had three in the issues division who were responsible for health alone. The question of policy advice in campaigns is ambiguous because there are numerous ways of getting it from specialists who are not part of a paid professional staff.
23. Indeed, one person who helped create the McGovern task forces wrote the Carter organization arguing that none should even be set up!
24. Xandra Kayden, *Campaign Organization* (Lexington, Mass.: D. C. Heath, 1978).
25. Part of this is the "precision of ambiguity" characteristic of all presidential campaigns. The only possible exception involved the absolute level of cuts Carter promised to make in defense spending. Carter and Ford disagreed over whether Carter had promised to cut $15 billion or $4 to $5 billion, but it is difficult to treat this as a serious reversal of his basic policy commitment to cut spending. After seeking to reduce the growth of the Defense Department's budget during the first two years in office, Carter abandoned his 1976 promise and sought large increases for the FY 1980 and 1981 budgets.
26. John W. Ellsworth, "Rationality and Campaigning: A Content Analysis of the 1960 Presidential Campaign Debates," *Western Political Quarterly* 18 (December 1965): 794-802. On the 1976 and 1980 debates, see *The Past and Future of Presidential Debates,* Austin Ranney, ed. (Washington, D.C.: American Enterprise Institute, 1979); Jeff Greenfield, *The Real Campaign: How the Media Missed the Story of the 1980 Campaign* (New York: Summit Books, 1982); Myles Martel, *Political Campaign Debates* (New York: Longman, 1983); and relevant sections of *Television Coverage of the 1980 Campaign,* William Adams, ed. (Norwood, N.J.: Ablex Publishers, 1983).
27. David L. Paletz, "Candidates and Media in the 1976 Presidential Election," in *Parties and Elections in an Anti-Party Age.*
28. Walter Dean Burnham, "Jimmy Carter and the Democratic Crisis," *New Republic,* July 3, 1976, 17-19.

Outsiders as presidents: the record of the Carter administration 4

> Why is it, she wondered, that men who spend their lives fighting priests end up giving prayer books as gifts?
>
> —Gabriel Garcia Marquez

Holding up the wall, cocktail in hand, Washington, D.C., in September—hot, stuffy, humid, soggy. Life here, literally, is a sponge. But it's business as usual at a crowded party on Capitol Hill.

"So you're writing a book. What about?" he asks.

"On the presidency, comparing campaign pledges to what they do in office, with emphasis on the Carter and Reagan presidencies."

"The Carter presidency?" Eyes roll back, a quiet sigh emerges, head turns, looking elsewhere in the room, as if to suggest, in a vaguely embarrassed way, that he can't believe there is anyone left in Washington still interested in such relics, particularly *that* relic. Has been. Over with. Done for.

But his attention returns. He is, after all, a liberal Democrat, a threatened breed in the Washington of 1981, and he was implicated, quite directly, since he worked for the Carter administration.

"Arthur Schlesinger and Tom Wicker were right," he says. "They were the most inept group to hold the White House since Warren

Harding and the most conservative Democratic administration since Grover Cleveland!"

A slight rumble in my stomach. The usual litany from liberals. I begin to feel the need to be a little nasty: "Does that include you and your role, too?" I ask.

Long pause. He stares at his glass, wondering, I muse, whether to respond or move on to more congenial company. A small grin breaks through; he looks up, an unexpected concession:

"Maybe. Yeah, maybe it does."

The avalanche of criticism heaped on the Carter presidency—in the media, from congressional and state leaders of his own as well as the opposition party, among ex-staffers, and obviously from his primary and general election opponents in 1980—has been formidable. To be sure, one reporter had it right when he insisted that Carter *was* an utter failure: after four years in office, Washington, D.C., still did not have a major league baseball team!

Others, who are sophisticated enough to know better, were considerably less generous. Few presidents of recent memory have been as frequently accused of promising so much and doing so little. Why? Perhaps Schlesinger and Wicker were right: Carter and his staff did commit a number of unconscionable political blunders, and they did pursue, in the final years, economic and defense policies that were clearly contradictory. These critics had and still have a lot of company.

Americans for Democratic Action (ADA), justifying their decision to desert an incumbent Democratic president in January 1980, summarized the basic complaint:

> Carter's failure to adhere to the basic tenets of the Democratic platform on which he ran . . . have eroded the vital differences between the two major parties and suggest that party principle and platform matter little to him.[1]

The attacks on the Carter administration, particularly from the liberal wing of his party but also from those like Washington senator Henry Jackson and New York senator Daniel Patrick Moynihan for his supposedly "left-wing foreign and defense policy," actually began within a few months of his taking office and culminated in the ill-fated effort of Edward Kennedy to deny him renomination in 1980.

In light of the overwhelmingly negative consensus of the "Washington community" about Carter, as well as his rejection at the polls, the central argument and major findings of this chapter may strike some readers as perverse. The chapter suggests that the Carter administration was neither as wayward as the ADA and other anti-Carter partisans asserted nor as heroic as the citizens of Plains, Ga., might believe. To accept this judgment, readers must take seriously a line from a recently absentminded *New Republic:* candidates run for the presidency, not canonization.

If one concedes the usual evasions and hedging that have been characteristic of every president since 1960—probably every president since the institution was invented—and the massive uncertainty of an inflationary economy that led to a sharp change in the administration's economic policy after 1978, the findings suggest that the substance of Carter's legislative and executive proposals were consistent with what "reasonable" analysts would have predicted from the promises of his campaign. The Carter administration was plagued by a large gap between presidential efforts to deliver on his promises and the scope of his actual legislative achievements. Much more than earlier presidents, *Carter ranks high on effort, low on eventual delivery.*

Responsibility for this gap cannot be attributed solely to Carter's problematic leadership or the political mistakes of his administration. His administration faced a world, political and economic, that was dramatically different from the world earlier Democratic presidents confronted.

Evaluating presidential performance requires suitable comparative baselines. Too much popular commentary is ahistorical, with presidential decisions being damned or praised without any realistic comparative benchmark. Thus, presidents like Roosevelt, Kennedy, or Johnson are lionized, depending on what aspect of their presidencies analysts are examining, as if each never suffered the bruising defeats of a more contemporary president like Carter.[2] We need more precise comparative measures of presidential effort *and* achievement, anchored in the particular political and economic context each administration faces.

First, this chapter examines some aspects of the Carter presidency relative to other administrations since Eisenhower's. For a quantitative overview of presidential effort and achievement, the reader should consult once again the material presented in Chapter 2.

Second, the emphasis is on programs sought and won and less on *specific* aspects of presidential leadership that characterized the Carter administration. At least most of the time. Substance and process are inevitably linked, so leadership will receive some attention. However, this is not a comprehensive treatment of the Carter presidency, in which the personal and political aspects would, of necessity, play a much larger role. Others, most recently and notably, Paul Light, provide skillful and compelling accounts of the determinants of agenda selection and success.[3]

Third, the chapter is linked to the central theoretical concern of the book—democratic accountability in the extent to which presidents follow through on campaign promises, those made personally in their speeches and position papers as well as those churned up in party platforms.

Finally, as noted above, an evaluation of Carter must proceed not only comparatively across time but also contextually *in* his time. Individual presidents face different environments, have different opportunities. This chapter is concerned with Carter's performance in the context of the specific electoral problems he confronted, the specific coalitional structure of the Democratic party he led between 1976-1980, the specific constellation of forces in Congress during his presidency, and the specific global realities he faced.

Understanding Carter's agenda, 1977-1978 _____

A momentarily famous Georgian who crisscrossed Washington for a brief period during the early days of the administration is reported to have once observed, "Jimmy, he campaigns liberal but governs conservative." [4] On the basis of two presidential campaigns and one term in office, it would be more accurate to say that he campaigned liberal *and* conservative and governed the same way. For liberal disbelievers, who certainly were the most vigorous of Carter's critics,[5] let me mention some actions that were broadly consistent with his "liberal" campaign promises. The administration:

> —proposed a combination guaranteed annual income/work incentive program that would fundamentally alter current welfare policy, guaranteeing a family of four an income of $4,200 per year and gradually reducing payments, when one or both household heads worked, by 50 cents for each dollar earned up to $8,400. The proposal was finally killed in Congress as "too expensive" after being considered off and on for 13 months. The administration resubmitted a scaled-down plan in May 1979 that passed in the House, stalled, then died in the Senate. Most opposition came from conservatives in Congress, although many progressives were put off by the plan's low income floors and enforced work components.[6]
> —submitted a 1977-1978 comprehensive economic stimulus package that raised by $21 billion federal spending for public service employment, doubling these jobs to 725,000; created 200,000 additional jobs through a $4 billion public works program; increased by $1 billion countercyclical revenue sharing; and created a $1.5 billion youth employment program for 200,000 jobs. The administration later reversed course, submitting an FY 1980 budget

that sought to reduce public service employment, but it is ironic that it had to fight the Senate Budget Committee, under the leadership of that old northern "New Dealer," Sen. Edmund Muskie, D-Maine, to prevent the Senate from cutting the administration's request by an additional 100,000 jobs. The FY 1981 budget sought further reductions in public service employment.

—fought attempts to convert college student loan programs into a "tuition tax credit" program and expanded family income eligibility to $25,000, removing the older income limit for low-interest federally guaranteed student loans. (It is unclear whether this struggle should be classified "liberal versus conservative," but most observers believe that private tuition credits would have a disporportionately negative impact on public educational institutions, the only ones that are reaching significant numbers of students from lower middle-class, working-class, and poorer families).

—sought, unsuccessfully, to develop a national urban policy, opting instead for a series of discrete programs that expanded by $1.2 billion the Urban Development Action Grant Program; assisted in providing a "permanent" solution to New York's muddled financial affairs by providing federal guarantees of $1.65 billion in loans; supported the passage of a Consumer Cooperative Bank; and targeted more countercyclical assistance to cities (instead of states).

—supported, unsuccessfully, a national no-fault insurance program.

—supported changes in the eligibility for food stamps that benefited more families.

—supported, unsuccessfully, the creation of a federal consumer protection agency.

—supported ("too little, too late, and too ineffectual," said one feminist leader) passage of the ERA; later supported extension of the constitutional deadline for passage.

—reversed the original position of the two highest ranking black officials in the Justice Department, Assistant Attorney General for Civil Rights Drew Days and Solicitor General Wade McCree. Both originally had supported a brief *rejecting* the argument that race was a constitutionally permissible criteria in the selection of students for admission to medical school. Affirmative action was not fundamentally altered by *Bakke*, in which the Supreme Court's opinion was supportive, more or less, of the administration position and *revised* Justice Department brief. In short, the White House courageously intervened against the position of the two top-ranking black officials to assure the future of affirmative action for blacks.[7]

—waged a successful four-year struggle in Congress to obtain a comprehensive Alaska National Interest Lands Bill, which the Sierra Club called the "most important conservation measure of the century." For conservationists, this bill is the single most important contribution of the Carter administration to protecting what remains of American wilderness, and its achievement is a lasting contribution to "progress as if survival matters."

—supported legislation that created, in addition to the areas in Alaska, 15 new National Park system units, increased substantially the number of wilderness and wild and scenic river units, and added 48,000 acres of watershed and redwoods to the Redwood National Park.

—supported a bill setting the first national uniform standards for strip mining.

—sought, unsuccessfully, to make the first comprehensive change in the National Labor Relations Act since Taft-Hartley that would have improved considerably the bargaining and organizing rights of labor.

—forwarded to Congress on June 13, 1979, after two and one-half years of planning, the "first" step of a national comprehensive health plan.[8]

Clearly, the Carter administration attempted to follow through on many of its most important campaign promises that mattered to liberals. The close fit between the campaign's domestic agenda and the presidential agenda for the first two years is illustrated by the data in Table 4-1. Of 10 major policy clusters, 7 were rated "High" by senior staffers who served in the Carter campaign and held important positions in the White House. All but two of the high presidential items involve liberal directions in policy; on the campaign agenda, all but one are liberal, depending on how one considers the energy development/conservation debate.

The quantitative data in Chapter 2 show that the Carter administration developed legislation or advanced executive orders that were "fully" or "partially" consistent with 65 percent of its campaign promises, a record that matched Kennedy (66 percent) and Johnson (63 percent) and exceeded Reagan (53 percent) or Nixon (60 percent). Carter's "good faith" is particularly evident in these data, and assertions that he was abandoning his campaign promises, assertions that were becoming widespread as early as late 1977—that is, before the deferrals and reversals of 1979-1980—were off the mark. In the first two years of his presidency, Carter's pledge-to-proposal ratio is high, consistent, and strongly "liberal" in content, but discontent with not only the process

Table 4-1   Domestic policy clusters ranked as high and low in the agenda of the campaign and in the Carter administration, 1977-1978[a]

Policy cluster	Salience on:	
	Campaign agenda	Presidential agenda during first two years
Unemployment and economic stimulus	High	High
Government reorganization and management	High	High
Welfare reform (Guaranteed National Minimum Income)	High	High
Tax reform	High	Low
National health insurance	High	High
Deregulation and regulatory management	Low	High
Energy development and conservation	High	High
Environmental protection	High	High
Labor law reform	Low	High
Consumer protection agency	High	High

[a] Rankings of "High" and "Low" were obtained in the following manner. On the basis of my own field work in the 1976 campaign and careful but nonquantitative assessments of reporting in *Congressional Quarterly, The National Journal,* and the *Washington Post,* I extracted 10 policy clusters that seemed to recur throughout Carter speeches and issue statements. I then asked three advisers who served in the campaign and who were later appointed to the White House staff to specify the salience of each item as "High" or "Low." The ratings were obtained independently at two times, once during May-July 1976 (in the campaign) and then in Dec.-Jan. 1977-1978. All three had to agree that a cluster was High; otherwise it was designated Low. Interestingly, only one item received two Highs from all three respondents. The rest were either consistently ranked High or ranked Low by at least two of the three respondents. Only one cluster not selected by me (urban development) was thought to be of equal importance by staff to those shown above.

but also the substance of administration programs was mushrooming among liberal Democrats. Why?

Consider again the points made about the inevitable subjectivity and conflicting expectations related to assessing presidential performance.

Group-anchored standards. Within three months of Carter's taking office, prominent leaders in the women's rights, organized labor, civil rights, and environmentalist communities were questioning the priorities and direction of his administration. By the end of 1977, these questions had turned into a fusillade of condemnation that Carter was "backing off," "caving in," "selling out" to nonprogressive forces in Congress and elsewhere. Some of this is an expression of the natural disappointment of campaign coalition partners who feel slighted when the rhetoric of campaigns must be fitted to the highly specific, detailed, legislative proposals of governing, proposals that always reflect political compromise. More important, such criticism stems from the imperative of group leadership. The internal pressures of leading many social change organizations require that leaders articulate and defend maximum demands. Otherwise, group members or competitors for leadership may come to believe that their own leaders, not the president, have "sold out." These pressures are intense in change-oriented groups, notably those who have not enjoyed a long, mutually beneficial relationship with decision makers in Washington.

Feminist organizations like NOW (National Organization for Women) and NWPC (the National Women's Political Caucus) clearly fit this pattern during the early years of the Carter administration. Naturally, they defined "progress" on Carter initiatives affecting women in a way very different from the White House. Assessing presidential fulfillment is an intensely political activity that depends as much on the internal power configuration of groups as it does on their relationship to the president himself.

Flexible presidential strategy. Presidents must make decisions not only about what bills to propose but also how to propose them, what resources will be committed to advance them, and what costs will be borne in committing those resources. In Light's phrase, presidents and their staffs operate on "a theory of legislative expense."[9] All proposals carry a political price tag, and some are more expensive than others. For example, the Carter administration committed substantial resources to advancing labor law reform as a major legislative priority in 1978, ultimately losing a bruising filibuster battle in the Senate. The bill sought to amend federal labor law on small but important technical questions, giving organized labor a stronger bargaining position with management. To the organized business community in Washington, particularly the Chamber of Commerce, already deeply suspicious of the administration, this move set off the predictable fire alarms, and the chamber, along with other national business associations, exploited a growing and sophisticated business lobbying effort in sustaining the filibuster.

At the same time, the administration resisted the AFL-CIO's call for raising the minimum wage to $3.00 (supporting instead a compromise increase to $2.65), deferred supporting the full employment provisions of the proposed Humphrey-Hawkins bill until November 1977 (reinforcing labor's suspicions, left over from the campaign, about Carter's lack of enthusiasm for Humphrey-Hawkins), and deferred proposing anything concrete on national health insurance until early 1979. AFL-CIO president George Meany had been fuming in private about Carter for months and publicly condemned the administration in a speech at the 1977 AFL-CIO's annual meeting, saying that the working person was no better off under Carter than Ford.[10] Senior Carter staff, however, saw the trade-off in a different fashion:

> The basic issue is not whether we support most of the things labor supports. We do! We had to make decisions about how much of our agenda could be dominated by labor-demanded bills in the first two years. Our decision to go with comprehensive welfare reform dictated that health insurance had to wait. Not forever, but just intelligently delayed. Our decision to go with labor law reform meant that we had to be very careful, damn careful, about trade issues. I don't understand them [the AFL-CIO]. They know this, but you would never know it by reading the morning papers. We're using up a lot of credit in the Senate on the labor [reform] bill. But we get no thanks from them!

Or consider the issue of public financing of congressional campaigns. The Carter administration backed public financing of congressional elections throughout its tenure. Early in the 1976 campaign, Carter committed himself to this and other election reforms as "necessary remedies to the maldistribution of influence in our elections," and each year the administration supported legislation to implement public financing. Indeed, in an otherwise rather spartan 1979 State of the Union address, the president focused on this reform as a major agenda item for the 96th Congress.

Between the commitment and the potential achievement was a complex and uncertain political "cost-benefit" estimate. The House Democratic leadership had been unable to obtain sufficient commitments from its own party members on the House Administration Committee and was convinced that forcing the bill out of committee and onto the floor was simply a flag-waving routine that would lose them future credit with moderate and conservative Democrats who opposed public financing. The leadership still publicly supported (in March 1978) a campaign financing bill, but the House refused to consider it and the bill was scuttled. Backed by the Democratic Study Group (DSG) and Common Cause, House reformers then sought in July to attach a relevant amendment to the Federal Election Commission authorization bill but, operating without the support of the Rules Committee, were defeated on the floor, 312-196.

Throughout this long episode, according to numerous staff and lobbying groups on the Hill, the White House declined to invest a major lobbying effort in support of reform, primarily because the administration believed the Speaker and Majority Leader, who said that it was a losing struggle and would cost important votes on other more highly valued legislative goals. The president, however, believed that public financing was still sound, long-range policy, and his support for it thus reappears in the 1979 State of the Union message.

Assessing Carter's performance, like that of any other president, requires that the observer distinguish between proposal and follow-through, which in turn depends on how presidents transact the costs and benefits of bargaining and priority setting.

Agenda volume, timing, and focus are three specific aspects of flexibility. Ironically, at the same time the Carter presidency was being condemned for not delivering on its campaign promises, it was being attacked for doing too much, for being obsessed with following through on all the president's pledges, rather than discriminating between them to establish clear priorities. Light's analysis of the first-year agendas of each president since 1960 casts doubt on the assertion that Carter supported too many major initiatives, that his legislative menu was excessively rich and complex compared to earlier Democratic presidents. According to Light's criteria, Kennedy requested action on 25 major domestic items, Johnson 34, and Carter 21; in other words, Carter requested *fewer* than either of his Democratic predecessors.[11] The criticism that he was overloading legislative dockets, widely reported and believed throughout the Washington community in 1977-1978, was erroneous. There are three explanations as to why this belief took such a strong hold on lawmakers and political activists.

First, the overall legislative agenda of the executive branch has grown by 60 percent since the Kennedy years. In 1977, the Office of Management and Budget approved 552 draft bills emanating from the executive branch, compared to 355 in 1961, Kennedy's first year. Many of these bills are routine, but some would be on the secondary list of the president's agenda. OMB clears only those bills that are "consistent with" or "in accordance with" the administration's goals and policy. Congress, however, manages these items as well as those that are higher on the president's agenda.

Second, a Democratically controlled Congress, which had been struggling against Republican presidents for eight years, was also "reforming" itself so as to maximize decentralized power sharing. Thus Congress inevitably would be more competitive with the presidency for agenda control in the late 1970s, even with a Democratic president. A significant increase in major, change-oriented proposals came on top of "business as usual" in a Congress long adjusted to fewer, less sweeping proposals from the White House.[12]

Third, both senior White House staff and leading congressional figures agreed that the administration failed to focus properly its energies and resources on the three or four most important goals of the first session. The lack of clear presidential priorities added to the normal confusion of a large, although not an exceptionally large, Democratic agenda.

Hamilton Jordan, Carter's informal chief of staff, initially refused to concede that presidential focusing was that important:

> His [Carter's] style is full-court press . . . he will be more successful than you think by working on all of them simultaneously. If he had started off saying "The Number One thing I want is the Department of Energy," everyone would have gone after that [trying to defeat it]. If you do a lot at once, you can slip some [good] things by—it works the same in domestic and foreign policy.[13]

Two months later, at the beginning of the 1978 session, Jordan still defended the "all at once" strategy, but he was much less confident about its political advantage to the president:

> I think the option would have been to set very limited goals and objectives this first year, and that was never in the cards. . . . If we had . . . we could be beating our chests now and claiming to have batted 1000 percent. Instead, we tried to do 20 or 30 things, and it is difficult to present a coherent picture to the American people as to what you are about and why you're trying to do so many things. . . . I don't think we have presented a very coherent picture.[14]

The failure to focus properly, to concentrate selectively on a *few large* items, and to deploy most of the president's resources to achieve them badly eroded the political credit of the Carter presidency. This erosion undercut his policy agenda because *in the presidency, process can swamp substance.*

The early political mistakes of the Carter administration have been extensively chronicled, analyzed, and reanalyzed.[15] Strategic errors in timing, missed opportunities, and mistakes in setting priorities characterized many (not all, of course) of Carter's first year initiatives. The appointment of Frank Moore, a newcomer to Washington and inexperienced in the nuances of congressional intrigue, as director of the president's Office of Congressional Relations proved a serious error, one that dogged the White House long after OCR's internal and external operations had noticeably improved.[16]

The forced resignation, in October 1977, of Bert Lance, the president's first director of OMB and one of his closest personal associates, contributed to Carter's "soft" public image. One study concluded that "an administration that began with such careful attention to imagery and a president who at first seemed such a 'master of the symbolic act' turned out to be an enormous symbolic failure." [17] Press stories, following the usual cycle of early cooperation during the "honeymoon" period and changing to antagonism as presidents find themselves "reading more and enjoying it less," amplified the negative fallout of the Lance scandal.[18] "Loss of control and lack of competence," Bruce Miroff concludes, "became deadly images that Carter and his aides would futilely combat for the rest of his term." [19]

Despite these setbacks, the substantive record of Carter's first two years in office was in fact modestly respectable. His presidential support scores, as assessed by Congressional Quarterly, although lower than Kennedy's or Johnson's, were considerably higher than those of his predecessor, Ford, mainly because party loyalty is still important in Congress, decentralized and contentious as it was and still is.

Many critics, however, apparently felt the same as one of those celebrated Germond-Witcover respondents, located in Rockford, Ill., who, when asked about the administration, said, "Jimmy Carter? Yes, he's a Democrat and I voted for him, but what the hell, he's turned out the same as the rest. He don't do nothing." Or, more precisely, the *other* things the administration began to do—supporting the deregulation of crude oil, abandoning welfare reform, reducing budgetary support for social programs in FY 1980 and 1981, increasing in real terms the defense budget and escalating cold war rhetoric, hedging on enforcement standards for the clean air and water pollution acts, continuing to support nuclear power options, among others—placed "progressives everywhere on a collision course with the Carter administration and the Democratic party." [20]

In late 1978, as the final portions of the FY 1980 budget were being completed, a senior White House aide observed:

> Inflation has wracked us. I'm a liberal Democrat and hell, there are things that badly need being done. We may still do them but I'm not so sure anymore. Hold the budget! Hold the budget! That's all I ever hear and it's been that way ever since we got here. The president is *not* a Keynesian. His background as a businessman and governor doesn't lead him there. And then, at first, the influence of Bert, and now Strauss and Blumenthal. I'm disappointed. For example, I go over to COPE and you know those guys—they've been around here a long time, they're tough, I look like a youngster compared to them, and they sit there, and pound the table and demand "when are you going to make good on the platform?" and I try to tell them what we've done, but what else can I say? They just don't believe me.

Selective reversals in the Carter agenda, 1979-1980 _____

As the 1980 election year opened, the Carter administration was being attacked by a broad segment of Democratic opinion leaders for having reversed its program commitments in two general areas, economic and defense policy. Carter was not unique in this respect. With the exception of Kennedy, every president studied in this period reversed himself in important policy areas, and all of them, including Kennedy, deferred action on segments of their original campaign agendas. The reasons for policy reversal or deferral can be found in the impact of unanticipated events during their early years in office (mounting inflation, in Carter's case), the political demands of governing rather than campaigning (shared power with Congress), and White House calculations about what issue positions will be electorally advantageous in a bid for reelection.

Keep in mind my observations about the content of Democratic *campaign* agendas. Because sluggish economic growth and recessions are more typically the economic problems to which Democratic presidential candidates have addressed their agendas, campaign promises are likely to reflect New Deal-style rhetoric. "God in His Infinite Wisdom," David Broder wrote, "did not make the Democratic party His instrument for dealing with Inflation." Until recently, Democratic presidential candidates since Kennedy have made promises that emphasize relatively high government spending, low interest rates, and a plentiful supply of money. While he was more concerned about inflation in 1976 than many earlier Democratic candidates, Carter's promised economic package was firmly in line with traditional Democratic principles. And the administration acted consistently with these principles during its first two years in office. Inflation, however, reached 13 percent in 1979 and threatened to hit 18 percent in 1980. Carter and his major economic advisers unsurprisingly concluded that it was time to alter their original economic commitments. Because they rejected the alternative preferred by some leaders in the liberal wing of the party and by the AFL-CIO— mandated controls on prices, interest, and profits and, if necessary, on wages—the administration's proposals were seen as "illiberal and inconsistent with the 1976 platform." [21]

Simultaneously, the Soviet invasion of Afghanistan fueled a growing fear inside and outside the administration about Russian expansionism and belligerence and was used by some advisers to persuade Carter to increase defense spending. Carter's FY 1980 and 1981 budget choices reflected these fears, and this, too, was an important reversal of his 1976 campaign pledge. The fact that many labor leaders supported the

renewed defense buildup, while denouncing the concomitant retrench-
ment in social services, is irrelevant. Factional disappointment with the
administration was growing among different groups in the Democratic
party for different reasons, but all could join in a general chorus of
criticism of his policy reversals. This is a classic no-win situation for any
president.

Democratic presidential agendas become increasingly unpredictable
when little consensus exists in the party coalition over appropriate
responses to problems (for example, defense and the Soviet threat), or
when uncertainty about cause and effect (for example, concerning
inflation) undermine the utility of older, party-based, consensual solutions. The shift in the Carter agenda, reflecting in part the resurrection
of cold war "imperatives" and "un-Democratic" economic problems, is
graphically represented by the data in Table 4-2.

The same three senior White House officials were asked to compare
those areas of high and low priority status in the two periods, and the
differences are substantial: of the nine policy clusters ranked high
during 1977-1978, five were ranked low for 1979-1980. Predictably, some
of these would be of intense concern to liberals in the Democratic party.
Tax reform, for example, was high on the campaign agenda but slipped
in 1978 because of the early and bruising defeats suffered by the
administration in Congress. Two other areas, national health insurance
and environmental protection, were still considered top priority in the
closing days of Carter's presidency. Four new areas, all "post-New Deal"
issues, had become central. Each adviser stressed the impact of foreign
policy crises like the 1978 OPEC oil squeeze, inflation, and the Kennedy
challenge as responsible for these shifts. Asked in early February 1980
whether this different emphasis might be interpreted as a reversal of
1976 campaign promises, one respondent laughed and replied:

> Of course! That isn't the point. How could he responsibly be saying and
> working on the same things in 1980 that we were talking about in
> 1976? We have delivered ... or at least broke our hearts trying. The
> world has changed. Voters are going to judge the president on the basis
> of his flexibility, his responsiveness to new problems, not just what he
> said he would try to do in 1975 and 1976. I'm still committed to some of
> our old concerns—tax reform, for example—but it's just going to have
> to wait. We're going to beat Kennedy and the decaying liberals around
> him, and we're going to reshape the Democratic party in the process.

The variation in the way the administration treated different
environmental and energy questions is instructive on this point. On
"old line" conservation issues, like the Alaska Lands bill or expanding
national park and wilderness areas elsewhere, the Carter programs, in
the words of one environmentalist, "were golden." The reason, in part,
is that a large, fairly stable, and visible coalition exists outside and inside

Table 4-2 Comparison of domestic policy clusters ranked as high and low during the Carter administration, 1977-1978 and 1979-1980[a]

	1977-1978 agenda	1979-1980 agenda
Policy cluster		
Unemployment and economic stimulus	High	Low
Government reorganization and management	High	Low
Welfare reform	High	Low
Tax reform	Low	Low
National health insurance	High	High
Deregulation and regulatory management	High	High
Energy development and conservation	High	High
Environmental protection	High	High
Labor law reform	High	Low
Consumer protection agency	High	Low
"New cluster"[b]		
Inflation	Low	High
Energy development[c]	High	High
Revenue sharing	Low	High
Budget reductions	Low	High

[a] See Table 4-1 for how these ratings were obtained. The same officials were interviewed both times.

[b] These four areas were mentioned by all three respondents, as well as others in foreign policy, particularly defense programs.

[c] All three mentioned "controlled" energy development (synfuels, Energy Mobilization Board, windfall profits tax), suggesting these went beyond the early concerns, although all stressed that the president was still committed to conservation strategies.

Congress and the Democratic party, and has existed for some time, in support of these policies. On the other hand, questions originating in the "new" environmental conflicts, like energy and air pollution control, lack a secure and unified coalition base in either the Democratic party or Congress. Thus, as always, the administration's recourse was to muddle through, adjusting here, reversing itself there, trying to retail solutions as if these problems were independent rather than interdependent, hoping to minimize their losses, but retaining a rhetorical commitment to the need for comprehensive problem solving. As was suggested earlier about complexity, this strategy, unless artfully employed, can increase rather than decrease organizational error, especially political error.[22]

On the other issues, either because of unanticipated external developments, as in the economy, or because of a reassessment during the first three years, the administration changed its agenda in dramatic fashion. For example, Carter:

—suggested in the FY 1980 and 1981 budget messages a clear departure from the 1976 pledge to "achieve an unemployment level of 4 percent or less by the end of my first term." The administration's fiscal and monetary policy was ultimately based on assumptions of increasing unemployment, higher interest rates, a tighter money supply, and projected recession.

—proposed cuts in the defense budget of $5 to $7 billion in the 1976 campaign, articulating a vision of further reorganization in domestic priorities to reduce the preeminence of military priorities. Beginning in FY 1980 and permeating the FY 1981 budget was a commitment to a "5 percent" *real* increase in defense spending.

—proposed taxing capital gains at the same rate as "other earned income," but signed a tax "reform" bill that actually *reduced* the pre-1976 rate of taxation on capital gains.

—opposed the deregulation of "old" crude oil throughout the campaign, but made deregulation of both oil and natural gas central in the administration's national energy plan.

—suggested consistently that a "large and comprehensive plan to rebuild the nation's railroads" would be undertaken, but sought to reduce AMTRAK service by approximately 43 percent.

—and whatever happened to that pledge to make the DNC Women's Division "a fighting feminist force"? (The DNC was practically bankrupt by 1980, although Carter was hardly the first incumbent president to ignore the national party committee.)

The list, perhaps surprisingly, does *not* go on endlessly. A count of *major* campaign-to-White House reversals suggests the administration backtracked in seven areas, took token action on five (enforcement standards for the Clean Air Act, the Water Pollution Control Act, and the Toxic Substances Control Act are examples) and failed to take action of any consequence in four areas. "Gun control legislation," Rep. Pete Stark, D-Calif., observed, "was not going to be a 'Profile in Courage' issue for Carter."

Carter's early attempts to redeem much in the campaign agenda, followed by selective reversals, drift, and deferrals, was true to the pattern mentioned earlier: selective reversal occurs after the midterm elections if incumbent presidents and their advisers believe that the trade-offs between pursuing the policy commitments of the last campaign and the next one substantially favor a shift away from the priorities and direction of the old agenda.

As early as 1978, senior White House staff, most notably Hamilton Jordan, were assuming that Ted Kennedy and California governor Jerry Brown would enter the primaries against Carter. Brown was considered an irritant, Kennedy a major threat. On January 17, 1979, a full 10 months before Kennedy announced, Jordan formally outlined a strategy for defeating him in a memo to the president, but only a small part of the memo reflected much concern with issues. Others in the White House, however, were concerned about the policy implications, clearly distinguishing between what they believed were the requirements for surviving a primary challenge from Kennedy and winning the general election against the Republicans. One observed:

> I consider myself a liberal but there is no way our policies, at least economically, are going to satisfy my liberal friends in Congress. *My friends are wrong;* no Democratic president, given what's happening in the economy, can return here in 1980 by pursuing their suggestions. We cannot spend more substantially on social programs; we can tax no more; we cannot allow the Republicans to pin that old label about being "soft on the Russians" on us. Wage and price controls are out of the question—politically speaking. We *can* do some things that will satisfy many in the party, but only *some* things. And they probably won't like that, anyway. *They* are wrong, politically and otherwise. Ted Kennedy, if he goes, just may defeat us in the primaries, because the primaries will overrepresent groups, like organized labor, who will not face current realities. Even if he has the charisma of Jesus Christ—and I think you know that he doesn't, Chappaquiddick and his personal life will eat away at that—it will be hopeless against the Republicans in the fall. If we are unable to sell Carter as a sober, thoughtful moderate on economic and defense matters, and the economy keeps racing out of control, Kennedy and his band will sink the Democratic party, and most liberals, to permanent oblivion in the fall. Mark my word!

The Carter campaign hardly "rescued" the Democratic party (to say the least!). Nor did Kennedy sink it.

More important, as this staffer's comments reflect, the Carter presidency was moving toward a reelection strategy that would emphasize an economic and defense agenda different from what they originally carried into office. What people *see* as reality *is* reality; even a much revised and more sophisticated New Deal economic agenda was no longer considered a viable electoral philosophy by liberal Democrats who worked for Carter's reelection. The incentives to challenge Carter among those in the party who disagreed with this electoral strategy, whether they won or lost the primaries, were thus established long before Kennedy announced during the first week of November 1979. Kennedy's challenge, from the viewpoint of agenda building, was a gamble on an untested hypothesis: *when the incumbent is faced with intense competition for renomination, agenda development is a trade-off between the electoral incentives to continue existing policies and the coalitional incentives to shift toward the preferences of the challenging faction.*

Another, perhaps obvious, factor needs mentioning in assessing presidential follow-through and its absence in the Carter administration. Although the American business community is diverse and pluralistic in its organization and policy preferences, Carter faced growing antagonism to his economic priorities from leading sectors of that community.

More than any other factor, business fears about the economic policies of Democratic presidents serve to retard, deflect, and sometimes undermine even moderately redistributive economic policy. "Business confidence," that old bogey of every Democrat since Andrew Jackson, is a formidable antagonist, all the more so because many Americans share the same fears as business owners and their sympathetic interpreters in the world of mass communication. One can reject the idea of a corporate structure united around the same policy configuration and still understand why redistributive policies usually will be resisted by most national associations that speak for business. The Carter administration was haunted by the fear of "losing business confidence" from the beginning, becoming more sensitive as inflation continued to spiral. The impact of this fear, which led to the appointment of a conservative Wall Street banker, Paul Volcker, as chairman of the Federal Reserve Board and to the dramatic attempt to balance the FY 1981 budget, helped push Carter's economic policies further away from what was promised in 1976.

The next point is even more basic: presidents face new issues, new problems, new demands that cannot be anticipated from the last campaign. The longer a president is in office, the more his agenda will be determined by current events. In Carter's case, one need only mention the rising tax revolt in the states and the resulting, if perhaps temporary, stampede to restrict property taxation.

Last, the governing coalition of the Carter administration became unstable over time because its electoral coalition was forged largely in the primaries, where candidate-centered, not party-centered, activities are emphasized. One consequence of this is to make political trust less durable and harder to achieve, a fact that in turn makes governing through coalition building more difficult. That the governing coalition of Carter was unstable, like that of Johnson after 1965 and Ford after 1975, is reflected in the behavior of one usually reliable Democrat—Edward M. Kennedy.

The Kennedy challenge

The Massachusetts senator had been the first choice for president of so many rank-and-file Democrats for so many years that his long-anticipated announcement in early November 1979 at Boston's Faneuil Hall seemed anticlimactic. Five months later, "Ted Kennedy emerged as the year's champion loser ... one of the longest-lived bubbles in American politics—the image of Edward Kennedy as a political superman—had been burst, quite possibly beyond repair." [23]

"Superman" he is not, but Kennedy remains a major spokesman for the chastened if recuperative liberal wing of the Democratic party. Obviously, the Kennedy "bubbles" are considerably more durable than one defeat might suggest.

From the viewpoint of agenda development in the Carter administration, Kennedy's decision to challenge the president represented a gamble with both negative and positive dimensions—negative in that the obvious divisiveness and struggle would weaken *any* Democratic nominee and, by implication, risk all Democratic policy alternatives; positive (for Kennedy and his partisans) because, if he won both the nomination and the general election, progressives would be free of the Carter "half-loaf" many had grown to hate. Apparently, starvation was preferable to malnutrition. Said one Kennedy staffer, who had taken leave from the AFL-CIO to join the campaign:

> What we stand for, have always stood for, is dying in the Carter administration. Are they better than the Republicans? Sure they are! That isn't the point. Carter is through politically; he will never make it back to the White House. Our choice is not between a half-assed Democrat like Carter and the Republicans because there is no chance that he can beat the Republicans. I signed on with Kennedy because not only is he better on the issues but he is our only hope politically in the fall.

This theme—mixing despair over the policy direction of the White House with alarm about the sinking electoral fortunes of the president—appears consistently in the justification of those who defended Kennedy's entry into the primaries. The point needs to be emphasized because it is clear that Kennedy's support among many well-placed Democrats was not based exclusively on policy or ideology. Colleagues, like Henry Jackson in the Senate and Paul Simon in the House, pleaded with Kennedy to run because they felt that Carter's renomination would precipitate a Republican avalanche. The polls were strongly supportive; Kennedy led Carter among all major constituencies in the Democratic party and in every region outside the South throughout much of 1978 and all of 1979. Carter, Kennedy supporters argued, was both a political *and* policy liability.[24]

So confident was the senior Kennedy campaign staff about the president's political vulnerability that, ironically, after announcing, Kennedy virtually ignored, during the first two months of his campaign, every policy area that supposedly distinguished him from Carter. No substantial issues staff was created; no position papers were prepared ("Everyone knows how the senator stands; what's the point?" said an aide); no task forces were created; no specific agenda was discussed or projected. "The most important issue in this primary campaign," continued the Kennedy aide, "is the utter failure of Carter to provide leadership, for our party or the country."

Roger Mudd's CBS interview, in which the senator mumbled ineptly through a series of questions about why he wanted to be president, unable to articulate a reasoned response to this "nonissue," set the stage for his early campaign failures. With a little help from Ayatollah Ruholla Khomeini, after Iranian nationalists took over the American Embassy on November 4, 1979, Carter and his organization deftly implemented a classic "incumbent strategy," sinking Kennedy first in the Iowa caucuses and then on through 24 of 34 primaries.

The unexpected electoral weakness of Kennedy and the temporarily soaring fortunes of Carter due primarily to the Iranian crisis (among Democrats, Carter's approval rating went from 37 percent in November to 62 percent in February, sliding back to 37 percent by June) combined to force a significant shift in Kennedy's strategy—or nonstrategy. Commented one of the senator's staffers:

> Iowa taught us a very big lesson. The senator could not alter the Iranian thing, but he could alter the terms of the debate. We had to reach our natural constituency, blue-collar workers, liberals, minorities, urban ethnics, with something other than attacks on Carter, and that something was Kennedy's commitment to the issues that have made the Democratic party the champion of the common man.

Others had underscored the importance of the Iowa defeat on Kennedy's thinking. One reporter wrote that "Iowa liberated Kennedy ... he told his advisers that he was going back to the clear advocacy of the liberal cause that had been his trademark."[25] Six days after Iowa, Kennedy delivered a speech at Georgetown University, outlining in more detail his commitment to liberal positions on wage/price/interest controls, gasoline rationing, and oppositon to the "helter-skelter militarism" of the Carter administration. The speech was beautifully crafted, not only from an issues standpoint, but also in tone, modalities, and delivery. The response among Carter's opponents was enthusiastic. Whatever the impact on voters—neither gas rationing nor government managed wage/price controls were positions voters enthused over in 1980—the new Kennedy strategy reinforced the ideological rationale of his challenge.

Liberals and other activists needed reasons and reinforcement to sustain Kennedy's challenge to an incumbent Democrat, and the Georgetown speech and much of Kennedy's behavior in the primaries thereafter gave it to them. Darrell M. West, employing a sophisticated content analysis of candidate comments reported in the *New York Times*, found that Kennedy substantially led the main Carter surrogates (Walter Mondale and Rosalynn Carter) in his references to "specific policy" and "general problems," with Kennedy referring to such items 72 percent of the time, Mondale 44 percent, and Rosalynn Carter 37 percent.[26] The president opted for an early "Rose Garden" strategy that kept him off the primary campaign circuit.

These findings should be placed in context. If one considers only specific policy, no 1980 candidate from the major parties and not even John Anderson, who ran as an independent, was very policy oriented in his campaign speeches. The figures are 16 percent for Kennedy and 13 percent for Mondale; by comparison, Anderson was 20 percent, Reagan 13 percent.[27]

However, the Georgetown speech and the candidate's subsequent stump rhetoric had the effect of reassuring anti-Carter liberals about Kennedy and about the agenda items that underlay his campaign. Particularly after Kennedy's crushing defeat in Illinois, an industrial state where the Democratic party is dominated by the very constituencies thought to be pro-Kennedy, his challenge to Carter had to be shown as based on something more than Carter's political vulnerability. West provides a useful quote from Kennedy delegate director Richard Stearns on this problem:

> We had been campaigning simply on dissatisfaction with the quality of leadership that Carter provided. I don't think there is anything particularly wrong with that theme, but in the midst of that rally for Carter because of the hostage and Iranian/Afghani crisis it wasn't that satisfying an answer. . . . The Georgetown speech was meant to explain and spell out the actual content. . . . It supplied the intellectual capital that basically sustained the campaign for the rest of the primary season. . . . It had the effect of putting . . . Kennedy to the left of Carter.[28]

After the defeat in Illinois in April and more often after the primaries ended in early June, the most persistent question asked of Kennedy was why he remained in the race. Many agreed with Washington reporter Dom Bonafede, who wrote, "The suspicion persists that he is seeking vindication not in a hopeless cause but in the judgment of history and is fighting today's battle for tomorrow's ... victory." [29] Or perhaps, as Elizabeth Drew suggested, "Quitting was not in his upbringing ... it appears that Kennedy and Carter really dislike each other, and what each thinks the other stands for, and this dislike has deepened as the campaign has gone on." [30] Finally, one can point to the losing struggle over the "open convention" rule—Kennedy and other anti-Carter Democrats tried to win support for releasing delegates previously pledged to Carter—as clear evidence that everyone likes the drama of uncertainty even when it was clear that Kennedy had lost. Various Kennedy people and others kept hoping that the bottom, somehow, sometime, would just drop out.[31] As the reader knows, Carter's "bottom" was made of solid oak—at least until November.

The impact of the Kennedy challenge

The question of why Kennedy continued in the face of certain defeat is unanswerable; no individual, perhaps not even Senator Kennedy, can answer it. More important for this analysis is examining the impact of Kennedy's challenge on Carter's policy agenda. Did Kennedy's bid, divisive and doomed as it was, move the Carter administration back toward supporting a more liberal agenda?

As usual, Jimmy Carter defies a straightforward and analytically convenient answer. Five important considerations need to be remembered. First, recall the earlier proposition from the agenda-setting framework. The "seasons" of presidential politics shape expectations about issue specificity and content, at least for challengers, with candidates remaining much less specific on issues in the primary stage, growing more specific as they move toward the convention and the platform-writing process. Second, the lack of control over external forces in the international and domestic environment makes seemingly long-held party positions less stable. Third, the continuing division within the Democratic party over appropriate responses to communist and/or revolutionary regimes in general, the Soviet Union in particular, was heightened because of the Iranian crisis and Soviet intervention in Afghanistan. Fourth, the increasingly bitter intraparty dispute over the relative importance of inflation versus unemployment in a stagflated economy complicated any easy definition of precisely what a "liberal response" might be, let alone what constitutes a "liberal agenda." Finally, Carter was the incumbent president, and, no matter how much his campaign themes and rhetoric might emphasize nonissues, ("A Family Man, A Man of Character, A Man of Peace—A Solid Man in a

Sensitive Job") presidents, unlike candidates, actually make policy and therefore cannot avoid being specific on many issues.

Consider the impact of the last factor, incumbency, first. The major arena of presidential decision making on domestic policy during the winter and spring of 1980 was the development of the FY 1981 federal budget. Money *is* policy, and the administration shaped its budget in direct response to both the Kennedy primary challenge *and* the impact of external events in the domestic and international environments.

Carter presented *two* budgets in 1980, one coming after the usual internal bargaining process in January and the other, a fundamentally revised budget, in March. The two were radically different in economic assumptions and policy choices. The first budget represented a classic amalgam of Democratic party interest group politics with marginal increases in most social and economic development programs and an important increase in real defense spending (beyond inflation). Budget I showed significant support here and there for most housing, environmental, energy (particularly solar), consumer, and income maintenance programs. Of course, given the persistence of 10 percent to 12 percent inflation rates, the first budget was still defended as "austere and disciplined." But the political rationale underlying it was, as economist Arthur Okun once said, "a middle-of-the-road, muddle-through, election year budget." For the White House, however, it offered a number of gambits to the Democratic liberal/labor coalition, drafted specifically to antagonize as few factions as possible, given Kennedy's continuing assault on Carter's "conservatism." One presidential assistant described the budget and the process that led to it this way:

> OMB and some Congressmen kept trying all year to make drastic cuts, even in entitlement programs, worrying about inflation, reminding us constantly about the president's promise to have a balanced budget by 1980. We just overrode them. We were not going to cut entitlements in an election year, no matter what the hell was going on in the economy, and, with Kennedy's yapping all over the country about the president's betrayals, we were not going to give him more ammunition. We did need to make some cuts, and we did, raising some hell here and there in Congress and among some liberals, but I feel the real pressure was coming the other way, from a more conservative direction, last November and December when final decisions were made. We held out for a budget that wouldn't kill us in the primaries—particularly the northern primaries.

The same aide then sighed (the interview took place after the second, greatly scaled down budget had been introduced in March) and said, "I call those the 'good old days.' "

Events dramatically challenged this characterization and the domestic agenda implied by it in late February when the cost-of-living index rose 4 points in one month, signaling a potential annual inflation rate above 18 percent. "That was it," he continued, "because there was no way we could keep holding back. The president was determined to respond, and respond *immediately.*"

The "emergency" economic shifts of March, coming as they did just *before* the Illinois and New York primaries, led to sweeping changes in the 1981 budget in every major social/economic program except defense spending, which was increased. Although various softeners were included—one $500 million amendment in added revenue sharing for distressed cities, supported by the administration, was called the "New York primary amendment"—the thrust was unambiguous: Carter was going to balance the budget at the expense of domestic social/ economic programs. He made sure that his cuts or program deferrals were cushioned by appropriate concern: "I am recommending cuts in programs that I support very strongly because we must reduce inflation." But from March on, despite the president's rhetoric, inflation was the primary hobgoblin, and the administration's decisions ran directly counter to the positions the Kennedy coalition supported. Of course, given the substantial reductions achieved by Reagan, even Carter's second budget now seems very liberal. Hindsight, however, is of no benefit in helping one understand decisions made in 1980.

For those who supported Kennedy on the grounds that his challenge would move the Carter administration in a more liberal direction, the lessons of this short budgetary history are mixed. In the first round, the administration overrode those who were urging deep cuts and did so, at least in part, to forestall Kennedy's rise in the primaries. By March both economic and political reasoning led the administration in the opposite direction. Balancing the budget and combating inflation, not shoring up labor and liberal support, were the major goals of the Carter administration.

In short, challenging an incumbent president on the grounds that one can influence his decisions in an important policy area assumes that all other factors will remain equal. When uncontrollable factors like steeply rising prices—carrying a greater political cost than rising unemployment—intervene, as they did in early 1980, the policy logic of the challenge can lose its force. If Carter's budgetary decisions provide a reasonably good test, progressives lost any hope of shifting the administration's economic agenda in late February. Moreover, on some specific alternatives for combating inflation like wage/price/ interest controls, the very fact that Kennedy supported them doomed these alternatives in the eyes of most of Carter's senior advisers. Commented one:

As you know, there's never been much support here for government-mandated controls. But there has been some. Those voices have grown progressively more quiet as Kennedy has grown more demanding in his call for controls. So you might say there has been a reaction formation: the more Kennedy supports them, the less we'll consider them!

Such are the ironies of challenging the president's domestic policy agenda through electoral politics. Are there other tests of this question, other decision arenas where the policy impact of the Kennedy challenge can be fairly assessed? One obvious place came three months later in the writing of the platform at the national convention.

Agenda building at the 1980 convention

Many observers of the 1980 Democratic convention can be excused for agreeing with Nelson Polsby's wry comment that, after the "open convention" rule vote on Monday, the rest consisted mostly of waiting "to see whether Senator Kennedy would embrace the ticket, and how happily." [32] Television commentary, in its usual preoccupation with the personally dramatic, monotonously repeated the themes of "will he, won't he" come to the podium (he did), "will he, won't he" hold the president's hand up in a show of unity (negative, he merely shook it), "will he, won't he" campaign for Carter in the fall (not much).

In their soap-opera way, of course, these questions probed an important issue of party organizational maintenance. The extent to which postconvention unity could be achieved, given the obvious divisiveness of the campaign and the numerous ways in which Kennedy declined to be gracious after losing at the convention, was an important concern. On one measure, perhaps the most important, the president benefited a great deal from the convention, despite dire predictions to the contrary. Reagan's lead over Carter at the beginning of the August gathering, estimated by a Gallup poll at 15 percentage points and by a Harris poll at 23, dropped to 1 percent in Gallup's and 3 percent in Harris's after the convention ended. Michael Malbin stressed the irony when he noted:

> To almost every neutral observer in New York's Madison Square Garden, the convention had caused Carter as many problems as it had solved ... but the constant criticism of Reagan in every convention speech clearly had a cumulative impact that had little to do with the subtle tea leaf variations observed by professional convention watchers. [33]

Carter's relative electoral strength, despite the constant assaults on his administration and policies, rose substantially after his contentious party evacuated New York.

Underneath all this, however, an important chapter in agenda building was being constructed. Factional leaders from the liberal wing of the party negotiated, cajoled, pushed, threatened, and finally imposed an extraordinary number of revisions on the final version of the 1980 platform. It is important to emphasize that the original platform, carefully written under White House direction, was hardly a reactionary document. Still, groups as diverse as gays, feminists, antinuclear and environmental activists, and orthodox labor officials understandably wanted planks closer to their preferences and moved in various ways to change the administration's draft. While they may have lost the war in the nomination process, they most certainly won numerous important battles over the party's agenda as it was reflected in the national platform. Informal negotiations between the White House and factional leaders, first during the drafting stage and then before the convention opened, led to significant changes, making the document more accept-able to liberals. The sometimes emotional struggle at the convention, along with politically astute concessions by Carter officials, resulted in the adoption of more (14 of 23) minority planks than at any convention in the twentieth century. Among the most important changes were:

—the first gay rights plank in the history of the American parties (compromise language was agreed to by the Drafting Sub-committee with Carter's support) [34];

—a commitment to "retire nuclear power plants in an orderly manner" (compromise reached between the administration and delegates supporting the Committee for Safe Energy's well-orga-nized antinuclear campaign during the full platform committee's deliberations);

—acceptance of six minority planks before the convention opened as part of a bargain with Kennedy involving scheduling and Kennedy's agreement to withdraw two others. Kennedy forces also agreed to withdraw support from two additional planks during the convention. The six accepted by the White House before the convention opened included:

1. a pledge not to cut funding for welfare, education, and other programs directed at assisting "the most needy in our society";
2. a pledge not to change the cost-of-living index in any way that would result in lower Social Security payments;
3. a commitment to have the federal government assume financial responsibility for state and local government wel-fare costs by the end of 1981;

4. language denying the newly created Energy Mobilization Board "fast track" authority to override environmental, public health, and safety laws;
5. a pledge to spend more on development of solar, wind, and other renewable energy sources than on synthetic fuels;
6. a commitment to give states and Indian tribes the power to veto sites they believed would be unsafe for disposal of nuclear waste.

—a compromise with Kennedy on four economic proposals and a labor-backed jobs plank. This agreement was reached because many of Carter's delegates supported Kennedy's economic program. The outcome permitted the White House to win in its opposition to wage/price controls, in exchange for losing three others on economic affairs. Altogether, the four planks included language committing the Democratic party to:

1. a $12 billion antirecession economic recovery plan;
2. a promise to take "no fiscal action, no monetary action, no budgetary action" that would cause "significantly" greater unemployment;
3. a statement of opposition to fighting inflation through a policy of high interest rates and unemployment;
4. pursuit of a jobs policy that guarantees "a job for every American who is able to work as our single highest domestic priority."

—challenges by feminists in the Democratic party to the administration in two areas—Medicaid payments for abortions and a proposal mandating that the DNC deny support to candidates who opposed the ERA—that were both successful.

"Kennedy," observed one reporter, "lost the nomination and won the platform." Almost, but not quite. The White House was able to fend off Kennedy partisans in three important areas. One challenged the president's decision to move ahead on the MX missile and was defeated on a roll call by almost 600 votes. The second substituted Kennedy's version of a national health insurance program for Carter's and was defeated by slightly more than 200 votes. (Carter supported the concept but sought slower implementation.) The third minority plank won by Carter forces would have prohibited the federal government from using oil import fees or gas taxes to "artificially increase the price of gasoline," which was bartered by Kennedy in exchange for Carter's support of the solar plank. In addition, the administration beat back a conservative effort to reverse the original document's commitment to freedom of choice on abortions. Carter forces prevailed in opposing two minority planks where Kennedy abstained—a commitment to charter oil companies federally and a promise to "pursue an immediate nuclear freeze."

Ironically, the defense/foreign policy language of the 1980 platform, considerably more strident in its argument for a defense buildup than it was in 1976, was never seriously challenged by Kennedy.[35] The platform contained conciliatory language, particularly in its commitment to human rights and the use of "moral principle, rather than force in international conflicts," but the shift to a more confrontational posture vis-à-vis the Soviet Union and the justification of 3 percent annual increases in defense spending during the Carter years are in sharp contrast to the rhetoric and commitments of 1976. Indeed, Democrats even fault the Nixon/Ford administration for a "steady decline of 33 percent in real U. S. military spending between 1968 and 1976," as if the party or the president had never questioned either the practicality or morality of large defense budgets.

In the end, however, Carter's formal statement to the convention made the essential point, reinforcing a feeling shared by most delegates:

> There was ... sometimes heated debate on the major domestic and foreign policy issues facing us. The end product is a strong and progressive platform ... the differences within our party are small in comparison with the differences between the Republican and Democratic party platforms.

Considering the unknowable

Does any of this now make a difference? After all, Carter and the Democrats were given exit visas from the White House shortly after they left Madison Square Garden. The obvious question, tantalizing and unanswerable, is whether the platform would have affected a potential second Carter term? Analyzing events that do not take place is a little like carrying the football into your own end zone: it ignites considerable emotion but no points. The Carter administration all but dropped the issue of a balanced budget for FY 1981 during the general election campaign, privately conceding to a strategy of not antagonizing Democratic factions or potential voting blocs. The highly trumpeted balanced budget of 1981 never came off, partly because of these piecemeal concessions, partly because of the incredible vagaries in economic projections, and supplemental appropriations. In fact, FY 1981 ended with an approximate deficit of $58 billion even after the Reagan administration had imposed some cuts.

Moreover, the fall campaign mandated that Carter turn to opposing Reagan, mobilizing Democratic and independent support through rhetorical appeals, and that intraparty warfare among Democrats end. Because my research and the supporting work of others demonstrate that both parties have implemented a major part of their platforms, one can assume that a second Carter term would not simply have abandoned all of it. The emphasis here should be on "part"; we can never know precisely which part Carter would have implemented, ignored, or scuttled. Precise as they are, platforms still permit a large measure of ambiguity. Carter's own response to the revised platform, imposed on him by an unprecedented rule change requiring candidates formally to declare their support of the platform and to explain any specific disagreements, was masterful in its imprecision. In those areas where he had reservations—the $12 billion antirecession jobs plan, for example—Carter wrote that he would "accept and support the intent" of the program, leaving out a commitment to specific dollar figures. He neither rejected nor accepted the specifics of the plan, leaving exact federal responses to be determined if and when he returned to the White House. Like all presidents, Carter preferred to keep some options open.

Of what impact on the Carter administration, then, was the Kennedy challenge? In real terms, the impact was blunted by the state of the economy. Inflation made it impossible to implement even the piecemeal concessions made to liberals in Budget I and led to a revision, Budget II, that ran counter to what most Kennedy partisans preferred. In New York, at the convention, where party, not governance decisions (except indirectly) were at stake, the challenge had a direct and substantial impact: the coalitional incentives to shift toward the preferences of the challenging faction were considerable, and the administration, with a feint here and an endrun there, made the shift.

Conclusion

Historians have many virtues. High on any list is their capacity to accept the paradoxes of history, particularly presidential history, with an enlightened shrug. Thus few historians would have been surprised when, facing a press gathering in Washington on June 3, 1982, Rev. Robert Drinan, president of Americans for Democratic Action, announced: Jimmy Carter will be "vindicated by history because he was extraordinarily good on many, many issues." [36] Of course, Drinan's comparative reference point was the presidency of Ronald Reagan, and one suspects that Atilla the Hun would fare better on a vindication scale constructed by the ADA.

The point, however, is important. Carter's harshest ADA-like critics must feel some nostalgia and regret over the consequences of the 1980 election. Starvation, it turns out, is a lot worse than malnutrition, even though the ADA, like most human organizations, would prefer to avoid both. Assessing presidential performance is inevitably a comparative enterprise, anchored in both what is desirable and what is possible.

Some of the Carter administration's most notable accomplishments—the pardoning of Vietnam War resisters, the Panama Canal Treaty, the Camp David Agreements, and the creation of more national parks and wildlife preserves than any president in history—surely would satisfy the sternest of liberals. Better than any analyst, Bert Rockman captures the essential dilemma in understanding Carter.[37] The president and most of his administration, Rockman notes, were "problem-solvers," not "generalizers." He continues, "Once the problem-solver is detached from his bureaucratically defined problems and placed in the role of a generalist, as the president is, the substance of his solutions becomes, without the anchor of a familiar ideology, largely unpredictable." [38] To be unpredictable does not mean that decisions will be made randomly.

> It is not that Carter has no value system; it is rather that his values do not fall along lines of immediate political comprehension. Skepticism and analysis . . . are at the core of what he values, but alone a problem-solving orientation like this cannot produce the political support necessary for governance.[39]

The fundamental shift in the administration's fiscal and monetary policies midway through the term was a classic "problem-solving" approach to the economic and political fallout of rampaging inflation—with one important caveat. The ideological breadbasket of this "solution" (tightening credit, reducing federal spending) was classic American business ideology, stemming from those old and powerfully rooted fears about the loss of business confidence. Accordingly, the traditional labor/liberal wing of the Democratic party, whose most cherished solution to inflation was increasing central government control, felt abandoned.

Similarly, the provocative behavior of the Soviets, first in the decade-long buildup of its military capability, then in its intervention in Afghanistan, forced the administration to accentuate publicly an anti-Soviet posture to accommodate those who demanded a more aggressive response. Again, these moves reflected a problem-solving framework ("After all, we're still pursuing SALT II," said one White House official), but with another important caveat. The responses were rooted in traditional Cold War assumptions about Soviet expansion, assumptions that were dormant in the president's outlook from the beginning. And again, the numerically small, but vocal, peace-oriented wing of the Democratic party felt abandoned.

The comparatively high rate of follow-through by Carter on his 1976 campaign agenda is ignored or forgotten by most analysts because of these policy shifts and the well-documented political mistakes associated with many of the administration's most carefully developed legislative proposals. The high effort/low delivery record of Carter was not, however, caused entirely by the administration's deficiencies in process management, the lack of Washington "know-how" so frequently emphasized in damning assessments of Carter. Rather, two large structural problems—unpredictability in the economy and unpredictability in the international system—undercut the administration's capacity to follow through on its original promises in a manner that would have satisfied leading elements of the Democratic party.

What is wrong with the "problem-solving" approach to governing is not only that it tends to ignore the political tasks of an effective presidency and that it is overly concerned with data collection, thoughtfulness, and policy skepticism, but in its laudable desire to resist "familiar" (in other words, New Deal/Great Society) ideological categories, it ignores the necessity of providing an alternative vision, one that might break through the unacknowledged ideological assumptions of problem solving itself.

Thus, another barrier to presidential achievement was the inability of Carter and his leading appointees to overcome the constraints imposed on agenda building by the mobilization of bias in American politics: the "values, assumptions, and beliefs" that restrict policy solutions to the usual contours of pluralist ideologies. But here the Carter administration reflected the larger bias of the political system itself. In rejecting conventional "liberal" solutions to inflation or to international conflict,[40] the administration failed to provide a useful alternative, reverting instead to time-honored "moderate" policies of fiscal and monetary balance, policies historically associated with "sensible" Republicans and moderate Democrats. Emerging political doctrines, such as the "neo-liberalism" of Sen. Gary Hart or the undeveloped but suggestive contours of a "New Age" politics that seeks to transcend and transform the old liberal-conservative conflict,[41] went unacknowledged and unexamined in the Carter presidency. The anemic attempt to develop the slogan "New Foundations" was jettisoned because it was so obviously hucksterism without content.

Perhaps all of us expect too much from the American presidency. The social, economic, and political conditions for a change in paradigm as fundamental as that envisioned by New Age thinkers did not and does not yet exist. Far more than gifted presidential leadership is required. Jimmy Carter should not be faulted for failing to usher in a comprehensive vision of a largely untested new order; change of this magnitude requires change among the citizenry long before we will see it in the presidency.

James MacGregor Burns distinguishes two broad styles of leadership, transformational and transactional.[42] Leaders like Lincoln and FDR, who meet Burns's transformational standards, are rare in every country. Carter, a moderate Democrat in outlook, analytically skeptical in style, needed, therefore, to excel as a transactional leader. Clearly, he and many of his senior advisers were deficient in this regard, and these limitations in process management—the art of the possible in a turbulent domestic and international environment—further undercut their ability to deliver on the promises of his campaign. Over time, agenda formation in the White House became more *reactive*, less a matter of planning and foresight.

Without a central strategic vision and the capacity to subordinate details to it, circumstances always will overpower leaders. Or, as in President Carter's case, presidential achievement will be confined to isolated breakthroughs, like Camp David or the Alaska Lands bill, while the list of blocked initiatives grows longer and more damaging to the president's reputation. Moreover, Carter himself grew less interested in domestic policy as time went on—he devotes fewer than 60 pages of his 600-page memoirs to a discussion of domestic issues.[43] Foreign policy dominates the latter stages of most presidential terms, and Carter's was no exception.

The Carter presidency was one of mainly decent intentions, some significant accomplishments, and some failures, but

> little of the self-centeredness that seemed part of every decision of some of his predecessors, such as the one who used to emblazon his monogram "LBJ" on everything within his sight, and the man who bugged himself (and others) in the name of history and titled his memoirs, "RN." [44]

Given what the United States had experienced in the 12 years before Carter, these are not insignificant accomplishments.

One final, perhaps melancholy, point is essential. Campaigning in 1980, Carter and his surrogates were justifiably proud of pointing to the fact that the nation had not been at war during his four years in office. However, the reemergence of a combative, anticommunist posture in his final years and the willingness to give it credibility by supporting costly and dangerous new nuclear weapon systems like the MX contributed to an uneasiness among many Democrats about the international prospects of a second Carter presidency. Two Democratic presidents have either been unlucky (the generous hypothesis) or misguided (the ungenerous hypothesis) in leading the United States into "wars against aggression" since World War II. Why are the negative consequences and human suffering of Vietnam now fading in a haze of nostalgia about the Johnson presidency?

For Democats, as well as others, the Marquez character (from *One-Hundred Years of Solitude*) whose question I pirated for the first page of this chapter should be taken seriously. The lover spurned by Amaranta Buendia is a nineteenth-century Latin American anticleric, who starts giving the catechism as a gift after he decides that war is a necessity.

Unjust wars ravage the integrity of democratic leaders and democratic societies, not only in the novels of Marquez but in the painful history of catastrophes like Vietnam. Fortunately, the United States was spared that type of tragic betrayal in the promise Jimmy Carter made "to keep America out of war." He kept his promise and in this century that alone is a monumental presidential achievement.

Notes

1. Americans for Democratic Action, "The Carter Record," Report to the membership, January 1980, 3.
2. John F. Manley, "Presidential Power and White House Lobbying," *Political Science Quarterly* (Summer 1978): 255-275; George C. Edwards III, *Presidential Influence in Congress* (San Francisco: Freeman, 1980).
3. Paul C. Light, *The President's Agenda* (Baltimore: Johns Hopkins University Press, 1982). See also Bert Rockman, *The Leadership Question: The Presidency and the American System,* (New York: Praeger, 1984); Stephen J. Wayne, *The Legislative Presidency* (New York: Harper & Row, 1978); and John H. Kessel, *The Domestic Presidency* (Boston: Duxbury Press, 1975).
4. The resilient Bert Lance. Despite the scandal he created in 1977, Lance reemerged as an important party figure in southern Democratic politics and, later at the 1984 Democratic convention, where Mondale's attempt to make him head of the Democratic National Committee provoked a major revolt. Mondale rescinded the decision and Lance withdrew from a public role in the Mondale campaign.
5. Carter was also subject to broadsides from conservatives in his own party, neo- and traditional. His fellow Georgian, friend, and first attorney general, Griffin Bell, attributes the failures of the Carter presidency to a cabal of Nader/McGovern/Mondale people. See Bell, *Taking Care of the Law* (New York: William Morrow, 1982).
6. See Lawrence E. Lynn, Jr., and David Def. Whitman, *The President as Policy-Maker: Jimmy Carter and Welfare Reform* (Philadelphia: Temple University Press, 1981); Ben W. Heineman, Jr., and Curtis A. Hessler, *Memorandum to the President* (New York: Random House, 1980).
7. Carter staff attributed this unlikely morass to a breakdown of communication and/or failure of nerve inside the Justice Department itself, particularly

in the McCree and Days operations, because the original anti-affirmative action brief was developed and aggressively pushed by a less senior member of the staff, reportedly a Nixon/Ford holdover appointment. The unanticipated argument of the original brief mobilized civil rights groups to protest and finally led to direct presidential intervention. For an analysis of more general concerns about Carter policy affecting blacks, see Robert C. Smith, "The Black Vote and the Carter Administration: The Political Payoff" (Paper delivered at the 1979 annual meeting of the National Conference of Black Political Scientists, Washington, D.C.).

 8. On the long internal struggle over national health insurance, see Heineman and Hessler, *Memorandum to the President*, and Joseph A. Califano, *Governing America: An Insider's Report from the White House and the Cabinet* (New York: Simon & Schuster, 1981).
 9. Light, *The President's Agenda*.
10. Barry M. Hager, "Carter's First Year: Setbacks and Successes," *Congressional Quarterly Weekly Report*, Dec. 24, 1977, 2641.
11. Light, *The President's Agenda*.
12. Ford submitted 110 proposals in 1975, and there was a combined Ford-Nixon total of 163 in 1974. Nixon's highest year, 1970, featured 210 OMB-approved proposals. One would need to go back to the Johnson years for a legislative agenda that exceeded 400 proposals per year. See Wayne, *The Legislative Presidency*, 168-172.
13. Elizabeth Drew, "In Office," *New Yorker*, Oct. 8, 1977, 173.
14. Dom Bonafede, "A Report Card on Carter—Lowered Expectations After One Year," *National Journal*, Jan. 14, 1978, 46.
15. More recently, see Nelson Polsby, *Consequences of Party Reform* (New York: Oxford University Press, 1983). Polsby is unremitting in his critical remarks, so much so that in a chapter-length survey, he fails to mention a single accomplishment of the Carter administration. Nor, in his lengthy parade of Carter horribles, does he note that obvious improvements—as in legislative liaison—were made after early 1978. His analysis combines wit, insight, and not a little malice in damning without qualification the Carter presidency. A less ferocious, although still critical, assessment is contained in Light's comparative study, *The President's Agenda*, or in James Fallows's lengthy review of the president's memoirs, "For Old Times' Sake," review of *Keeping Faith*, by Jimmy Carter, *New York Review of Books*, Dec. 16, 1982, 3-11.
16. Eric L. Davis, "Legislative Liaison in the Carter Administration," *Political Science Quarterly* (Summer 1979): 287-301; Davis, "Congressional Liaison," in *Both Ends of the Avenue: The Presidency, The Executive Branch and Congress in the 1980s*, ed. Anthony King (Washington, D.C.: American Enterprise Institute, 1983), 58-85.
17. Bruce Miroff, "The Transformation of a President's Image: Press Depiction of Jimmy Carter's First Year in Office" (Department of Political Science, State University of New York, Albany, 1982), 26.
18. The cycles of presidential-press relations are developed in Michael B. Grossman and Martha Joynt Kumar, *Portraying the President* (Baltimore: Johns Hopkins University Press, 1981).
19. Miroff, "The Transformation of a President's Image," 28.
20. One of the salvos from the first meeting of a coalition of labor and liberal organizations called by the UAW's Douglas A. Fraser. Reported in the *Washington Post*, Oct. 18, 1978.

21. Joseph L. Rauh, Jr., as quoted in the *Washington Post,* Sept. 12, 1979.
22. Michael Malbin traces Carter's moves in the adoption of a national energy plan and notes that the administration finally succeeded in getting a bill passed when it dropped its earlier insistence on a comprehensive and analytically consistent plan. He concludes, "[I]f one looks at energy in incremental terms, the Carter administration can in some sense be called a success. Those were not the terms on which the administration asked to be judged, however. It came in asking for a comprehensive plan involving a radical shift in outlook. It went out, not with a plan, but with a set of incremental changes that followed existing patterns of thought. There is nothing wrong with incremental policy change.... What was wrong was not the way the system worked, but the way the president worked the system." Although I agree with Malbin, my point is somewhat different: in the absence of a working congressional majority ready for comprehensive change, it is unlikely that even gifted presidential leadership can break through the considerable barriers to achieving it. Of course, the president's on-and-off commitment to mobilize support outside Congress did not help. See Malbin's excellent essay, "Rhetoric and Leadership: A Look Backward at the Carter National Energy Plan," in *Both Ends of the Avenue,* 238.
23. T. R. Reid, "Kennedy" in *The Pursuit of the Presidency 1980,* ed. Richard Harwood et al. (New York: Putnam, 1980), 67.
24. Ibid., 71.
25. Ibid., 76.
26. Darrell M. West, "Rhetoric and Agenda Setting in the 1980 Presidential Campaign," *Congress & The Presidency* (Autumn 1982): 1-21.
27. Ibid., 5.
28. Ibid., 13.
29. Dom Bonafede, "How to Win—Or Lose—The Presidency," *National Journal,* Sept. 12, 1980, 1681.
30. Elizabeth Drew, "A Reporter at Large (The Presidential Campaign)," *New Yorker,* Sept. 8, 1980, 41.
31. Predictably, blocking coalitions like this involve unlikely bedfellows. The "open convention" move was just as much engineered by neoconservatives connected with Sen. Henry Jackson as it was by Kennedy backers.
32. Nelson Polsby, "The Democratic Nomination," in *The American Elections of 1980,* ed. Austin Ranney (Washington, D.C.: American Enterprise Institute, 1981), 37-61.
33. Michael Malbin, "The Conventions, Platforms, and Issue Activists," in *The American Elections of 1980,* 107.
34. Some gay activists wanted larger commitments but relented during negotiations with White House platform representatives. See Malbin, "The Conventions, Platforms, and Issue Activists," in *The American Elections of 1980,* 121.
35. One Kennedy adviser defended the senator's abstention on the nuclear freeze proposal on grounds that it was unwise to open a division between Kennedy and other, more hawkish anti-Carter Democrats.
36. "ADA Flays Reagan, Pines for Carter," *Washington Post,* June 4, 1982, 3.
37. Bert Rockman, "Constants, Cycles, Trends, and Persona in Presidential Governance: Carter's Troubles Revisited" (Paper delivered at the 1979 annual meeting of the American Political Science Association).
38. Ibid., 41.
39. Ibid., 42.

40. I am not sure there is a conventional liberal solution to international conflict because liberals have been divided on this type of issue since the beginning of the Cold War. What I intend here is to emphasize the peace-oriented wing of American liberalism and its consistent opposition to Cold War defense policy.
41. Uneven in quality but thoughtful examples of this philosophy are provided in Mark Satin, *New Age Politics* (New York: Delta, 1978); Willis Harman, *An Incomplete Guide to the Future* (New York: Norton, 1979); Paul Hawken, James Ogilvy, and Peter Schwartz, *Seven Tomorrows* (New York: Bantam, 1983); and Walter Anderson, ed. *Rethinking Liberalism* (New York: Avon, 1983).
42. James MacGregor Burns, *Leadership* (New York: Harper & Row, 1978).
43. Fallows makes this point and explores the implications in his review of Carter's *Keeping Faith*. Presidential memoirs are not the most reliable gauge of these matters. My interviews suggest that Carter moved from a primary emphasis on domestic policy during the first 18 months to primary emphasis on foreign policy in the remaining portion of his term. The Reagan presidency also reflects this shift in presidential attention and interest.
44. Edward Walsh, "A Flawed Presidency of Good Intentions," *Washington Post*, Jan. 18, 1981.

Presidential campaigns from the West, conservative style: the promises of Ronald Reagan

5

> *That cabbages grow in dung is something I have always taken for granted.*
>
> —C. G. Jung

In the beginning was The Speech—Family, Work, Neighborhood, Peace, and Freedom.[1] And the superb precampaign organization, Citizens for the Republic, staffed by some of the most capable political professionals in the Republican party, supported and financed by some of the richest, nourished in the belief that they were the wave of the future.

And the long years as a successful, if mediocre actor, confident in the Hollywood and television worlds of half-reality/half-fantasy, resonating in the image of the Good Guy from *Kings Row* or *Death Valley Days*, glamorous but comprehensible and hence comfortable for large parts of the American middle class, particularly the Republican middle class, the Great Communicator.

And the eight years as governor of California, sometimes vindictive and vicious, as in the National Guard assault on the "People's Park" of Berkeley, but coming out of those years in a hazy patina of having been, despite his rhetoric, a pragmatic Republican. Most of the time.

Unfortunately, however, there also was a problem. Ronald Reagan was the undisputed leader of the conservative faction of a minority party. True blue, flags flying, bells ringing American conservatism.[2]

Sixteen years on the mashed potato circuit, suggesting or implying that American troops be committed all over the globe, that world communism had to be confronted before it "landed at Long Beach," that labor unions were undermining the American spirit, that Social Security was a fraud, that "fascism was the basis of the New Deal," that unemployment was necessary if inflation was to be stopped (pre-supply-side Reaganomics!), and on and on. With Sen. Barry Goldwater as their guide, many Republicans, not to mention most Democrats, and an army of sophisticated observers, believed that Reagan was unelectable—Jimmy Carter's "favorite opponent."

The problem was not the candidate ("a little old but beautiful," said one GOP operative) nor the organization and its considerable resources, nor his Hollywood background. The problem was the conservative agenda that Reagan first needed to defend, then might attempt to enact. His emerging campaign agenda seemed so far beyond what is electorally defensible in centrist-oriented American presidential politics that Reagan's well-known ideology, many believed, surely would drag him under. All those who argued this position overestimated the negative impact of conservative ideology on electoral outcomes and underestimated the flexibility of conservative agenda building in presidential campaigns.

This chapter sketches the way the Reagan coalition framed a future policy agenda, emphasizing the substance of what emerged during the seasons of 1980 campaign politics. Reagan did not become more centrist on the basic issues during the campaign—a claim repeatedly made in the press—so much as skillfully exploit the ambiguities of his fundamentally conservative outlook. Thus, the campaign was able to finesse his conservative ideology, emphasizing matters of style rather than substance. His organization was equally skillful in using both back and front channels to hold the core of his conservative support while expanding that support dramatically in the general election.

In addition, the platform-building process of 1980 enabled the Reagan organization to use supply-side rhetoric to overcome internal party conflict and circumvent the party's oldest and thorniest political/economic problem, a long-standing public fear about recessions associated with Republican administrations. Voters, as always, needed to invest considerable energy and effort in sorting through his campaign rhetoric to uncover much detail about the candidate's future agenda. If they were willing to make the effort, however, some was there; many of the programs sought by President Reagan were telegraphed in his 1980 campaign. His policy promises, even those communicated in the back channel, however, lacked the depth and specificity of Carter's in 1976.

Agenda formation and
Reagan's nomination

Like Jimmy Carter, the former governor of California was considered an outsider. Unlike Carter, he was not an outsider in his national party. Quite the contrary. Over the years Reagan had carefully courted Republican activists through extensive speaking engagements, financial support of GOP congressional candidates, and participation in other party-building activities. After barely losing the Republican nomination to Gerald R. Ford in 1976, he emerged as a graceful "party regular" for the campaign, helping in various small ways to keep Ford competitive against Carter. Neither Reagan nor his closest advisers were antiparty in the style of some of the Carterites.

Further, Reagan's basic values were closer to a majority of Republican activists than Carter's were to most active Democrats. Except among the dwindling band of GOP progressives and moderates, Reagan's ideology had become "mainstream Republicanism" in the 1970s, a fact that helped him enormously as a candidate and, just as important, later as president. When Republicans worried about their eventual nominee, it was not so much about what he believed, but about the negative electoral consequences of what he believed. The difference is important and helps explain why the Californian was so enormously popular among his fellow partisans. He was the unquestioned front-runner among Republicans during the entire four years before his nomination, and for good reason. Huge majorities of those most active in the party agreed with his conservative principles and admired his political style.[3]

So far as the outsider label fits, it does so because Reagan had never been part of the Washington scene, as were George Bush, Howard Baker, Gerald Ford, and even John Connally, and because his conservatism was seen as beyond the bounds of what makes candidates "presidential." The Reagan organization thus faced two problems in coalition formation. First, it needed to overcome the concern about lack of experience, particularly in foreign policy where his inexperience was associated with potentially dangerous unpredictability. "Running against Washington," a favorite pastime of both Republicans and Democrats, was not the issue; the challenge was in overcoming the collective strengths of Ford-Baker-Bush, all of whom had a reputation for moderation, and for "knowing how to change what's wrong because they had been there before."

Second and more important, the Reagan team needed to show that it could solidify its coalitional base among the conservative Republican activists who provided its foundation and at the same time expand the coalition to independents and others after the primaries and convention. One senior staff member explained it this way:

> We were in a delicate position. His position on the issues during the primaries was not going to help us any more than it already had. Hell, everybody knew where he stood. What we did *not* need were the lengthy position papers, rigid commitments, long policy commentaries. Our problem was keeping him from getting too specific or too detailed about issues. Play up his natural strengths among Republicans. Early on, John Sears and others decided that the best thing to do was keep him off the usual campaign trail, emphasize the media and his front-runner status, let the pack cut itself up, and concentrate on planning for the convention and the general election. Even after the disaster in Iowa, and John being fired, our basic thrust in this regard was the same—stress his warm and self-assured leadership, keep the organization going, *ignore but not antagonize the Far Right.* Our best asset was the candidate himself, his style, his skills, his integrity, and that Carter and the Democrats were the real issue for Republicans. [Emphasis added.]

Accordingly, the Reagan campaign developed few serious issue or position papers during the primaries, relying on three- or four-paragraph press handouts under the campaign committee's imprimatur, "Reagan for President." A comparison with Carter's strategy in 1976 is instructive. The Carter organization attempted to reach northern Democrats and labor and liberal activists through extensive back-channel communication in the form of position papers, specialized articles, and so forth, while emphasizing nonissue stylistic appeals in the front channel (mass media and direct audience contacts). Carter became more liberal *and* more specific in the back channel as he moved through the primaries. Reagan, on the other hand, had *considerable incentive to fudge on the issues because there were no additional coalitional incentives to deliver.*

Conservatives were the dominant group within his coalition, as well as the most active in the party. Moderates were a clear minority and split among Ford, Bush, Baker, and Anderson. Emphasizing party unity for the coming battle against Democrats and deemphasizing past issue commitments were obvious parts of what Charles O. Jones aptly labels Reagan's "trifocal strategy." [4] Later, in the platform deliberations and more dramatically during the general campaign, Reagan's strategists changed direction; they began to emphasize centrist-like rhetoric on a host of issues, from Social Security to civil rights to questions involving labor and blue-collar workers. This shift occurred, however, *after* they had consolidated their strength in the nomination struggle, specifically after the Illinois primary in mid-March. It was mainly a shift in rhetoric, *not* a shift in specific issue commitments.

Of course, they needed to keep reassuring their core of conservative supporters, and it was here that signs of Reagan's future agenda as president were most evident. Variations on The Speech were used as a substitute for detailed campaign position papers. With the exception of a major speech on the economy, delivered in September 1980 and accompanied by an extensive "Fact Sheet," minimal amplification was provided in their brief press handouts.[5] Reagan reassured his audience throughout the primaries that he was committed to "conservative principles and conservative programs," employing all the charm, one-liners, down-home examples of welfare cheats and frauds, and attacks on liberal do-gooders that had won him such positive response among like-minded Republicans for so many years.

The Reagan team's formal press releases on issues, although truncated, retained the essential commitments but embellished them with considerably more sober, careful, qualified, and ambiguous language. The following are an illustrative, although not comprehensive, collection of these commitments, drawn primarily from the press releases. They represent the most extensive policy record of the campaign that is available, ambiguous as the statements are.

The releases stated Reagan's position

—against abortion, supporting a constitutional amendment to protect the "right to life":

> I personally believe that interrupting a pregnancy is the taking of human life and can be justified only in self-defense—that is when a mother's life is in danger.... I support enactment of a constitutional amendment to restore protection of the unborn child's right to life.... In the meantime, I am opposed to using federal tax money to pay for abortions in cases where the life of the mother is in no danger. *Reagan for President, "Abortion," undated.*

—against court-mandated busing as a means of helping achieve school desegregation:

> It is time we removed control of our schools from the courts and federal government and returned it to local school boards where it belongs, I [oppose] court-ordered compulsory busing. *Reagan for President, "Busing," undated.*

—against federal "guidelines" or "quotas" in affirmative action, apparently supporting voluntary programs:[6]

> [W]e must not allow this noble concept ... of equal opportunity to be distorted into federal guidelines or quotas which require race, ethnicity, or sex—rather than ability and qualifications—to be the principal factor in hiring and education.... Instead, we should make a bold commitment to economic growth, to increase jobs and education for all Americans. *Reagan for President, "Affirmative Action," undated.*

—against the Equal Rights Amendment, insisting nevertheless that he supported equal rights for women:

> I do not believe that the Equal Rights Amendment to the federal Constitution is the answer to the problem. The amendment would not

itself redress inequalities in rights, and, by increasing the courts' "legislative" power, could do more harm than good. Instead I will ask the existing National Commission on the Status of Women to submit annually a list of federal laws which subvert women's equal rights. I will then work with Congress to revise or repeal those statutes, or to enact new equal rights legislation as required. *Reagan for President, "Equal Rights for Women," January 1980.*

—against "excessive environmentalism" that "endangers" economic growth, supporting a transfer of "primary responsibility" for environmental regulation to the states:

To achieve a sound environmental policy, we should reexamine *every* regulatory requirement with a commitment to simplify and streamline the process. Moreover, we should return to the states the primary responsibility for environmental regulation in order to increase responsiveness to local conditions. [Emphasis added.] *Reagan for President, "Environment," January 1980.*

—against "special" gay rights ordinances:

While I do not advocate the so-called gay life-style, all citizens have equal rights before the law ... an employer should not be subject to special laws (such as the gay ordinances passed in some cities) which, in effect, would compel him to hire a person because of that person's sexual preference.[7] *Reagan for President, "Homosexual Rights," April 1980.*

—against the abolition of school prayer in public schools, supporting a constitutional amendment to permit "voluntary" prayer:

I will support a constitutional amendment restoring the right to hold voluntary prayer in our public schools. *Washington Post, Feb. 19, 1980.*

—against "inexcusably large" federal deficits, supporting legislative remedies, and, "if necessary," a constitutional amendment to balance the budget:

Balancing the budget is essential.... I support a requirement that the federal government balance its budget except where temporary periods of war or national emergency require otherwise. My preference is that the balanced budget requirement be implemented legislatively, but, if it is necessary, I would support a constitutional amendment to that effect. *Reagan for President, "Balanced Budget Amendment," January 1980.*

—against federal inheritance and gift taxes:

I favor elimination of federal estate (inheritance) and gift taxes ... the estate tax, the gift tax, and the carry-over rule have no place in the U.S. tax code. Their elimination should be top priority. *Reagan for President, "Taxation of Inheritances," undated.*

—against antimerger legislation developed to reduce vertical and horizontal monopoly:

I would enforce our sound and effective antitrust laws ... however, the current proposals before Congress do not make economic sense ...

often a merger is the only viable alternative for companies in financial difficulties. *Reagan for President, "Antitrust," January 1980.*

—against further handgun controls:

I yield to no one in my concern about crime . . . gun controls do not prevent crime . . . handgun controls could lead to further firearms controls . . . while we are facing a serious crime problem, gun control is an unrealistic and dangerous proposal. *Reagan for President, "Gun Control," undated.*

—against peacetime draft or draft registration:

I strongly oppose universal service, which rests on the assumption that people belong to the state. . . . Moreover, I oppose military draft in peace-time. . . . Finally, I oppose the establishment of a standby registration system, which would not speed U.S. mobilization in time of emergency, would require a large, costly bureaucracy, and would be seen—quite likely, accurately—as a first step toward a peace-time draft. *Reagan for President, "Registration, The Draft, and National Service," January 1980.*

—against phasing out nuclear power as an energy source:

Nuclear power plants do cost more to build, but once built, they operate more economically than oil-, gas-, and coal-fired plants . . . properly operated, nuclear plants are among the safest means of energy production. . . . We have no choice but to continue to operate and construct nuclear power plants. *Reagan for President, "Nuclear Power," January 1980.*

—against the "windfall profits" tax on oil and natural gas:

[T]he so-called "windfall profits" tax, which actually has nothing to do with profits but instead is a per-barrel tax on domestic production, would greatly reduce U.S. energy supplies . . . by so drastically reducing U.S. oil output, the windfall profits tax would increase our reliance on foreign oil. . . . The consumer would end up paying the tax every time he goes to the pump. *Reagan for President, "Windfall Profits Tax," undated.*

—against "unnecessary" government spending, supporting the "control" of government growth in expenditures, employees, new programs by cutting nondefense expenditures and balancing the budget "without depriving the poor or needy":

[W]aste, duplicative agencies, and counterproductive programs consume . . . federal tax dollars. By cutting such unnecessary spending, we can balance the budget without depriving the poor or needy. We can provide a better government, rather than a bigger, more expensive government. *Reagan for President, "Government Spending," January 1980.*

—against hospital cost containment controls:

[S]uch arbitrary limitations . . . make it inevitable that hospitals would be forced to reduce their services . . . instead we will control hospital costs only when we control inflation . . . and controlling inflation means eliminating federal deficit spending and excessive increases in the money supply, not enacting arbitrary "cost control." *Reagan for President, "Hospital Cost Containment," January 1980.*

—for a 30 percent across-the-board reduction in personal income tax rates, phased in over three years; accelerated depreciation schedules for business; indexation of personal income tax rates to inflation after the rate reduction is accomplished:

> (Multiple sources; the Reagan team's best-publicized promises.)

—for transferring "general" welfare programs back to the states and localities, along with the tax resources to pay for them:

> [E]liminating this layer [federal agencies] alone would save tax dollars, usable both to increase benefits and reduce taxes . . . since states and localities are closer to welfare recipients, they could maintain tighter controls over waste and fraud. *Reagan for President, January 1980.*

—for transferring "general" educational programs back to the states and local school districts and . . . abolishing the Department of Education:

> Since 1962 . . . per-student costs have increased and test scores fallen virtually in proportion to the rise in federal spending. . . . We should transfer general federal educational programs back to the state and local school districts, along with the tax resources to pay for them. *Reagan for President, undated.*

—for the "immediate" elimination of all price controls on oil and natural gas and . . . the abolition of the Department of Energy:

> I favor the immediate elimination of all federal price controls on oil and natural gas . . . eliminating DOE . . . would be an important first step toward solving the energy crisis. *Reagan for President, "Energy Price Decontrol" and "Department of Energy/Allocation Rules," January 1980.*

—for accelerating federal deregulation and giving Congress veto power over "all" federal regulations:

> [A] successful deregulation program must be one of action, not just words. We should, on a broad scale, reevaluate regulations, identify unnecessary ones, and eliminate them . . . we should establish a "sunset" procedure for regulations with substantial impact and give Congress veto power over all federal regulations. *Reagan for President, "Federal Regulation," undated.*

While these papers articulated what he was against and sometimes what he was for, they gave analysts little idea of *how* he might pursue these commitments, *when* (the first year? the second? if he ran for election again?), or what the precise *magnitude* of the proposed change would be. For example, Reagan resisted specifying how much his defense buildup might cost. Would the defense budget increase by 5 percent? 8 percent? 15 percent? Or would the child nutrition program fall into the category of "counterproductive" federal activities and be eliminated? Or would "unnecessary expenditures" for it simply be reduced? If so, by how much? In construction, these documents fulfill beautifully Benjamin Page's conditions for the "art of ambiguity."

But as powerful symbolic rhetoric, they provided the needed cement for conservatives, leaving enough room to maneuver and for qualification later and reinforcing their willingness to support and actively work for his candidacy. And they do provide rough if ambiguous guidelines about the shape of his future agenda.

Most reporters, Darrell West notes, ignored these items while covering Reagan during the primary campaign, neither digging further to explore how he might implement such positions, and with what consequences, nor pressing the candidate to become more specific about them.[8] Ironically, the media were critical of George Bush for policy vagueness, although West's content analysis of their campaign speeches found Reagan *less* specific than Bush (13.4 percent and 15.5 percent, respectively, of their statements deal with specific policy). West notes that "journalists applied different standards to the candidates. Campaigners (such as Reagan, Mondale, and Kennedy) who were well known and had compiled track records on the issues over time, were insulated from media criticism about ambiguity."[9]

There were reasons other than variations in campaign experience and political familiarity that explain this behavior, however, reasons stemming from the norms governing media coverage of presidential campaigns. One reporter put it bluntly:

> How many times can we write that he's against abortion or the other things you mention? Reagan's position on the issues is not the story. Nobody but the single-issue nuts gives a rat's ass about "the issues." All these guys, Reagan, Bush, Baker, Connally, believe basically the same thing. Anderson is different, but he's already gotten more publicity than he deserves. The only story worth writing is whether Reagan can make it and how.

This is a classic defense of the norms associated with front-channel communication; as always, the horse race was *the* story. During the general election, highly critical questions were raised about Reagan's policy positions—partly out of guilt and partly because Carter staff people, Jody Powell and Patrick Caddell, waged a vigorous personal campaign accusing reporters of defaulting in their responsibility to cover Reagan with the same "intensity" they presumably were devoting to Carter. CBS, particularly, zeroed in on four or five apparent shifts in his positions, graphically showing viewers a comparison of Reagan's statements "then" and "now." Such emphasis on the candidate's policy promises was the exception, however, and it did not provide much depth about his future agenda, inconsistent or not. Media reporting about future policy was more typically, and inevitably, relegated to other places.[10]

Reagan's primary campaign thus reflected most of the attributes of the seasons of presidential politics. The emphasis was on overcoming potentially negative concerns about personal attributes (his age, for example) and reiterating goal-oriented rhetoric that would reassure conservative Republicans while not alienating independents and disgruntled Democrats on the broad contours of his future policy agenda. As the campaign moved closer to the convention and to the necessity of producing a platform, pressures were mounting on the Reagan coalition to grow *more* specific, *more* conservative, and *less* conservative in many of these areas of future policy, contradictory as these points may seem.

At the convention: building the platform

Republican political managers historically have prided themselves on being able to plan and run an efficient, well-organized national convention, one designed to maximize the advantages of television ("A family event where everyone ends up smiling") and minimize the disadvantages (Gerald Ford telling Walter Cronkite, much to the astonishment of Reagan's senior staff, that, yes, he might consider the vice presidency). Disdainfully referring to the "usual Democrat catastrophe," as a "model of how they run government," one RNC official predicted:

> You won't see any of that in July. Certainly we have some conflicts and disagreements but we've been pointing to this since 1977. Reagan's staff have been involved at all levels but they've allowed us to make the basic decisions. That includes the platform. The draft has emerged out of three years of careful study and consultation by our advisory councils, and we are more united this year than at any time since 1972. Oh, there may be a wild delegate here and there, but most don't want to embarrass the candidate or the party, no matter how strong they may feel. *We know how to settle our differences in private!*

So concerned with negotiating out of the limelight were Republican officials that the platform chairman, Sen. John Tower of Texas, through executive director Roger Semerad, decided to revert to pre-1976 Republican practice and close the committee and subcommittee deliberations to the public. The committee promptly overrode him, voting to keep the sessions open. Semerad, however, refused to permit distribution of the platform draft to reporters and others not on the committee. Since committee members always meet shortly before the convention, divide up into subcommittees, and then go over the staff draft line by line, this was tantamount to inviting 250 reporters to a press gathering and then refusing to talk. Delegates intent on modifying the document, however, were free to talk with anyone they pleased. Anti-ERA and antiabortion members of the Human Resources Subcommittee did so with abandon, as did their opponents, passing out copies of numerous amendments and proposed changes, in addition to the staff draft. As Michael Malbin points out:

> The result was predictable . . . [since] the Human Resources Subcommittee was about the only place reporters could figure out what was happening . . . Tower's decision ensured that the press could not cover anything [other than the struggle over ERA and abortion] if it had wanted to. Thus, Tower's worst fears were realized; days of negative headlines about the big fights over two issues, with almost no coverage of the bulk of the document.[11]

So much for settling one's differences in private!

The long struggle over the ERA plank, in which the Republican platform abandoned its 40-year support for the Equal Rights Amendment and ultimately approved language that neither opposed nor supported it, has been well told and need not be repeated here. From the viewpoint of using the platform to expand Reagan's coalitional support to include moderates, the committee's decision to abandon ERA and the process that accompanied the abandonment, squandered a carefully worked out compromise developed before the convention. Quite surprisingly, given the candidate's clear opposition to the amendment, the staff draft of the Republican platform included a back-handed endorsement of it. The draft read:

> We reaffirm our Party's historic commitment to equal rights and equal opportunity for women, a commitment which made us the first national party to endorse the Equal Rights Amendment. We are proud of our pioneering role and do not renounce our stand.

Equally surprising, this language was cleared by Martin Anderson, Reagan's primary lieutenant for domestic policy, before the convention. When asked whether the candidate might have to renounce this plank later in the campaign, one aide explained:

> Not really. His position is well known and he can say that, of course, he supports equal rights for women, just not the amendment, but that many in his party are divided about the means for achieving equal rights and he respects their right to differ. The plank does not commit him to doing anything about it.

Perhaps. But it is unclear whether this position would have helped or hurt him any more than the final plank and the associated disharmony in the party did.

Malbin contends that the Reagan team came into the convention with three strategic goals: maintaining enthusiasm about his candidacy, reaching out to moderate Republicans who were considering Anderson, and building on Reagan's appeal to normally Democratic blue-collar workers. In effect, the *specific* commitments of the platform, as amended, permitted them to accomplish the goal of reinforcing conservative loyalty. The selection of George Bush for the vice presidential nomination, along with extensive back-channel communication with dissatisfied moderates, particularly Republican women worried about the ERA and other matters, helped keep most of the moderates in line. And the upbeat, progress-through-economic-growth rhetoric of the platform, combined with the candidate's careful avoidance of anti-New Deal sloganeering, ultimately sustained the impression of a positive agenda for economic change that would appeal to wavering Democrats and independents.

For the out-party, there always is a temptation to emphasize attacks on the incumbent and downplay creating an alternative program agenda that is specific and comprehensive. No matter how much this appealed to some of Reagan's managers, pressures mounting inside his own coalition prohibited it. Leading members of the "New" and "Old" Right did have an agenda, and the platform gave them an opportunity to pursue it. The coalitional incentives to deliver on policy commitments, as Carter had learned in 1976 and 1980, were immense, particularly on social and foreign policy/defense issues. Ultraconservatives in the Republican party, like Jesse Helms, might concede a point here or a sentence there, but they were not going to be distracted from their goals by pleas for party unity, attacks on the Carter administration, and the rhetoric of supply-side economics.

By contrast, moderates were unable to alter the conservative thrust of the platform, even losing on the questionable judicial selection clause, which stated: "We will work for the appointment of judges at all levels of the judiciary who respect traditional family values and the sanctity of innocent human life." This item provoked intense consternation among moderate Republicans. Sen. Charles H. Percy of Illinois, in a bit of overstatement, labeled it "the worst plank I have ever seen in any platform by the Republican party." And Mary Dent Crisp, former co-chair of the Republican National Committee, an ERA supporter, and an opponent of the judiciary plank, delivered a fiery speech on television denouncing the anti-Equal Rights Amendment and antiabortion clauses before the convention actually adopted them. All of this was of no avail; moderates did not even have sufficient votes to force a roll call on the floor, and the 1980 platform, as amended, was adopted by voice vote on July 15.

Combined with Reagan's long-standing commitments, the platform represented a substantial alternative to any Democratic administration. The GOP platform also accurately mirrored Reagan's projected economic program; in terms of current policy, supply-side economics may be passing into one of many campaign has-beens, but in 1980, the dramatic promise of this untested theory became the foundation of the party's proposed economic programs.

William Greider, writing in the *Washington Post*, neatly caught the shift:

[T]he Republican party has played the national scold for 40 years, the permanent nay-sayer ... counting pennies at the national Treasury came before Social Security ... now, they were the ones preaching growth and prosperity. They were the party of progress and hope and it was the Democrats, in the person of President Carter, who had become the scolds. Forget the caricature, elect Ronald Reagan and let the good times roll. [12]

Supply-side theory bypassed the old GOP economic dilemma. Scrap the Phillips Curve; unemployment need not be the "painful but necessary" cost of controlling inflation. Rather, push through a version of the Kemp-Roth bill, lowering tax rates 30 percent in three years; eliminate "wasteful" domestic social programs, but retain that elusive "safety net"; halt the growth of government; and the American free market—through the resulting savings, investment, and growth—will create jobs, reduce interest rates, cure inflation, and permit a balanced federal budget. In addition, supply-side economics would provide the revenues for financing the large and expensive new weapons systems that Reagan promised as part of his plan to increase defense capabilities. Greider concluded that "Kemp's plan [now Reagan's and the party's] was called irresponsible, and many mainstream economists, including Republican economists, agreed." [13]

However, no amount of criticism, inside or outside the Republican party, could undermine the basic *political* logic of the supply-side thrust. It was consistent with a post-convention strategy of expanding the party's coalitional base to include blue-collar workers and others threatened by increasing unemployment rates, trying to overcome in a spectacular way the long-standing public fears about the association of Republican presidents and economic hardship. Conversely, it did little damage, except among monetarists and other lonely figures in the GOP, to the older free market "magic" that traditional leaders in the party had espoused. And it certainly jelled with the candidate's seemingly inexhaustible personal optimism and his managers' drive to present the candidate's and the Republican party's economic promises in an upbeat, positive light. "Laffer lightens our load," observed one sardonic Republican.

With a brilliant if illusory political side step, the Reagan coalition avoided dealing with painful trade-offs between economic complexity and uncertainty, on the one hand, and the policy and electoral claims of the *anti*-New Deal coalition, on the other.

Implied in the promise of a 30 percent cut in tax rates and explicit in the promise of substantial capital gains and corporate tax cuts, was a considerable "redistribution" of resources back to the wealthy. To those in the top tax brackets, supply-side economics is a bonanza because a 30 percent rate reduction for families in the $100,000 and above brackets is both absolutely and relatively worth more than a comparable cut to families with annual incomes of $25,000 or less. When combined with reductions in government support for the poor and near-poor, Reagan's economic agenda promised to slow government's growth in sustaining the country's existing, if modest, framework of assistance to the needy. But this was a shift in the magnitude of governmental commitment, *not* a counterrevolutionary attempt to dismantle the major pillars of the Positive State. Indeed, the Reagan coalition consciously and carefully avoided labeling it "anti-New Deal."

There is no evidence that large proportions of the electorate understood or responded to the nuances of supply-side versus "old-side" Republican economics. Various postelection studies demolish the contention that voters cast a ballot in the general election because they supported the specifics of Reagan's proposed economic policies—the most generous estimate would be fewer than 10 percent.[14] The Reagan coalition used supply-side to circumvent internal party opposition and to create harmony among the most active Republicans. They also employed it in a media campaign that sought to overcome traditional public fears about "Republican recessions," hoping to create a general belief, free of details, that Reagan and the GOP would do a "better job in handling the economy." In this, they were partially successful; 21 percent of the American electorate thought Republicans would do better in dealing with inflation and unemployment, compared to 10 percent who chose the Democrats. *Almost 70 percent reached another conclusion* (the GOP would do well in one area, the Democrats better in another, both parties would be disasters, and so forth.)[15]

How cynical was the original supply-side commitment? Two years later, after presiding over a $103 billion deficit for FY 1982, Reagan helped push through a $98 billion tax *increase,* and the administration seemed to be discretely abandoning many (not all) of the elements of supply-side economics. David Stockman's *Atlantic* "confessions" suggest that some around Reagan harbored serious doubts about the workability of this economic theory but held back in the belief that it could be fine-tuned if and when they won the election.[16] The question of whether Reagan's supply-side commitment was a cynical expression of elec-toral calculation is unanswerable when applied to his belief system or motivation; in fact, one need not be naive in reaching a generous conclusion because it is obvious that he has championed other ideas that also lack complexity. Moreover, the president and his party took a considerable risk by actually following through on a large part of this promised economic package in their first year. It is, therefore, safe to assume that *he* believed what he said during the campaign, even if some of his more thoughtful advisers were colluding in a campaign equivalent of the Big Lie.

As in the Carter campaign, the Reagan forces faced well-organized partisans who needed to be assured about the candidate's "loyalty to party principles" in the writing of the platform. Unlike Carter's team, Reagan strategists believed (correctly) that there was enormous potential good will toward Reagan *as a Republican* and that his programmatic concerns were important but secondary. Thus the two candidates faced very different circumstances in calculating how they could negotiate a platform that was consistent with building unity for the fall campaign and a good prediction of what the candidates might do later in office.

The Republicans' 1980 version did contain a number of fairly specific promises about what Reagan would do if he were elected. Compared to its Democratic counterpart, however, the GOP version is shorter and less specific. Indeed, compared to other successful candidates, Reagan himself made fewer concrete promises.

Reagan in the general election

Reagan's greatest asset in the 1980 campaign was that he was not Jimmy Carter. He was not the incumbent, forced to defend an erratic economic program in the face of extraordinary uncertainty about inflation and an impending recession. He was not saddled, or potentially blessed, with the explosive hostage situation in Iran. He was not given to quasi-sermons about discipline, sacrifice, and public "malaises"—except, of course, when it involved "welfare chiselers," and others unfortunate enough to have missed the train to Hollywood.

Like James David Barber's portrait of the model candidate floating in the historical rhythms of the "politics of conciliation," Reagan seemed "one of the most agreeable men with whom I ever came in contact, courteous and cordial ... a star who winged it—flew way beyond his capabilities on the strength of his personal showmanship." [17] The quote is not about Reagan, however, but about an earlier "actor," Warren G. Harding. The lineage is direct and obvious.

Ironically, the Carter forces campaigned on the assumption that *his* greatest asset was that he was not Ronald Reagan. And Reagan had given them plenty of targets, having indulged during his political career in sometimes irresponsible statements on everything from the use of nuclear weapons to potential "blood baths" if student protesters continued to engage in demonstrations at the University of California. The strongly anti-Reagan thrust of the Carter campaign floundered in part because Carter was unsuccessful in persuading many voters that there was an association between Reagan-the-dangerous-ideologue and Reagan-the-personable-human-being, particularly Reagan-the-personable on television. Whatever doubts voters entertained about the ex-governor of California were eclipsed by the widespread dissatisfaction with Carter's performance in office. The outcome of the 1980 election was much more a rejection of the incumbent than it was an affirmation of the challenger.

Reagan and Republican strategy

Republican challengers since the New Deal have framed campaign strategies for the general election that embrace certain recurring elements. Reagan was no exception to this generalization. First, because Democrats outnumber Republicans in the voting population, even in a period of declining partisanship, it is imperative that any Republican deemphasize his party attachment and stress themes that will reach independents and potential defectors from the Democrats. Second, the ideological homogeneity of the Republican party, with its strong and active conservative majority, is an organizational asset but an electoral liability. Thus all Republican presidential contenders inevitably modify their natural conservative rhetoric in seeking to broaden their appeal. A third element in the strategy involves the relative trade-off of the domestic/economic versus the foreign/defense policy question. The GOP has held a slight advantage on foreign policy questions since World War II during those times when the main concern of voters is focused on America's role abroad rather than at home. The 1980 election was an exception to this: voters were much more likely to trust Carter on questions of international affairs and somewhat more likely to believe that a Reagan presidency would do better on management of the economy.[18]

The situation was similar to that of 1964, when Barry Goldwater was feared because he might too frequently "shoot from the hip"; regrettably for Goldwater, he was also mistrusted on domestic social/economic issues as well. Thus the Reagan campaign needed to exploit its advantage on economic issues (blaming the incumbent and reiterating supply-side assumptions were the two chosen methods) and to overcome fears about the candidate's belligerence in world affairs. Finally, the question of White House leadership—more accurately, denunciations of "weak and vacillating" leadership—is a universal target for all challengers, and the Carter administration had provided a moveable feast. Republicans have proved just as skillful in exploiting it as the Democrats when they have been the out-party.

The Reagan campaign moved in classic fashion after the Republican convention to implement a strategy that embraced each of these elements, adding, of course, some different twists that reflected those aspects of 1980 that were unique. From the viewpoint of agenda formation, one important goal of the campaign was to present Reagan as a "moderate," not antagonistic to the "great achievements" of FDR. Lou Cannon, certainly one of the oldest and most astute Reagan-watchers in the business, wrote an internal memorandum for his editors at the *Washington Post* in late September noting:

> [I]t is useful to look at Reagan's emergence as a born-again New Dealer not as a sudden shift in strategy but as the third act in a long drama in which Reagan is the central player. There has never been any doubt that Reagan would campaign as a centrist in the general election campaign ... there has always been a distinction between Candidate Reagan in the primaries and Candidate Reagan in the general election.[19]

So far as issues received much attention from the mass media, the "September Shift" was the most voluminously covered. Many reporters seem to believe that the only story about policy worth covering is whether the candidates are consistent across time. Inconsistencies, "flip-flops," lapses in the candidate's memory are frequently pounced upon ("There he goes again, lying to the American people!") and explained using a hypothesis of the worst-motive variety. Cannon, incidentally, did not and does not follow this path in his analysis of Reagan. Inconsistency may be newsworthy, but it represents a partial truth. Lost in the desire to portray candidates as evasive and manipulative is the other part, the substance of policy, the details, practicalities, and implications of the candidate's new, or old, positions.

If Reagan had begun to view the political universe in the manner of a moderate like Sen. Charles Mathias—or even Howard Baker—then this certainly would have been big news. What shifted, however, was not so much the candidate's ideological commitment, but his rhetorical style and his approach to presenting positions on a few selected issues. Reagan did not become a moderate Republican, let alone a "New Dealer." Rather he skillfully shifted the tone and content of his symbolic rhetoric. The blue-collar strategy, for example, represented less a shift on most policy questions involving labor or the economy (with the possible exception of three issues to be discussed) than it reflected a conscious effort to change his presentational style. As an actor, he is exceptionally capable of playing these different roles, but then so are most candidates who manage to win a major party nomination. Consider his final remarks in the Cleveland debate with President Carter:

> Next Tuesday, all of you will go to the polls . . . and make a decision. I think when you make that decision, it will be well if you would ask yourself, are you better off than you were four years ago? Is it easier for you to go and buy things in the stores than it was four years ago? Is there more or less unemployment in the country than there was four years ago? Is America as respected throughout the world as it was? Do you feel that our security is as safe, that we are as strong as we were four years ago? [20]

This approach, followed by the candidate throughout the general election campaign, left precisely what Reagan would do about these questions unanswered, open-ended. The candidate could be seen in front of a shut-down steel mill, or listening sympathetically to the plight of unemployed workers, or proudly discussing the "constructive role" of labor unions and his own presidency of the Screen Actors Guild without fundamentally altering the specific positions with which he was long associated.

Or he could appear to alter a few specific stands, as Carter and every other candidate had done in the past, and still retain the consistency of the overall thrust of his future agenda. Typically these minor changes received most of the attention because they were newsworthy in the sense of being "new" information. Lost in this emphasis was the basic consistency of the candidate's world view. His overall agenda, just like Carter's, was to be found in what remained stable, tested, developed, and bargained over by the time the conventions ended, not what changed during the general election. Reagan's positions on some of the issues of importance in his blue-collar strategy are good examples of these themes.

The Davis-Bacon Act, long championed by labor and opposed by Reagan as far back as his days as governor, reflected a "pseudo-shift" in his position. Davis-Bacon essentially mandates "prevailing wage" rates for construction workers involved in projects using federal funds. As late as October 1980, Reagan's campaign headquarters was still releasing a statement on his behalf, reading, "I think the Davis-Bacon Act has outlived any usefulness it once may have had and should be repealed." [21] Cue-card summaries for each of his debates, including the one with Carter a week before the election carried the same message. [22] However, on the campaign trail, Reagan seemed to shift his position by adopting the following qualification:

[W]hile I still believe it has outlived its usefulness and should be repealed, why, of course, I will first take a look at how it is being administered to see if anything can be done to take care of the problems, before supporting its repeal.

Had the candidate truly changed his mind on this issue? The media reported widely that he had, primarily because of the emphasis on ferreting out deviations from consistency that marks one of the norms for covering candidates, but it should be clear that future action about repeal was left intentionally ambiguous.

A similar approach was used for Section 14 (b) of the Taft-Hartley Act—support of a state's authority in establishing right-to-work laws, usually considered harmful to labor unions. Reagan said, "I believe that each state should be able to decide whether right-to-work laws are desirable for its workers." He was fond of suggesting that *"perhaps we should consider* whether national legislation would help the working men and women of America" [emphasis added] but, when pressed, would deny that he intended to propose legislation altering existing law. Rather, he reiterated his belief in the "workers' freedom of choice"; in other words, he supported a state's right to choose right-to-work options, a choice that organized labor has sought to eliminate since it was enacted after World War II.

Another issue area that was subject to considerable attention because it seemed to prove that Reagan was moving to the center, was handled even more ambiguously by the candidate than the two already mentioned. During the primaries, the candidate revived an old antilabor bugaboo in an apparent suggestion that labor unions should be subject to antitrust laws: "Labor has become so powerful ... they should be subject to the same restrictions that are imposed on business and industry.... We should *look very closely* at whether they should be bound as businesses are by the antitrust laws." [23] [Emphasis added.] In the general election campaign, however, the Reagan organization declined to write a more comprehensive statement, and the candidate, when asked, merely said that he "was not proposing full-scale legislation," just saying that it "was something that might be looked at." [24]

Do any of these "shifts" constitute a more "moderate" approach to those issues of most concern to labor in the 1980s? Organized labor had a very different view. The AFL-CIO summarized a long set of policy differences with any future Reagan administration involving:[25]

—his hostility toward Davis-Bacon; maintaining 14 (b) of the Taft-Hartley Act; and ambiguously flirting with the idea of bringing unions under the antitrust laws;

—his opposition to *common situs* picketing legislation (permitting unified labor strikes on construction sites);

—his support of legislation that would deny food stamp and other welfare benefits to legally striking workers and their dependents;

—his opposition to the Humphrey-Hawkins Act, which prescribes but does not mandate a national policy of full employment;

—his active opposition to the United Farm Workers and other agricultural workers in their long struggle to organize many of California's farm employees;

—his early opposition to Medicare and then more recent opposition to a federally supported comprehensive national health insurance plan;

—his long-time opposition to minimum wage and his ("first step") advocacy of a legislation exempting "young people" from the current minimum wage;

—his commitment to "reorganizing" OSHA (rather than abolishing it);

—his advocacy of large cuts in virtually every major social/domestic program created since the Kennedy years that was designed to benefit those with few economic resources;

—his record as governor that included opposing collective bargaining for teachers; cutting the state's disability insurance programs; suspending workers' rights to hearings in some workers' compensation programs; and his repeated efforts to cut back on job-creating public works projects.

In short, organized labor treated the Reagan campaign's "blue-collar strategy" as a subterfuge, which, at least in part, it was. Of course, Reagan and his senior policy advisers believed that they, rather than organized labor, knew better what blue-collar workers "really wanted," and they were partly correct: a substantial minority—*not* a majority, as is frequently and erroneously reported—of blue-collar workers voted for Reagan. This belief does not make Reagan different from other conservatives. Herbert Hoover and every Republican candidate since has questioned whether the economic liberalism of organized labor is in the best interests of blue-collar workers.

What made Reagan *seem* different is that, compared to his outlook *20 years earlier*, he was now less strident in opposing some of the social/economic programs created in Democratic administrations since the New Deal. Neither the candidate nor his advisers, in fact, had changed their basic beliefs about what was appropriate for economic justice in the United States.[26] Supply-side economics, with its emphasis on growth through tax incentives *was* different from the old-time, belt-tightening ideology so long associated with conservative Republicanism.

But on most specific issues affecting the current and future economic fortunes of the lower middle class, as well as those at or near the bottom of the income structure, the Reagan coalition made only minor and ambiguous concessions.

The fact that a Republican presidential candidate in the 1980s could say some decent things about FDR, was supportive of Social Security, and not in favor of selling TVA to the private sector was taken as evidence that he was moving toward the middle of American politics! Concerned liberals who feared that he was going to "repeal the New Deal" also did little to clarify what his actual agenda might be if the Republican succeeded in the election. That the Reagan administration has made no legislative effort to alter laws like Davis-Bacon *may* stem partly from the electoral incentives of competing in a general election, both the last one and a future one. Much more powerful factors arise from the realities of governing, where blocking factions inside and outside Congress would have inflicted heavy damage on other parts of the Reagan program had the administration actually championed legislation to undermine the existing protections of labor law. Reagan, like all presidents, has made basic decisions about what he can accomplish. He is flexible enough, both as a candidate and as president, to keep his feet, in his own words, from being cemented into concrete.

So, like Carter's in 1976, the Reagan forces focused most of their energies during the general election on exploiting claims about the incumbent's failure as a "strong leader," deemphasizing partisanship, and avoiding the development of more concrete policy alternatives. They continued to repeat, through advertising, in speeches, and in the debates, that the candidate was not antilabor, that he was not anti-Social Security, not anti-New Deal, not antiminority or anti-equal rights, that he was not reckless in foreign affairs, but that he would "make America strong again." Thematically, the Reagan coalition used front-channel communication to do what the front channel does best: to build belief in his character, style, and leadership potential, reiterating in thousands of different ways that

> the only real long-term solution to unemployment is to stimulate economic growth, thereby creating enough private jobs for all those seeking work. This increased economic growth can best be achieved by a comprehensive program of tax rate reductions and deregulation of American industry, to restore America's incentive to produce.[27]

And of course:

> I would like to have a crusade today, and I would like to lead that crusade with your help. And it would be one to get government off the backs of the great people of this country and turn you loose again to do those things that I know you can do so well, because you did them and made this country great.[28]

The role of issues staff in the campaign

Organizationally and in policy terms, Reagan's agenda was established and solidified at the Republican convention, and the general election campaign was of little additional importance in predicting his future behavior as president. This was also true of Carter's 1976 campaign and appears to be a common pattern in the seasons of presidential campaign politics. While Reagan's domestic "Policy Development and Research" and "Policy Coordination" staffs grew during the general campaign (from 19 to 26), they were a small proportion (6 percent of approximately 450 full-time paid staff) of the campaign's resources. "Firefighters, not policy analysts," said one, "is what we are." He continued:

> As a group, we've spent much more time documenting the problems and snafus of the Carter administration than we have developing comprehensive policy initiatives. The Advisory Councils of the RNC, the separate reports of people in Congress, plus whatever Martin [Anderson] really wants is where you'll find the real action on policy. That's the way it should be. The candidate's positions are well known by everybody, including the press.

The internal life of this part of Reagan's campaign mirrored other presidential operations in an important way. Virtually all of its energy was devoted to servicing the background needs of the mass media and organized group constituencies, with a few back-channel policy papers written for smaller publications. Unlike Carter's 1976 issue personnel, very few of Reagan's policy development people were specialists in public policy. Most came out of backgrounds of public relations or media, and they did not go on to form the nucleus of Martin Anderson's first Office of Policy Development in the White House, as for example, Carter's campaign issue staff did under Stuart Eizenstat. Anderson was on the plane during most of the campaign, and the issues staff was not as racked by the tensions associated with "The Fear of Not Flying," as the Carter group had been in 1976.

Since the overwhelming majority of voters is unconcerned with the details of public policy, and neither the candidates nor the mass media are predisposed and/or organized to alter this, the most important contribution of an issues staff is its ability to refine and extend the policy themes of the candidate for smaller audiences. Here Reagan's staff failed because the campaign's strategy was intentionally based on avoiding highly specific, detailed policy information. While the papers issued under "Reagan for President" did contain some additional details and did telegraph the *general* direction of his future agenda, they were, on the whole, considerably less specific than Carter's had been four years earlier. For this reason, front-channel communication dominated the campaign's policy thrust, and much of what was actually published ignored or briefly skimmed the essentials.[29]

Finally, the limited role the general election season plays in agenda formation was reflected in the design and belated formation of Reagan's domestic and economic policy task forces. Their formation was belated because most were not fully created until late October, two weeks before the election, with the president's press release carefully noting, "I look forward to carefully examining their recommendations *after* the November election." [30] [Emphasis added.] Their importance stems less from what they did during the campaign than in their preliminary role during the transition.

Under the operational guidance of Darrell Trent, the domestic groups were coordinated by Martin Anderson, who in turn reported to Ed Meese. Twenty-three task forces were created with 329 "advisers," including a unified "Economic Policy Coordinating Committee," chaired by George P. Shultz. The committee was composed of the chairs of each of the six economic task forces plus six other individuals.

Like Carter's operation in 1976, these task forces were blue-ribbon committees, carefully screened for political loyalty and conservative representativeness, and operating under a mandate not to make any of their deliberations public—before or after the election. Campaign task forces like these provide individuals an opportunity to advance their policy goals and their own political ambitions, and for that reason alone, they are important to the future of the president's agenda. In turn, candidates use them to "pay off" important individuals in their coalition, and the task forces serve the candidate as *one of many* sources for basic ideas in their future legislative programs. They are clues about *who* may be important in a candidate's potential administration, and by inference, what policy will be pursued, since the "who" and the "what" are linked. But they are clues, nothing more.[31] These domestic groups were paired with 25 foreign policy and defense working groups with a total membership of 132, coordinated by Richard Allen, who in turn was also funneling ideas through Meese. This arrangement, Anderson and Allen through Meese, was duplicated in the early days of the Reagan White House, then abandoned when his first secretary of state, Alexander Haig, and his first assistant for national security affairs, Allen, were forced out. Anderson also departed after the first 18 months, and the White House policy machinery shifted notably from this original campaign framework.

On election day 1980, President Jimmy Carter conceded before 10:00 p.m. EST, and Ronald Reagan and the forthcoming "Reagan Revolution" were now responsible for creating much more than a handful of press releases or policy task forces.

Conclusion

Summarizing the dominant opinion of most influential commentators one month after the election, Richard Harwood wrote:

> The American electorate on November 4, 1980, rendered a judgment of incompetence on President Carter, on "liberalism," and on the federal establishment in Washington ... there could be no doubt that the economic and foreign policies of the liberals had been found wanting.[32]

Like most of us, he got one-third of it right. Without question, the perceived "incompetence" of the incumbent was a major factor in the voting decision. And equally without question, few Americans in fact "rendered a judgment" about liberalism. Data from the University of Michigan's 1980 National Election Study show that in October, one month before the election,[33]

—42 percent of the electorate "didn't know" whether Reagan or Carter could be thought of as liberal, conservative, or anything in between;

—52 percent were unable to say whether Reagan favored policies that would reduce inflation or reduce unemployment (for understandable reasons, given the candidate's rhetoric);

—35 percent "didn't know" whether Reagan believed that expenditures for domestic services should be cut, remain the same, or be increased, and another 16 percent believed that he favored *not* making any cuts;

—substantial majorities opposed cuts in domestic programs like education, housing, unemployment compensation, and food stamps;

—31 percent "didn't know" whether Reagan believed that détente with the Soviet Union was "important" or a "mistake," and another 16 percent apparently thought he supported détente.

—only on defense spending did the electorate begin to approach the conditions assumed in a Harwood-like analysis. Here 48 percent believed that Reagan would increase defense spending, while 30 percent didn't know, and 6 percent thought he believed that defense spending should be reduced. Carter, who in fact had moved in his FY 1980 and 1981 budgets to increase defense spending, was perceived by 35 percent as believing that cuts should be made.

Just as observers tend to underestimate the amount of issue information that is available in campaigns (if one is willing to scratch for it), so too they tend to overestimate the consistency of public opinion in rejecting or supporting the broad ideologies and programs that candidates advance. Liberalism and conservatism are (sometimes) useful summarizing concepts for those who are most informed and active in the political arena. They are less useful in examining the ideas, opinions, and desires of most American adults. Most voters do have political belief systems; they simply do not use them in a manner that is consistent with elite definitions of what constitutes a well-organized and comprehensive ideology.

Political scientists and others have long disputed the reasons for this relative ignorance (or genius) in the American electorate. Which is more responsible—the psychology of voters or the behavior of candidates and parties? The Reagan campaign was effective in working both sides of the street. Reagan frequently responded to the electoral environment in a nonissue way by emphasizing themes of leadership style and rhetorical claims about the necessity "for a change." Simultaneously the campaign's presentation of "the issues" undermined voter rationality because the candidate remained intentionally ambiguous about the direction, timing, or magnitude of many of his commitments. The 1980 campaign reflected the nature of campaigns generally, serving as both the cause and effect of the electorate's confusion and ignorance about public policy.

For the Reagan campaign, as for others, the drive to mobilize voter support for future presidential action, independent of the direction and content of that action, held a powerful and compelling logic; they could act *as if* they had a mandate without having to persuade competitors, in Congress or the media, for example, that it was true. Certainly this is what happened during the first year of the Reagan administration. The legitimacy of a presidential mandate is least likely to be challenged during the president's first year in office, particularly if he is elected in what influential observers report, erroneously in this case, as a "landslide."

The fifty-one percent of the popular vote Reagan received constitutes a landslide only on television, which feels compelled to report the news in a visually dramatic way. On election night, therefore, the public was treated to gobs of blue, representing Reagan victories, moving steadily across the screen, east-to-west, "as state after state falls to the Reagan bandwagon." Soon the entire map was a sea of blue, with a few uncooperative red islands like Georgia, Minnesota, and, dreaded enemy, Washington, D.C., resulting in a "landslide of historical proportions." No need to explain to viewers that what they are seeing is the accumulation of electoral college votes, that the components of mass voting behavior are complex and only rarely specifically ideological, that the rejection of an incumbent (which it was) does not thereby constitute majority endorsement of the challenger's political agenda. Viewers cannot handle the complexity!

So, combined with the Republican takeover of the Senate, which certainly was of historic significance, "the gates were opened," said one Reagan official, "and we knew that we had to move everything we could before they closed again."

What "moved" grew directly out of the campaign's policy agenda, ambiguous as much of it was, where the coalitional incentives to deliver—on policy and personnel—required that the cabbages go to Republican conservatives.

Which specific cabbages and which specific conservatives were questions still to be decided.

Notes

1. The origins and distinctively American class context of "The Speech" were skillfully traced by Nicholas Lemann in one of the best examples of interpretive journalism during Reagan's first 100 days, "The Speech: Reagan's Break from the Past," *Washington Post*, Feb. 22, 1981. On Reagan generally, see Lou Cannon, *Reagan* (New York: Putnam, 1982).
2. The objection that "conservatism," like "liberalism," is a meaningless concept is a recurring claim in political discourse. Of course, frequently they *are* meaningless, simplifying, and misleading, but the persistence of these terms suggest they have some utility in distinguishing the broad orientation of political leaders to public policy. If such concepts did not exist, we would be forced to invent them. An elaboration will be found in A. James Reichley, "The Conservative Model of the Presidency" (Paper delivered at the 1981 annual meeting of the American Political Science Association) and A. James Reichley, *Conservatives in an Age of Change: The Nixon and Ford Administrations* (Washington, D.C.: Brookings Institution, 1981).
3. On conservatism as the preferred ideological outlook of a substantial majority of Republican activists: David Nexon, "Asymmetry in the Political System: Occasional Activists in the Democratic and Republican Parties, 1956-1974," *American Political Science Review* (September 1971): 716-730; Warren J. Mitofsky and Martin Plissner, "The Making of the Delegates: 1968-1980," *Public Opinion* 3 (October/November 1980): 40-42; John S. Jackson et al., "Herbert McCloskey and Friends Revisited: 1980 Democratic and Republican Party Elites Compared to the Mass Public," *American Politics Quarterly* 10 (April 1982): 158-180.
4. Charles O. Jones, "Nominating Carter's 'Favorite Opponent,'" in *The American Elections of 1980*, ed. Austin Ranney (Washington, D.C.: American Enterprise Institute, 1981), 61-98. Other useful studies of the 1980 election include Paul R. Abramson, John H. Aldrich, and David Rohde, *Change and Continuity in the 1980 Election* (Washington, D.C.: CQ Press, 1982); *The Pursuit of the Presidency 1980*, ed. Richard Harwood et al. (New York: Putnam, 1980); Jack W. Germond and Jules Witcover, *Blue Smoke and Mirrors* (New York: Viking, 1981); Stephen J. Wayne, *The Road to the White House*, 2d ed. (New

York: St. Martin's, 1984); *The Election of 1980*, ed. Gerald Pomper (Chatham, N.J.: Chatham House, 1981); *The 1980 Elections and Their Meaning*, ed. Ellis Sandoz and Cecil V. Crabb, Jr. (Washington, D.C.: CQ Press, 1981); and *The Hidden Election*, ed. Thomas Ferguson and Joel Rogers (New York: Random House, 1981).

5. Ronald Reagan, "A Strategy for Growth: The American Economy in the 1980s" (Address to the International Business Council, Chicago, Sept. 8, 1980) and "Fact Sheet—A Strategy for Growth," released Sept. 9, 1980.

6. This must be inferred since it is unclear, absent guidelines, that any option other than a "voluntary" one is possible.

7. Reagan's interpretation of the impact of gay rights ordinances is disputed by local officials where protective statutes have been enacted. His language about gays, other than in this misleading assertion about the effect of current laws, was surprisingly moderate in tone. Is he a "closet tolerant," perhaps because of his long years in Hollywood (Ben Wattenberg's suggestion) or because his political friendship network includes prominent people who are gay, or because of the growing electoral sophistication of gay activists, or indeed because of all three factors? Reagan's stance in 1980 was analogous to Carter's in 1976—"benign neglect." The Democrats adopted a more positive commitment in their 1980 platform, supporting the first gay rights plank in American party history. It is clear that this issue has broken through the mobilization of bias in a rather short time and may become a secondary but important and conflictual agenda item for both parties over the next few years.

8. Darrell M. West, "Rhetoric and Agenda-Setting in the 1980 Presidential Campaign," *Congress & the Presidency* (Autumn 1982): 1-21.

9. Ibid., 13.

10. The three most accessible sources are *Congressional Quarterly Weekly Report*, which presents a careful description and summary of candidate and platform positions by major policy area (economy, energy, foreign policy, and so forth); *National Journal*, which focuses on fewer areas but usually in greater depth; and, since 1976, Ralph Nader's Citizens Research Group, which has produced extensive "policy profiles" of major candidates, biased, of course, by Nader's policy preferences, in a series titled "Selecting A President: A Citizens' Guide to...." Important national interest groups (Chamber of Commerce, AFL-CIO, League of Conservation Voters, American Conservative Union, among others) also produce in-depth policy profiles of use for those with more specialized interests. The most comprehensive study of the role of television in the 1980 election will be found in *Television Coverage of the 1980 Presidential Campaign*, ed. William C. Adams (Washington, D.C.: Ablex, 1982).

11. Michael Malbin, "The Conventions, Platforms, and Issue Activists," in Ranney, *The American Elections of 1980*, 107.

12. William Greider, "The Republicans," in Harwood, *The Pursuit of the Presidency 1980*, 167.

13. Ibid., 169.

14. Gregory Markus, "Political Attitudes During an Election Year," *American Political Science Review* (September 1982): 538-560.

15. Abramson, Aldrich, and Rohde, *Change and Continuity*.

16. Reprinted with additional analysis in William Greider, *The Education of David Stockman and Other Americans* (New York: E. P. Dutton, 1982).

17. James David Barber, *The Pulse of Politics* (New York: Norton, 1980), 225-226.
18. These motifs are reconstructed, embellished, and reaffirmed in a workshop format involving principal campaign strategists and prominent journalists: *1980 in Retrospect*, ed. Jonathan Moore (Cambridge, Mass.: Ballinger, 1981). Two broader scholarly studies of presidential campaign strategy are John Aldrich, *Before the Primaries* (Chicago: University of Chicago Press, 1980) and John H. Kessel, *Presidential Campaign Politics: Coalition Strategies and Citizen Response* (Homewood, Ill.: Dorsey Press, 1980).
19. Lou Cannon, quoted in "October," in Harwood, *The Pursuit of the Presidency*, 291-292.
20. "Debates," in Harwood, *The Pursuit of the Presidency*, 399.
21. "Davis-Bacon Act," press release, Reagan for President, January 1980.
22. "Issue Box Scores—Reagan-Carter-Anderson," *Television Debate Briefing Book* (Washington, D.C.: Republican National Committee, undated.)
23. Citizen's Research Group, *Selecting a President: A Citizen's Guide to the 1980 Election* (Washington, D.C.: Public Citizen, 1980), 93.
24. *Congressional Quarterly Weekly Report*, Oct. 12, 1980, 1126.
25. "Reagan as Governor, 1967-75," AFL-CIO, COPE Summary Study, 1980.
26. A point made repeatedly by Reagan staff in my interviews.
27. "Federal Jobs Program," press release, Reagan for President, Jan. 31, 1980.
28. "Debates," in Harwood, *The Pursuit of the Presidency 1980*, 399.
29. See Robert Sahr's case study of energy for a good example: "Energy as a Non-Issue in the 1980 Coverage," in Adams, *Television Coverage of the 1980 Presidential Campaign*.
30. "Task Forces," press release, Reagan for President, Oct. 23, 1980.
31. Others disagree. Thomas Ferguson and Joel Rogers, for example, trace the corporate linkages of Reagan's major advisers in considerable detail, seeking to establish that mobilization of bias (class interest) was deeply imbedded in his campaign, and, by inference, would be just as characteristic of his administration. As the reader might surmise, there were no closet Democratic Socialist Organizing Committee members (or even ordinary old liberal Democrats) stashed away in any of these task forces! More is needed than what they provide if the precision and inferential power of quasi-radical analyses like theirs are to have greater impact; for example, tracing the *specific* policy preferences and *specific* operational responsibilities of ex-Wall Street executives on the *specific* decisions of governmental agencies responsible for regulating and/or shaping financial activities. See their analysis and that of their contributors, who are concerned with other aspects of the campaign, in *The Hidden Election*, ed. Ferguson and Rogers.
32. Harwood, *The Pursuit of the Presidency 1980*, 326-327.
33. Summarized from data presented in Markus, "Political Attitudes During an Election Year."

Conservatives as presidents: the record of the Reagan administration

6

Them as has, gets.

—Americana

Two years into the most conservative presidency since the 1920s, one of the New Right's magazines, *Conservative Digest*, published a series of articles under the economical title, "Has Ronald Reagan's Presidency Been Captured by Wall Street-Big Business-Corporate Executive Suite-Big New York/Houston Law Firm-Eastern Liberal and/or Establishment-Non Reaganite Republicans?"

Only in America!

That Reagan and most of his advisers took the 1980 Republican platform and his long-held, if somewhat contradictory and not inflexible, version of "conservative principles" seriously should not be in dispute, the protests of Richard A. Viguerie, Paul M. Weyrich, and the New Right notwithstanding.

The first year of the administration, particularly, was an extraordinary combination of political audacity, effective planning, gifted leadership, and swift execution, all geared toward implementing a significant part of its conservative economic agenda. Of course they gambled, with conservative as well as moderate Republicans, not to mention a more broadly based voting constituency, that their economic policies, combined with an antiregulatory, antigovernment administrative assault, would succeed. Defining "success" requires multidimensional, time-sensitive, and ultimately normative considerations. Judgment is deferred until later in the chapter.

The decision to move rapidly on the economic and regulatory component of Reagan's agenda in the first year and to defer temporarily full-scale action on the so-called social component was a political calculation, not a philosophical one. Like all presidents, Reagan was more comfortable with some parts of the platform than with others, more intensely committed ("stubborn" became a media cliché early in his presidency) in certain areas, willing to reverse direction here and there (tax deductions on interest income or draft registration are examples) but the coalitional incentives to deliver on a large part of his agenda, social and economic, were substantial. The president said it best, even if his assumptions about why he defeated Carter were wrong:

> I ran on the platform; the people voted for me on the platform. I do believe in that platform, and I think it would be very cynical and callous of me to suggest that I'm going to turn away from it.[1]

Nevertheless, like Carter's, Nixon's, and Johnson's, the Reagan administration, in fact, "turned away," deferred, scuttled, or reversed direction on some parts of its campaign agenda and the 1980 Republican platform, while holding fast to others. Sorting out which is which, and why, is the principal task of this chapter. Like the analysis of the Carter presidency, this will not be a comprehensive examination of the Reagan administration's performance. The primary emphasis here is on domestic programs sought and won, on the content of the campaign-related legislative and administrative action. And, as in the Carter chapter, I am concerned with the specific political context in which the Reagan presidency has developed, the varying effects of the specific domestic and global environment he has faced. Evaluating presidential performance requires that the analyst use comparative standards as well as judgments about events that are unique.

Ordering the Reagan agenda: the economic imperative _____

Although he promised less in terms of numbers than Carter or some other candidates, what Reagan pledged was far-reaching in the consequences it predicted. Recall again the "catechism" of the economic package pushed through in those heady days of 1981—we can cut taxes, substantially reduce nondefense spending, restrict monetary growth, increase defense expenditures, retain the "safety net" for the "truly needy," and provide American industry with regulatory "relief." The result will be an economy that will reduce unemployment *and* in-flation, bring interest rates down, increase savings and hence in-vestment, promote sustained growth, increase government reve-nues through growth—all of this leading to a balanced federal budget.

Twenty-one months from the day this package was introduced in February 1981, the economy was in a severe recession, with sharply higher unemployment rates and mounting business failures. Neither business savings nor investment had increased; industrial capacity was functioning at 71 percent; and FY 1982 ended with a federal deficit of $110.6 billion. Fiscal year 1983 ended with a larger deficit, $195 billion, and virtually every authority was projecting comparable deficits for FY 1984 and 1985. On the other hand, both nominal interest rates and inflation had declined, the latter primarily because of the recession and the absence of severe pressure on energy and other costs characteristic of the 1970s. The Federal Reserve Board's tight money policy, at least until mid-1982, also was responsible for sustaining the recession, thus slowing inflation.

Most economists agree that the recession and high interest rates overwhelmed any immediate response of business investment or con-sumer spending to lower taxes. The tax cut, combined with deficit spending, was an unacknowledged neo-Keynesian element in supply-side economics that helped prevent the recession from lurching into deeper and more painful depths. As recovery began in mid-1983, with unemployment falling consistently through early 1984 and industrial capacity climbing to 80 percent, most economists noted that the boom of the "boom or bust" cycle was a classic consumer-led recovery in the Keynesian mold. The ironies were not lost on critics of the president's anti-Keynesian rhetoric.

Whatever the long-run consequences of the administration's early economic policies, it is clear that, foolishly or not, it attempted to redeem a large portion of its campaign commitments about economic strategy. In doing so, paradoxically, the administration undermined its capacity to deliver on all of the promised consequences. Because most voters *focus on outcomes rather than means*, Republican congressional candidates paid the price in the midterm elections of 1982 when Democrats scored a 26-seat net gain in the House and came close to unseating five seemingly invulnerable GOP senators. "It could have been much worse," observed one RNC official, "but if it had been, the president might as well have retired." A similar logic, however, fueled the president's optimism about his reelection chances two years later. The economic recovery of late 1983 and 1984 was used by Reagan strategists to keep voter concern focused on "second-stage" outcomes rather than means, a strategy that depended on overcoming the negative public reaction toward "first-stage" outcomes in 1981-1982.

Budget cuts

Reagan campaigned on a platform of not only stimulating the private sector through tax policy but also of imposing substantial reductions in nondefense program expenditures. His administration—under the leadership of the highly energetic David Stockman, enjoying a Republican Senate (there had not been one since the 1950s), and counting on a cohesive Republican phalanx in the House to overcome a fragmented Democratic opposition—pushed through major cuts in a wide variety of social/economic programs during the budgetary struggles of 1981, 1982, and 1983. Congress increasingly resisted some initiatives—the outright abolition of the Legal Services Corporation, for example—but the administration forced reductions across programs in education, employment, job training, housing, and social services, presumably those outside the "safety net" of the Social Security system.[2] Stockman's oft-repeated commitment to cutting those with "weak claims rather than weak clients" was laudable and believable. Still, analysts estimated that 70 percent of all the reductions in FY 1982 and FY 1983 in fact affected the poor and near poor in America.

Henry J. Aaron of the Brookings Institution estimates that:

> real nondefense spending other than on social contract entitlements, e.g. Social Security, Medicare, etc. will fall $37 billion between 1981 and 1984 and another $27 billion by 1988 under the president's proposed FY 1984 budget.[3]

The promise of Reagan as a campaigner and the intent of Reagan as president were to "eliminate wasteful federal spending" and "counterproductive" programs. The impact of that highly ambiguous promise has been felt in countless programs targeted primarily on low income groups. One study, comparing the Reagan administration's FY 1983 budget with what was actually spent in FY 1981, noted there was a $40 billion reduction in *real* dollars stemming from cuts in the following programs: food stamps; Aid to Families with Dependent Children (AFDC); Supplemental Security Income (SSI); subsidized housing; Medicaid; employment and training; compensatory education; financial aid for needy students; social services; community services; child welfare services; legal services; low income energy assistance; the Women, Infants, and Children program (WIC); maternal and child health; primary health care; and free and reduced price school lunches.[4]

Actual federal spending for some of these programs has not been cut more dramatically for a simple reason: after 1981, and more aggressively after the 1982 midterm election, both Republicans in the Senate and House Democrats found effective ways to challenge some of the administration's budget priorities. Indeed the Senate Budget Committee simply abandoned the White House's FY 1983 and 1984 budgets, the latter much less ceremoniously than the former. One senior staff member put it directly, "Everyone around here knew the president's FY 1984 budget was dead in the water before it got to Congress."

Ironically but predictably, the administration attempted to dodge responsibility for making social program cuts that were consistent with the president's campaign rhetoric. A two-year review of accomplishments, issued by the White House Office of Public Affairs in January 1983,[5] took pride in claiming that "federal medical, nutrition, and housing assistance to the poor is 28 percent higher in FY 83 than it was in FY 80." [6] But this rise was due to inflation and automatic increases in the number of beneficiaries under Medicare and because of congressional modification of the administration's original budgets. The White House report stated:

> In fiscal 1983, spending by the Department of HHS [Health and Human Services] alone will be 36 percent of the total budget ... and the federal government will support such services as the following:
> —95 million meals per day;
> —medical assistance;
> —housing assistance for more than 10 million Americans;
> --food stamps for more than 20 million low-income people;
> —higher education assistance for almost 5 million students;
> —the Old Age Survivors and Disability Insurance provides monthly cash payments up to $729 to 28.8 million people who are 62 or over.[7]

And so on. Of course neither the president nor his advisers were pleased by the intensity of opposition attacks on their budget priorities. "He behaves like Ayn Rand but wants to be remembered as Santa Claus," observed one tart critic. It is indisputable that Reagan's budget reductions increased the pressure on America's poor and near poor, groups most vulnerable to the pain of economic uncertainty.

Virtually every objective study of his successive budgets, including some sympathetic to the administration's budgetary and macroeconomic goals, reaches the same conclusion.[8] Combined with the administration's tax program, the Economic Recovery Tax Act of 1981 (ERTA), the impact of these policies reduced the income, in services and cash, of those families with incomes less than $10,000, while increasing dramatically the real income of households earning $80,000 and more. The Congressional Budget Office (CBO) estimated that in 1983 the tax and budget program would *cost* those families earning less than $10,000 an average of $240, while the gain for those at $80,000 and more would be $15,130.[9]

Compensating for increases in Social Security taxes, the Urban Institute concluded that the net effect of ERTA's across-the-board reduction would be to provide modest short-term increases in the purchasing power of the broad middle class, substantial gains for higher-income families, leaving those at the bottom worse off than they were in 1981.[10] ERTA also cut capital gains taxes from a maximum rate of 28 percent to 20 percent and reduced the top rate on unearned income from 70 percent to 50 percent, both of which increased disproportionately the income of the well-off. As the president's 1982 *Economic Report* bluntly asserted, "income redistribution is not a compelling justification in the 1980s for federal taxing and spending programs." [11]

Rejecting even the redistributive *possibilities* in policy (neither American party has ever sought tax policies that would lead to fundamental redistribution) is conservative to the core, leaving the administration open to broad-scale and damaging criticism about "fairness" and "harshness" in its taxing and budget-cutting initiatives. No matter how hard Stockman and others worked to introduce some considerations of social equity into the decision-making framework, various factors, including the administration's aggressive drive to increase defense spending beyond what even many conservatives thought was reasonable, reduced their capacity to do so. The principal casualties of the Reagan program remained "weak clients." Said one administration offical:

> Dave Stockman did everything but resign in trying to carve out the groups who have grown fat on the federal budget and who don't really need it. Oh, sure, we knew there would be real short-term suffering for those less well-off. They were suffering already under inflation. It was impossible! Organizational power, here and in Congress, just won't let it work. We had to give and give constantly, in negotiations. Oh, we got a few but not many.

Stockman, as early as the spring of 1981, was concerned about the looming future deficits that were the inevitable result of growing entitlement budgets, the administration's tax cuts, and defense increases. Nevertheless, he was characteristically optimistic and pugnacious in his interviews with William Greider about his capacity to reduce projected defense spending:

> I put together a list of 20 social programs that have to be zeroed out completely, like Job Corps, Head Start, women and children's feeding programs, and so on. And another 25 that have to be cut by 50 percent: general revenue sharing, CETA manpower training, etcetera, etcetera. And then huge bites that would have to be taken out of Social Security. I mean really fierce, blood and guts stuff—widows' benefits and orphans' benefits, things like that. And still it didn't add up to $40 billion. So, that sort of created a new awareness of the defense budget.[12]

The "awareness" about the need to reduce defense spending Stockman hoped for never materialized; both the defense budget and federal deficits went up at a steep rate. The president had kept his campaign promise, but the process and consequences were beyond the capacity of talented managers like David Stockman to control.

Deregulation and business

In addition to budgetary, tax, and monetary initiatives, further deregulation of the business sector was considered a major part of Reagan's economic package. Throughout the campaign, he denounced the growth of federal regulation, saying that "it is the government's duty to protect us from each other, not from ourselves or from our own inability to use common sense in dealing with others . . . we should, on a broad scale, reevaluate regulations, identify unnecessary ones, and eliminate them." [13] Focusing on environmental policy, for example, he suggested that "we should re-examine *every* regulatory requirement with a commitment to simplify and streamline the process . . . and return to the states the primary responsibility for environmental regulation in order to increase responsiveness to local conditions." [14] [Emphasis added.] The candidate also supported the right of Congress to veto federal regulations, a position the administration abandoned once taking power.

The justification for moving quickly in this area was reinforced by Reagan's first chairman of the Council of Economic Advisers, Murray Weidenbaum, who had long decried the costs to "productive investment" that stemmed from governmental "social" regulation and by the ideological commitment of most of Reagan's top appointees in agencies with regulatory responsibilities. From Anne Gorsuch Burford at the Environmental Protection Agency (EPA) to James C. Miller III, who initially headed the deregulatory team and then became chairman of the Federal Trade Commission (FTC), Reagan appointees moved to implement the president's deregulatory rhetoric.

Within weeks of taking office, Reagan announced the formation of a Cabinet-level Task Force on Regulatory Relief, chaired by the vice president, whose responsibility was to review all major regulatory proposals, assess those currently in force, and suggest executive and legislative remedies. One month later, the president issued Executive Order 12291 establishing, among other things, that OMB would henceforth provide centralized review of all proposed major rules (assisted by the newly created OIRA, the Office of Information and Regulatory Affairs, attached to the Task Force). Unlike budget policy, this was a battle to be waged administratively rather than legislatively. [15]

What happened after the initial flourish? According to the most comprehensive study of the administration's early regulatory policies:

> The claims of cost savings have been skeptically received for a number of reasons.... Even more problematic is determining what industry anticipated to be the costs of these future regulations [that were rescinded]. Calculating the savings that resulted from reduced enforcement is even more difficult.... The plain fact is that no one really knows how widespread compliance with regulations was even before the Reagan regulatory relief program began. Enforcement programs have lacked strategic goals and measures of success. Thus we do not have a baseline against which to measure change. The effort has cut costs, though by an unknown amount, and appears to have convinced businessmen that the regulatory game has changed.[16]

Because the administration opted for an administrative rather than legislative strategy for the regulatory agenda, it left itself open to later challenge and subsequent reversals in Congress, through the courts, and by groups, such as the trucking industry, the Teamsters, consumer affairs specialists, and environmentalists, who were deeply unhappy with the specific application of deregulatory guidelines. OMB itself has been challenged in the federal courts, and assessments of the administration's efforts stressed the formidable opposition to the president's strategy. According to one observer:

> Industry has gotten some "relief" from regulation but much of this has come from budget cuts and [administrative] shifts that curtailed enforcement of federal rules. Such changes are easily reversed, and more permanent "reform" through statutory changes has thus far eluded the president. Efforts to translate the [deregulatory] spirit into law have been notably unsuccessful [on environmental issues] ... as a result 9 of EPA's 10 major laws remain intact, with efforts to revise them bottled up in Congress. Last week, the administration threw in the towel on the 10th, the "Superfund" hazardous-waste bill.[17]

Analyzing the specific contours of the administration's regulatory policy would require an agency-by-agency, area-by-area assessment that weighs economic and social costs and benefits. This is far beyond what is entertained here. Because the Reagan campaign did not specify precisely what it would do or when, with what qualifications, and under what circumstances, it is impossible to conclude precisely whether they have or have not redeemed their campaign promises on economic deregulation. But in a general sense, it is clear they moved in the anticipated direction, even if the political and policy outcomes are still to be decided. The Urban Institute studies pointed to contradictions in their regulatory policies such as increasing the federal reporting requirement for local government agencies on AFDC and intruding into the family affairs of millions of Americans with HHS's "letter to the parent" contraception requirement. Inconsistency, however, is not a monopoly of conservative Republicans.

The general pattern

Certainly the president attempted to redeem a large part of his proposed economic agenda during his first two years in office. The major exception was the second year tax increase; the White House tried to suggest that it was a tax "reform," a suggestion ridiculed by some of Reagan's most steadfast supporters in Congress. But the larger part of those campaign promises—a glittering fantasy called supply-side economics—faded in the reality of a harsh recession, even if the White House was claiming vindication by pointing to the later recovery.[18] Stockman, an early advocate of supply-side whose belief ebbed the longer he was in OMB, acknowledged the administration's dilemma:

> Let's say that you and I walked outside and I waved a wand and said, I've just lowered the temperature from 110 to 78. Would you believe me?... I don't believe in the momentum theory anymore. I believe in institutional inertia. Two months of response can't beat 15 years of political infrastructure.[19]

Nor, apparently, economic infrastructure. That old-time Republican religion, tight money, enforced mainly through the efforts of the Federal Reserve Board, helped bring down inflation, but the trade-off in unemployment and in business failure that the Republican coalition had sought to circumvent was a reminder of the vagaries of economic management through the intervention of government.

By mid-1983 there were signs everywhere that the recession had, as economic journalists love to write, bottomed out, with recovery well underway. First and second quarter earnings were up, the growth rate was rising at a rate exceeding administration projections, retailers were replenishing stock, and, of course, the president's approval rating, which had fallen by January 1983 below Carter's during a comparable period in his administration, was improving. Naturally the White House staff was upbeat, despite continuing problems of unemployment, high federal deficits, and fears that the Federal Reserve Board might choke off the recovery by forcing interest rates back up too quickly.

The boom-and-bust cycle of America's postwar economy, which Reaganomics had promised and failed to end, seemed to be in full swing once again. Managing the economy without these cycles assumes that federal policy makers truly have control over the process, a dubious assumption. Of course, government policy helps shape the contours, but economic "command and control" has proved to be as difficult for conservative Republicans as it has for liberal Democrats. Had Reagan's campaign statements not been as specific about what means the administration planned to use to control the economic cycle, one would be justified in dismissing the promises about ending unemployment and inflation (ends) as functionally or programmatically meaningless, the useless rhetoric of presidential electioneering. However, the statements were specific about means, and, related or not, the short-term result was the most severe recession since the 1950s, which, in turn, helped bring down inflation. This is a cruel and bitter trade-off, one that supply-side promised but failed to avoid. If the administration is held accountable for the recession, is it justifiable also to reward it for the recovery? Only if one ignores the double-sided nature of the promises—to stimulate growth without inflation *or* recession—made in 1980.

The short-run political gains of the 1983-1984 economic recovery were considerable, indeed essential to the Republican party's reelection prospects. The long-run consequences, particularly if projected future deficits force deeper cuts in domestic social programs, will continue to damage those in America least able to protect themselves.

The other three-fourths of Reagan's campaign agenda

So single-minded were the Reagan forces in pursuing their economic program during the first year that large numbers of their most conservative supporters, concerned about busing, abortion, school prayer, the "Family Protection" bill, and patronage, were in open rebellion by early 1982. The "James A. Baker III-Richard Darman-David Gergen" conspiracy theory, favored by many New Right activists because it held that the president's natural conservative instincts were undone by his senior staff, was in full swing by February 1982. Despite the intense pressure put on the White House personnel office by Lyn Nofziger and his staff in screening senior appointees for their Reaganite/conservative bona fides—pressure that both centralized White House control and slowed senior level appointments—unhappiness grew among conservative activists.[20] They believed that pragmatic White House officials were selling out on conservative policy. Said one leader of this unhappy faction:

> They are pulling back, giving in, reversing themselves. Not that I expected everything. As a political party, the Republicans are just like the Democrats, they have to kowtow to pressures. Even the president is too flexible, too likely to not force things he believes in. Baker has been saying for months to "have patience," that "he's with us," that "we'll get what we want," but my patience is wearing thin. Either you have a real conservative vision and the courage to go for it or you don't.

Over the next few months, the administration attempted to redeem some of its other campaign promises and to shore up conservative support through action on other parts of the agenda.

On May 2, 1982, the Justice Department issued a letter through Attorney General William French Smith backing a bill sponsored by Sen. Jesse Helms, R-N.C., and Sen. J. Bennett Johnston, D-La., that effectively would have stripped federal court jurisdiction over busing as a "last-resort" remedy for desegregating public schools. The bill never became law.[21]

On May 17, 1982, the president transmitted to Congress a proposed constitutional amendment to allow voluntary and vocal prayer in the public schools. Reagan later devoted one of his weekly radio shows to advancing the amendment and gave a few speeches seeking support, but the school prayer issue was given ambiguous support in the White House during the first three years of the administration. The amendment was lost in a 1982 struggle between Helms and Sen. Orrin Hatch, R-Utah, over abortion. An effort to pass another version was resumed in early 1984 but was defeated in the Senate. The president continued to support an amendment during the 1984 campaign.

On June 22, 1982, the White House forwarded to Congress a bill providing for federal tax credits up to $300 per child per year for nonpublic school tuition. While this hardly would have permitted "lower and middle-income parents the option which wealthier parents have always had," as the White House claimed, it was certainly a beginning.[22] Strongly opposed by public education groups, the legislation remained submerged under a sea of congressional opposition. Around the same time, the Justice Department and White House decided to lift the IRS ban on tax deductions for private schools that practice racial segregation, a decision that naturally caused an uproar. The administrative ruling was later withdrawn, but the Justice Department continued to oppose the IRS ban, finally losing in court when the Supreme Court held that the IRS's long-time policy in prohibiting such deductions was constitutional.[23]

The administration hedged for months over what to do on its anti-abortion promise, primarily because it was an issue over which leading Republicans were divided and because major right-to-life groups disagreed over whether to push for a constitutional amendment or legislation that would deny federal courts the right to review antiabortion statutes. The situation in the Senate, with Hatch favoring a states'rights constitutional amendment and Helms supporting a multipurpose legislative package that would have denied federal funds for abortion and stripped the Supreme Court of jurisdictional authority over school prayer, grew bitter and divisive. In April 1982, the president sent a letter to antiabortion leaders urging them to unite around one of the two measures before Congress and suggesting that he would then "bring the full weight of my office" behind the preferred option. That agreement never emerged; pro-choice forces mobilized an effective blocking coalition, using the support of civil rights and civil liberties groups, Planned Parenthood, and the American Bar Association, which opposed Helms's plan to limit court jurisdiction, and effectively killed any antiabortion amendment in the 97th Congress. One commentator observed, "while the Right ran around like Keystone Cops, its opposition was coalescing, gaining members, raising money, and organizing." [24]

Nanette Falkenberg, executive director of the National Abortion Rights Action League, originally believed that an antiabortion amendment would pass and was directing most of her organization's resources toward state-based activities to stop it. As it grew clear that her pessimism was wrong and that an effective blocking coalition could be put together with the help of moderates like Sens. Bob Packwood, R-Ore., and Lowell P. Weicker, Jr., R-Conn., as well as conservatives like Barry Goldwater, R-Ariz., Falkenberg and others aggressively organized their supporters, outside and inside the Senate.

The administration did intervene, from midsummer through early fall, using its congressional liaison team and others in trying to bring unity to the efforts. "It was too late and too disjointed," said one Republican Senate staff member. "They pulled a lot of strings, I guess, but I don't think they were willing to really play hardball. Too many irons in the fire, and this fire was blazing!"

Balancing the federal budget, less important to the New Right than to many old-line Republicans, was nevertheless mentioned repeatedly by them as part of the president's early failures. In mid-July 1982, the president was still publicly supporting the proposed constitutional amendment mandating a balanced budget, even though Stockman and all his main economic advisers had revised their projections, edging closer and closer to acknowledging the reality of what their budget, tax policy, and a slumping economy were helping to create—sizable and unending deficits throughout the Reagan administration's tenure. Reagan had campaigned in support of "legislative relief" as his first preference, support of a constitutional amendment if that failed. Because his own policies were helping to create the failure, even White House staff had a hard time keeping a straight face when asked about the obvious contradiction. One responded to my question by saying, "What did you ask? I didn't hear it."

I dutifully repeat the question.

"I still can't hear you!"

The "Family Protection" bill, originally sponsored by Sen. Paul Laxalt, R-Nev., and supported in the 1980 Republican platform and by the president in the campaign, proved even more elusive than the balanced budget. Like the lost ark, it appears to have been plausible only as a summer movie, now lying forgotten among other ruins. The same White House aide, when asked about the legislation, laughed and said, "Never heard of it!"

The legislative record

The failures on the other part of Reagan's agenda help place in context the quantitative data on the administration's comparative performance. The fact is that Reagan's overall legislative record in seeking to redeem campaign promises is less substantial than his predecessors', including Jimmy Carter's. While the administration was justifiably praised for its dramatic first-year legislative victories, the resiliency of challenging factions and the Reagan team's errors of commission or omission eventually undermined their ability to sustain that initial momentum in Congress.[25] The administration reversed Carter's strategy; they subordinated action on other promises to their overwhelming desire to win on Reagan's economic package, and thus scored lower in overall promise-to-performance effort.

Remember that the quantitative measures are an assessment of presidential effort, not achievement, comparing the extent to which legislation or executive orders meet the spirit of campaign promises along a continuum from Fully comparable to Contradictory. (See pages 37 and 38 for the categories.) Reagan proposed action consistent with more than half of his promises—53 percent, which is obtained by adding the Fully comparable and Partially comparable classifications.

Compared with Carter (65 percent), Nixon (60 percent), Johnson (63 percent), and Kennedy (67 percent), the Reagan presidency does not have a pledge-to-effort ratio that is remarkable. A judgment like this requires perspective: most recent presidents would gladly have conceded a less impressive overall legislative record for the major victories Reagan gained in 1981, victories that dramatically shifted economic and defense priorities and were unmatched in their magnitude since Johnson. Unlike the Carter administration's, *the performance of the Reagan administration was one of high and focused achievement during 1981 and 1982, sporadic effort and low achievement thereafter.* The administration fared slightly better on those items classified as Fully comparable, equal to Nixon's and Kennedy's record, but running slightly behind Johnson's and Carter's.

On the other hand, accusations that the administration had defaulted or reversed direction across a wide variety of policy fronts are misguided. Only 7 percent of the administration's actions can be classified as Contradictory, and only 9 percent as No action. Their success at converting effort to achievement did go down. The declining capability of the administration vis-à-vis Congress is also reflected in Congressional Quarterly's Presidential Support scores, which dropped from 82 percent to 72 percent during 1981-1982 and then to 67 percent in 1983.

Of course, Reagan achieved an unusually high first-year score for a Republican president facing a divided Congress. The falloff was inevitable. The trade-offs that presidents face in dealing with Congress on their campaign agendas—between the degree of policy consensus in the president's party and the strategic location and resources of blocking factions—reasserted itself very quickly after the initial successes. David Broder wrote in early 1982 that "the mandate that led to last year's swift recasting of long-entrenched economic and military policies is now a year older and the paint is peeling." [26]

Indeed the "paint" began to peel quickly for those the president most counted on, members of his own party, particularly in the Senate but also in the House. By the end of 1983, every single legislative item of his social agenda had been blocked, frequently through the leadership of Republicans like Weicker and Packwood; and challenges to the administration's economic and defense spending priorities also were gaining momentum among more conservative Republicans. Thirteen Republican senators from northeastern and midwestern states sent a letter to Stockman at the end of the *first* session of the 97th Congress in 1981 warning the administration that they would not sanction further reductions in domestic spending, saying "we cannot support any future budget that exacts such a heavy toll" in their regions.[27] The signers included not only the predictable voices but also conservatives like Richard Lugar, R-Ind., Robert Kasten, R-Wis., and Alfonse D'Amato, R-N.Y.

The Senate Budget Committee, led by Republicans, unanimously rejected the president's FY 1983 budget after months of prolonged negotiation with the White House, fashioning their own version, which they then pushed through on a near party-line vote of 49 to 43 on the floor. In August Congress overrode Reagan's veto of a $14.2 billion supplemental appropriations bill, with Republicans ridiculing the president's claim that it was a "budget-buster," pointing to large increases in military spending backed by the administration and to the fact that it was $2 billion under his total request for additional 1982 spending.[28] The FY 1984 budget and the 1985 budget originally sponsored by the administration were rejected more harshly than 1983's, with the Senate Budget Committee again formulating its own version in the first budget resolution. In the House, a rejuvenated Democratic majority, strengthened by their midterm victories, reasserted itself against Republican opposition on numerous floor votes.[29]

Reagan and his supporters were learning, sometimes bitterly, sometimes philosophically, what every president learns about moving from promise to fulfillment: the power to redeem campaign promises is a shared power, shared both with Congress and with important power configurations outside the national arenas.

'New Federalism' initiatives

The fate of the president's New Federalism proposals, a comprehensive plan to decentralize program responsibility to the state level, further illustrates the potency of blocking factions that capitalize on both national and local resources. This was one of the administration's most dramatic initiatives and one that was ultimately buried under a deluge of political and policy opposition.

Defended by F. John Shannon, assistant director of the Advisory Committee on Intergovernmental Relations, as "an all-out attempt to deliver on a promise to get Washington off the backs of state and local government,"[30] the proposals were unveiled in the president's 1982 State of the Union message. The plan sought to swap responsibility for Medicaid in return for the states' gradually assuming full control of AFDC, food stamps, and 61 smaller programs, including vocational education, low-income energy aid, child nutrition programs, alcohol/ drug abuse/mental health assistance, airport grants, primary highway funding, bridges, water and sewer grants, and urban development. Since Reagan campaigned to return a number of (unspecified) welfare, education, and other programs to the states "with the revenues to pay for them," an immediate critical area of contention centered around whether states would, in fact, have sufficient revenues to assume responsibility for these programs. After 16 months of prolonged and contentious negotiations with governors and key members of Congress, most officials had concluded they would not benefit from either the major program swap or the assorted "turn-backs," and the administration shelved its comprehensive plan.[31]

"In a single stroke," Reagan had proclaimed in his 1982 address, "we will be accomplishing a realignment that will end cumbersome administration and spiraling costs at the federal level, while we ensure these programs will be more responsive to both the people they are meant to help and the people who pay for them."[32] Noble sentiments, both as a reflection of the administration's commitment to redeem the president's campaign rhetoric and from the viewpoint of the predicted goal of program responsiveness.

The New Federalism proposals emerged from a high-level staff group in the Office of Policy Development (formerly called the Domestic Policy Staff under Carter and the Domestic Policy Council under Nixon and Ford), OMB, Treasury, and the Office of Intergovernmental Affairs and were funneled through Baker's Legislative Strategy Group. Linda Demkovich, the *National Journal's* astute reporter, observed that the

> New Federalism package is a little like purgatory for both the President and the 50 governors. It's not quite heaven but it's certainly a lot better than hell. . . . [Reagan] would just as soon turn over all three programs [Medicaid, food stamps, AFDC] . . . [and this] would get the federal government almost entirely out of the welfare business.[33]

Tempting as the option of turning over all programs might have been for some in the White House, it was never seriously considered—for obvious reasons. Not only does such a "solution" reflect a profound indifference to the fate of millions of people, but it would have pushed the Republican party far out on a political limb that many feared was already collapsing. Two other internal sources of concern about the final proposal were evident from the beginning.

First, the institutional framework selected for decentralizing program finance and management was the states, not local governments, and this was seen by some in the White House as a failure of nerve and vision, as well as abandonment of Reagan's commitment to include local governments. Said one staffer:

> I'm here because I believed the president was serious about decentralizing power and responsibility in this country. The rich possibilities of community decision making and participation, which should be at the heart of any proposal like this, are ignored. This is substitution, one unresponsive bureaucracy for another. We should have done more to explore fundamental change, but we didn't. We are suffering from a failure of nerve, of imaginative rethinking, and the New Federalism program reflects it.

The decision to focus all swap and turn-back authority at the state level also guaranteed the eventual and sustained opposition of most mayors. Second, and more important in the development of Reagan's New Federalism proposals, there was an inability to separate program management from the administration's drive to force budget cuts across the board in domestic programs, a device that every governor, Democratic or Republican, knew would affect each state's revenue situations adversely, New Federalism or not. Projections of the revenues to finance the programs came from OMB and Treasury, but these figures were mistrusted by governors as well as key members of Congress.

Richard Williamson, presidential assistant for intergovernmental affairs, was charged with major political responsibility for selling the program to state officials, and he spent enormous time and energy muting the criticism that the administration was "selling a pig in the poke." Ultimately, the administration abandoned its insistence on swapping food stamps and made a number of other concessions. Nevertheless, the teams assembled in the White House, OMB, and Treasury to push the plan through Congress and win the acceptance of state officials failed.

Organized opposition to many of the specifics of the Reagan administration's New Federalism proposals increased as the combined effects of the recession, cutbacks in federal grants to the states, and the constitutional requirement for balanced state budgets imposed on governors and state legislatures the pain of belt-tightening measures, which were in turn related to the administration's own economic policies. Between mid-1981 and mid-1983, 32 states increased taxes and reduced state spending; 42 states imposed hiring freezes; 27 approved across-the-board budget cuts; 11 increased income taxes; 19 increased general sales taxes; and a substantial number upped cigarette, alcohol, and gasoline taxes.[34] These were external environmental factors that inevitably undermined the initiatives of the administration in institutional decentralization.

The New Federalism programs, along with the administration's first year economic blitz, were the domestic campaign proposals behind which Reagan and his team put the full political weight of his presidency. Without question, New Federalism represented a sustained, thoughtful, imaginative attempt (even if one disagrees with its thrust) to redeem the anti-Washington rhetoric of the president's campaign. Unlike the White House's on-and-off commitment to items on the social agenda, the administration should not be faulted for "symbolic posturing" in its commitment to move these proposals through the dispersed power structures of American politics.

In early 1983, Williamson was reassigned "at his own choice" to become the U.S. representative to the United Nations in Vienna, Austria. Ironically, many Democratic mayors publicly expressed regret at his departure because he had become their major champion inside the White House, despite their opposition to most of the New Federalism proposals and Williamson's solid New Right credentials (he had managed Philip Crane's presidential bid).[35]

One White House staffer summarized the lessons of the administration's failures this way:

What have we learned from this? A lot! If you are serious about decentralization, you've got to do it piece-by-piece, program-by-program, year-after-year. This runs counter to everybody's instincts here, [in the White House] but it's the only way it will ever get done.... And you can't have Dave Stockman or whoever's at OMB, muscling you all the time, trying to make horrendous cuts in revenue sharing and other programs that impact state budgets. Our own governors knew that our programs would have been political "kamikaze" for them.

The Reagan agenda and the administrative presidency

Richard M. Nixon was more suspicious of and harsh in his dealings with professional civil servants than any other modern president, but he reflected a basic attitude that others have harbored in less destructive ways since Roosevelt. Once, ruminating privately with John Ehrlichman, Nixon complained: "We have no discipline.... We never fire anybody. We never reprimand anybody. We never demote anybody. We always promote the sons-of-bitches that kick us in the ass." [36]

An unending anti-Washington rhetoric inconvenienced by facts (fewer than 15 percent of federal employees actually work in Washington, for example) has been characteristic of the American political culture since Thomas Jefferson first moved to town before the War of 1812. Conservatives habitually seem obsessed by the belief that every federal agency is overrun by recalcitrant managers who try to subvert whatever new policy direction their administration might adopt. And liberals frequently seem persuaded that "the bureaucracy" is a monolith of habit and prudence, universally antagonistic to political change. The facts suggest that both perspectives are false. [37]

Considerably less vehement than Nixon and generally more sophisticated in their understanding of the administrative process, Reagan's political managers still believed that a major tool for recasting policy could be achieved through centralized political control of the departments and bureaus of the federal apparatus. One put it quite forthrightly: "The only way we're going to get conservative policy is to get conservatives in complete control of the departments. I'm here to make sure that happens."

Of course the belief that they would be in "complete control" is an illusion because it assumes that all government activity can be cast in conservative/liberal terms and because the constitutional authority for the direction of departments is intentionally shared with Congress and the federal courts. The parameters of choice, however, are considerable, and political managers can help shape precisely how laws will be applied, when, where, and why. In this sense, the administrative presidency is a potent tool in helping presidents redeem campaign agendas. For reasons discussed in Chapter 1, my analysis excludes detailed consideration of the impact of personnel on policy. Some discussion is nevertheless essential in understanding the successes and failures of the Reagan administration.

White House staffing policy and its effect on the subsequent actions of major departments like Interior, Justice, Education, Labor, and Health and Human Services, and of some important "independent" agencies like the Environmental Protection Agency, the Equal Employment Opportunity Commission, the U.S. Commission on Civil Rights, the Occupational Safety and Health Administration, the Office of Personnel Management, among others, were reflected dramatically in the transition from Carter to Reagan.

The original Cabinet was dominated by "sensible, establishment Republicans," who, with the exception of James Watt, were not ultraconservative ideologues. Jeane Kirkpatrick scrambled the usual continuum because she had been a nominal Democrat, moderately progressive on domestic policy, but ideologically "hard-line" in foreign policy. Only one Cabinet secretary, Samuel Pierce at Housing and Urban Development, could be considered close to whatever was left of the "liberal" wing of the Republican party. The result: considerable grumbling and dissatisfaction among well-entrenched conservatives in and around, but not restricted to, the New Right.[38]

Conservatives were nevertheless able to reassert themselves through the centralized White House staffing system, relying on Lyn Nofziger and his allies to enforce standards of ideological acceptability and personal loyalty to the president in the selection of sub-Cabinet positions. Centralized screening of staff was pursued more vigorously by the Reagan team than by any president since the "new" Nixon (after 1972) because they had "learned from the mistakes of Carter" and because the coalitional incentives to deliver to conservatives on matters of patronage were taken seriously. The result: enforcement and implementation policies shifted sharply to the right in many agencies, in areas as diverse as civil rights and affirmative action, conservation and environmental regulation, and education and business regulation.

As a candidate, Reagan occasionally seemed to differentiate between "government" and "government employees" as the source of his "problem in Washington." Many senior civil servants believe these distinctions were lost when the Reagan team took office. The highly publicized moves by the administration first to freeze employment, then to reduce the federal workforce through reductions in force; the wholesale cuts in nondefense agency authorizations entertained in the

FY 1981, 1982, and 1983 budgets; the firing of all inspectors general in the major departments (a few were reappointed); the various threats to use the Senior Executive Service provisions of the Civil Service Reform Act of 1978 to reassign "uncooperative" managers, or to consign them to trivial tasks within the agency; and the aggressive posture of Donald Devine, the director of the Office of Personnel Management, in politicizing OPM and in seeking to alter federal pay, promotion, retirement, and fringe benefits—all of these reinforced Reagan's anti-Washington image.[39]

Within six months of taking office, White House political aides began worrying about what strategies were appropriate for overcoming the belief that the president was insensitive to the needs of minorities (blacks and Hispanics) and women. Their early concern mushroomed into a series of highly publicized moves such as the creation of a presidential task force on legal equity and presidential speeches before professional women's associations ("two steps forward and three steps backward," lamented one assistant after a clumsy Reagan performance before the International Federation of Business and Professional Women) [40] and sending William Bradford Reynolds, head of the Justice Department's Civil Rights Division, on a 1983 tour of Mississippi with Jesse Jackson to assess the need for additional federal voting registrars and monitors (additional registrars and monitors were sent). Despite signing an extension of the 1965 Voting Rights Act, which he did with considerable reluctance,[41] the president's enforcement and personnel policies in the Justice Department, EEOC, and the U.S. Commission on Civil Rights reinforced the opposition of every major civil rights organization to the Reagan presidency. Similarly, the administration's active enmity toward affirmative action for women or minorities in employment and education was consistent with its campaign rhetoric, even if Reagan sought to deflect the political consequences by stating that he supported the "noble goal of equal opportunity."

James Watt and Anne Gorsuch Burford are passing into history as the chief bugbears and unwilling membership promoters of American environmental organizations. Watt's resignation in late 1983 probably left some environmental leaders both relieved and disappointed. The Sierra Club's membership almost doubled in the first two years of the Reagan administration, from 180,000 in 1980 to more than 300,000 by 1982. The Reagan team viewed its large majorities in the western states as a mandate to reverse the resource protection thrust of the Carter administration's general, but hardly uniform, policy. From the beginning, the key strategy was administrative, not legislative. Using the discretionary provisions of land management bills like the Federal Land Policy and Management Act of 1976; the 1980 Alaska Lands Act; the

1977 Surface Mining, Control and Reclamation Act; and the Water Conservation Fund Act of 1965, the Interior Department and the EPA sought to alter, modify, and shift the enforcement of these land-use and safety laws in a way that maximized development and private control and minimized preservation and federal regulation. The result: sometimes successful, as in the cutback of national park expansion and land acquisition efforts or in water policy planning, and sometimes blocked by Congress or the federal courts.[42] One long-time conservation lobbyist observed:

> I don't know where we would be without Udall, Seiberling, Burton, and some others in the House. Or even McClure in the Senate, who turned out to be more accessible and reasonable than I ever thought he would. Watt and his people, despite all the right-wing bombast, are no dummies. He keeps us going every day, all the time. We're just better off, organizationally in Congress, and with our legal defense staff in the courts, than we were even three or four years ago. It *is* wearing, and sometimes discouraging. You just have to keep going even though it's no longer the big legislative victory; it's month-to-month guerrilla warfare!

In ways small and large, the Reagan team sought to use the considerable powers of an administrative presidency to implement the promises of his 1980 campaign. Typically those promises were not very specific. Considerable latitude, even reversal from what one might predict is possible—in fact, probable. Conservatives in office, like their liberal counterparts, must contend with the imperfections of reality, a reality that is based on shared power.

Selective reversals in the Reagan agenda

Aage Clausen will not object, I presume, if I recast one of his best lines: if you had a quarter for every time a political scientist observed that Ronald Reagan is a shrewd politician, you would have been a millionaire within 30 days of his inauguration. Of course, Reagan and most of his top political advisers have been shrewd. On any scale of political and organizational "shrewdery," the Reagan White House gains high marks from most outside observers, despite stumble-bumble mini-disasters like the 1981 Social Security firestorm or the decision to reverse IRS policy on tax deductions for racist schools. Foreign policy decision making was another matter, rarely demonstrating a comparable level of political sophistication.

But some Washington commentators seem to confuse political skillfulness with the assumption that the White House systematically avoided serious and sustained public doubts about the wisdom of Reagan's leadership and major policies. Nothing could be further from the truth.[43] Reagan started his presidency with public approval ratings lower than any of his predecessors in this study, sank further as the 1982 midterm elections approached, and began his third year with approval ratings lower than Carter at an equivalent period. His subsequent improvement during the third and fourth years, differing dramatically in this respect from Carter, began as the economy improved. They were shrewd and organizationally sophisticated, certainly, but neither Reagan nor his team has gone unscathed by the negative public reaction to many of their policy and political choices.

The Reagan administration *did* prove flexible on some of its seemingly cherished campaign agenda items. "He likes to win," an explanation that has been repeated in various guises is true, but it is unclear *how* true, under what circumstances, and with what costs to their own program integrity. One administration strategist put it this way:

> Look, we're not in the business of committing political suicide. There are swamps everywhere and one of our jobs is to try and keep the president out of as many as possible. Sometimes he listens, sometimes he doesn't . . . and we're not always right. He has well-honed antennae himself; he knows when to push and when to pull back, when to drive hard and when to wait it out.

The Reagan White House developed a sophisticated strategy for overcoming the political costs of reversal and deferral, particularly deferral. Reagan permitted some of his more controversial proposals, the social issues, for example, to slide on and off the agenda, without seeming to alter the rhetoric of his conservative principles in supporting them. The White House packaged this stance as proof that he is still a "strong" leader, undercut by a willful Congress that is dominated by irresponsible Democrats.

The strategic contrast with Carter is dramatic. Carter's shifts in policy *and* rhetoric on economic and defense policy served to reinforce mass beliefs that he was a "weak" leader, changing course whenever events and circumstances dictated, even though this was a simplistic and misleading caricature. Unfortunately for Carter, there was enough truth in the caricature to make it believable, as the numerous memoirs of his senior staff demonstrate.[44] Reagan's political challenge, like every president's, was to demonstrate that he was flexible without appearing to concede that he was abandoning his principles. Although Reagan and his team have reversed direction or deferred action on various campaign promises, they have done so in ways that caused as little political damage as possible.

The coalitional differences between the parties

The coalitional structures of the Democratic and Republican parties differ fundamentally; hence Carter and Reagan faced different threats and opportunitites in dealing with their respective party coalitions when considering agenda shifts. Unlike the situation Carter faced in 1980, there was no challenger like Edward Kennedy on the GOP horizon, ambitious and well positioned to exploit party discontent; no Republican equivalent of organized labor, unhappy about the general direction of "their" party's president and willing to gamble on an alternative; no equivalent bloc (equivalent in their combined factional power) of minority, feminist, intellectual, "cow country," and southern conservative Democratic dissidents, whittling away at his coalition, and seriously looking for an alternative. In short, the Reagan administration had not so much to worry about their own party coalition as they had to worry about seeking ways to broaden it, both to govern and to gain reelection.

Reagan's potentially fiercest internal critics—the New Right and whatever is left of the moderate-to-liberal wing of the party—were unable to mount a credible electoral challenge against him in 1984. Thus active New Right discussion about undertaking such a venture in the Republican primaries petered out quickly. Moderate Republicans are a distinct minority within the party and were equally unable to mount an effective primary challenge. Whatever Reagan and his team had done, he was still the preeminent conservative Republican, in rhetoric, tone, and policy, supported by large majorities of his party cohorts. With a conservative in office, defending his deferrals and reversals in carefully chosen conservative rhetoric, Republicans, fearing a political catastrophe, muted their criticisms and remained "team players."

These coalitional differences help explain the contrasting responses to the Carter and Reagan presidencies on shifts or deferrals in their campaign agendas. Also, the absence of a dramatic shift by Reagan in economic policy, despite considerable adjustments and alterations, dampened, even if it did not eliminate, criticism among those who helped him win nomination. The Reagan administration opted to sustain very high levels of unemployment, waiting until the midterm elections approached to begin giving token support to a modest jobs bill (a "handup, not a handout"), and keeping attention focused on initiatives to reduce domestic program spending. They did, however, assent to the Federal Reserve Board's expansionary policy, begun in late 1982, "so long as it does not drive up interest rates." The unacknowledged neo-Keynesian element in supply-side theory, the stimulus of the 3-year tax cut, reinforced their belief that it was possible to ride out the recession and sustain their overall strategy.

The move to increase taxes

The most bitter Republican opposition to White House initiatives centered around the impact of the administration's economic policies on long-term federal deficits and from Reagan's first clear campaign reversal, (actually, partial reversal)—the 1982 tax increase. The administration, hoping that a low-inflation recovery would be underway before the 1984 elections, saw no need for a *fundamental* alteration in party policy on macroeconomic strategy, even though they were overly optimistic in their projections about the timing of the recovery. Republicans have ridden out (or been ridden out by) recessions for years. The political trick has been to avoid the "Hoover Problem" with modest counterrecessionary measures, to shift the attention of the electorate to other areas, and to hope for recovery before the next election. With the deficits rising, however, and revenues not rising as much as the administration had projected, some "adjustment" to supply-side economics was inevitable.

Nudged along by Sen. Robert Dole, R-Kan., chairman of the Senate Finance Committee, the "Tax Equity and Fiscal Responsibility Act" cleared Congress in August 1982, after three months of intense party and ideological wrangling. The adminstration's decision to support, then actively lobby for the bill came as a result of the urging of Dole and his allies in the administration. Dole's case was strengthened by the increasingly gloomy OMB estimates about future deficits. The bill sought to recover an estimated $98.1 billion during fiscal years 1983-1985 through a combination of increased compliance, reductions in business tax write-offs, and increases in excise and employment taxes. The $98.1 billion figure was approximately 24 percent of revenue foregone by reductions won in the 1981 Economic Recovery Tax Act.[45]

Opposition to the bill was led by prominent Republican conservatives like Jack Kemp, R-N.Y., Newt Gingrich, R-Ga., and Mickey Edwards, R-Okla., chairman of the American Conservative Union. Despite an intense White House lobbying campaign, including group and individual visits with the president and his advisers at Camp David, 87 Republicans voted against the bill (103 supported it); the vote was the most substantial public crack in House Republican unity of the Reagan administration. One provision, mandating the withholding of 10 percent of interest and dividend income for tax purposes, contradicted a specific plank in the 1980 Republican platform. Senator Kasten later led a successful filibuster against this provision and congressional action was deferred for future decision.

Agenda deferrals and trade-offs

The Reagan administration's other policy reversals caused less rancor among Republicans, although some led to bitter denunciations by disappointed factions within his electoral coalition. These include:

—the decision to continue draft registration, a reversal of one of the candidate's few authentic libertarian positions;

—the promise to support greater congressional authority in using the legislative veto against administrative regulations, a promise later rendered moot by the Supreme Court;

—the support of block grants "for any valid purpose *local* governments might choose." [Emphasis added.] The New Federalism proposals bypassed "local governments," giving authority to states;

—the support of modified hospital cost containment provisions (in the prospective payment reimbursement regulations);

—the decision to support a national holiday commemorating Martin Luther King;

—the promise "to explore" the "many ways" of extending "health care coverage to those persons who are inadequately covered"; instead, the administration focused all of its energies on containing health care costs.

As this lists suggests, the administration did not openly and absolutely reverse itself on very many of its campaign promises, partly because Reagan made fewer concrete promises than most earlier candidates and partly because the administration opted for a strategy of deferring or not acting rather than clearly repudiating their commitments.

The range of deferrals is shown by the data in Table 6-1, where a comparison of the importance of various policy clusters, moving from the campaign agenda through four years in office is presented. Of 10 campaign policy clusters ranked "High" in salience by senior staff during the campaign and their first two years in office, only 3 were considered of equal importance by 1983 and 1984. All three social issues (abortion, school prayer, busing) were given mixed ratings in the second half. Inflation ("with qualification; it's our best issue"), business tax incentives, environmental deregulation, New Federalism, and the commitment to abolish the Departments of Energy and Education were ranked low in priority during the second half of the administration.

Table 6-1 Comparison of domestic policy clusters ranked as high and low during the campaign and during the Reagan administration, 1981-1982 and 1983-1984[a]

	Campaign agenda	1981-1982	1983-1984
Policy cluster			
Reductions in federal spending (nondefense)	High	High	High
Inflation	High	High	Low
Tax cuts (personal)	High	High	High
Tax cuts (business)	High	High	Low
Deregulation and regulatory management (business)	High	High	High
Deregulation and regulatory management ("environmental balance")	High	High	Low
Abolish Departments of Energy and Education	High	High	Low
"Social" issues (abortion, prayer, busing)	High	Mixed[d]	Mixed[d]
New Federalism (decentralizing major welfare programs)	High	High	Low
Unemployment	High	Mixed[d]	Mixed[d]
New Clusters[b]			
Medicare/Medicaid/Primary costs	Low	Low	High
Education	Low	Low	High
International trade[c]	Low	Low	High

[a] Rankings for this table were obtained in the same manner as for Carter. I extracted 10 policy clusters that occurred throughout Reagan's campaign speeches. I then asked three advisers who served in the campaign, all later appointed to the White House staff, to rank each as "high" or "low." All three had to agree that a cluster was high; otherwise it was ranked low. The ratings were obtained in September-October 1980; September 1981 and November 1982; and February 1984. The final year rankings are based on two respondents because the third had left the White House before the last interviews were completed.

[b] Not salient in the 1980 campaign.

[c] Although this is an "international" issue, the two advisers emphasized its domestic components.

[d] The Social issue cluster proved to be the hardest for these respondents. All agreed that they were high during the campaign; one ranked them high during the first two years, one ranked them low, the third felt only the antiabortion activities were high on the White House agenda. The two split on the rankings for 1983-1984. Similar conflict existed about unemployment.

The shift in the White House agenda reflects the response to varying degrees of political defeat: on the social issues, New Federalism, environmental deregulation, and the promise to abolish two Cabinet-level departments, blocking factions inside and outside Congress proved powerful enough either to beat the administration directly or to deter a serious effort by the White House to redeem these promises. The absence of a full-scale White House effort to overcome these countervailing pressures helped mobilize New Right discontent with the administration, reinforcing the belief that the Reagan White House *had* been captured by "establishment Republicans" bent on reversing the conservative "mandate" of 1980.

The White House refocused attention on the school prayer issue and religion in politics again early in 1984. School prayer supporters divided over whether the proposed amendment should permit vocal prayer (the president's position) or silent prayer (Senator Hatch's and others' preference). The vocal option was defeated in March by the Senate, but it is clear that prayer-in-the-schools will continue to bubble as a potentially divisive issue for some time.

There was considerable skepticism among Senate staff during the 1984 debate over whether the administration was seriously interested in winning the Senate vote or more concerned with keeping a potential campaign issue alive. Predictably, many prayer advocates were disappointed because they felt the president had not started lobbying the Senate early enough. Gary Jarmin, head of a group called Christian Voice Moral Government Fund, was quoted: "He [Reagan] should have launched a full-court press 10 days ago. It's a case of lost opportunities. If they had invited those guys to the White House a lot earlier we might have won them." [46]

Reagan still supported action on the three major social issues (at least rhetorically) and, strategically, he used the option of reemphasizing this commitment when he went before sympathetic groups. Despite the reemergence of religion-in-politics as a 1984 campaign issue, some have suggested that the social agenda pursued by the New Right, embraced and defended by the president in 1980 and again in 1984, reached its zenith in the late 1970s and has been declining since. [47] Crusades of "cultural defense" like this are recurrent in American history, likely to ebb and flow as circumstances dictate. Reagan faced here what others have faced before: *selective reversal occurs when the president and his aides come to believe that the trade-offs between pursuing the policy commitments of the last campaign and the next one substantially favor a shift in the priorities and direction of the old agenda.* If a shift on the social issues is contemplated, Reagan will do so through artful, if perhaps ambiguous, "deferral," rather than by more forthright disavowal.

The administration's changing concern with three other areas—
additional tax cuts for business, inflation, and, once again, in matters
affecting environmental deregulation—occurred primarily because the
deepening recession increased the tensions in the president's economic
agenda. Supply-side and its promise of prosperity through economic
growth could no longer be used to evade the political costs associated
with high unemployment, tax concessions to the wealthy, and public
concern over environmental health. These factors undermined the
legitimacy of further anti-public sector moves in such policy areas. But,
circumstances permitting, similar initiatives could be renewed in the
future.

The departures of Burford and Watt and the appointments of
William Ruckelshaus and William P. Clark gave the White House an
opportunity to repair their sagging political fortunes among an important segment of the citizenry concerned about the environment.

Three policy clusters, according to data from my White House
interviews, remained high on the Reagan agenda across all time periods:
cutting nondefense domestic spending, keeping the 3-year tax rate
reduction in place, and assisting in various ways the deregulatory
campaign for business in areas other than those concerned with environmental protection. Simultaneously, three "new" clusters—health
care spending and cost containment, education, and some aspects of
international trade—were thought to be of major importance for the
White House agenda as of mid-1984. Political considerations saturated
budget decision making in all of the administration's agenda-setting
priorities.

Overcoming the widespread belief that the president and the
Republican party support policies that are inequitable and serve the
interests of the few rather than the many, and to do this without losing
the support of those in their coalition for whom the terms "equity" and
"social justice" are distasteful, is the administration's most difficult
political challenge. It is unclear that they can accomplish this without
increasing the contradictions between the rhetoric of a conservative
president's promises and the reality of future domestic policy achievements.

Conclusion

A. James Reichley faults modern scholarship on the presidency for
assuming that conservative presidents have served mainly as correctives
or consolidators, generally governing in a manner to tidy up after bursts
of creative liberal activism. Reichley argues:

It seems a mistake to regard the conservative model of the presidency
wholly or primarily in terms of its function as a foil or corrective to its
liberal alternative. Conservatives have positive ideological goals and
assumptions of their own, and these had best be taken into account
when we seek to determine where a conservative administration . . . is
trying to lead us.[48]

His warning seems particularly appropriate for understanding what the
Reagan administration has attempted to accomplish and where and why
it has succeeded or failed.

In one important if misguided sense the administration has functioned as a "consolidator"; liberals who believed that Reagan would seek
to "repeal the New Deal" were wrong. The belief was part hysteria, part
a reaction to his rhetoric *in the 1960s*. By 1980, Reagan was neither
seeking nor promising to undo the basic institutions of the Positive
State. His New Federalism proposals, had they been enacted, would
have shifted the form of service delivery in a radical way but, one
surmises, if they had fundamentally altered policy substance, they
would have caused an anti-Reagan backlash of striking proportions.

With these qualifications, the Reagan presidency nevertheless
sought a series of major changes in existing policies and institutions. I
believe their initiatives have been attempts to promote Reichley's
definition of four major conservative goals: 1) the belief that the market
generally provides the best means for making economic decisions and
distributing economic rewards; 2) that responsibility and administrative
control over government services in social policy should "whenever
feasible" rest with state and local government; 3) that "traditional"
moral values involving the family and personal behavior should be
encouraged (legislated?) by government; and 4) in foreign policy, that
"national interest" rather than "moral values" should govern U.S.
conduct in world affairs.[49]

Defense and foreign policy have a habit of sneaking up on books
like this, despite the best of intentions. Something similar seems to have
happened to the Reagan presidency after the 1982 midterm election. The
relative reordering of domestic and foreign policy questions in the
priorities of the president's agenda is not unusual or unique to Reagan.
Of the past five presidents, Johnson, Nixon, and Carter clearly reflected
this shift, although for different reasons. The change in priorities is not
inevitable (consider Eisenhower) nor is it always a matter of presidential
interests (Nixon had a clear preference for foreign policy from the
beginning). The international system is considerably less predictable but
simultaneously more attractive for activist tendencies in the presidency
once domestic policy has "settled down" into its normal pluralist thrust
and counterthrust.

Reagan's preoccupation with returning American foreign policy to a bipolar confrontation with the Soviet Union was bound to intensify arenas of potential conflict at some point, not only with Russia but with U.S. allies throughout the Third World and at home. The campaign emphasis on strengthening the American defense posture and regaining superiority (or extending it, depending on which strategic estimates one believes) has led to dramatic increases in the defense budget, stop-and-go arms negotiations with the Soviets, and militarily backed policies in Central America and the Middle East. Reagan's 1981 defense budget called for 12.4 percent and 14.6 percent real increases in defense spending during FY 1981 and 1982. Congressional opposition reduced these increases after 1981, but the White House was still projecting an increase in real budget outlays averaging 9.4 percent annually from 1982 to 1984.[50] The Defense Department's new 5-year plan notes that national defense as a percentage of total federal outlays will increase from 24 percent in 1981 to 34 percent in 1988.[51]

Was any of this consistent with Reagan's 1980 campaign promises? Yes and no. That Reagan would push for substantial increases in spending was clear from his general support of weapon systems like the MX, the B-1, and the plan to increase the Navy from 450 to 600 ships— all items he pledged to support if elected. During the campaign, the Reagan strategists carefully avoided specifying precisely what spending increase they would support. Carter suggested that their general budgetary figures underestimated what would be necessary to implement their plans (Carter himself was proposing a 5 percent real increase).

In fact, they grossly overestimated the net impact of their projected cuts on federal deficits, and part (not all) of the reason stems from their commitment to large defense increases and sizable tax reductions. The media did not push Reagan hard enough for details about how much he would advocate spending on defense or what the impact of this preference might be on total government spending. Clearly Reagan has sought to implement his hard-line—I. M. Destler refers to it as "maximalist"[52]—rhetoric in defense and foreign policy. One unintended consequence of the administration's defense and international policies has been to play midwife to a born again antinuclear and arms control movement in the United States and Europe, reflecting a depth and breadth of public concern unmatched in 10 years. Neoconservatives (usually Democrats!) also have suggested that the administration's lack of prudence in forcing steep increments in defense expenditures actually undermined a "national security consensus" that had emerged by 1980.[53] True or not, all public opinion surveys reflected a sharp drop in public support for Reagan's defense increases as the disparity between domestic cuts and defense increases received more attention in Congress and the mass media. So, the pursuit of one of the recurrent conservative goals in foreign policy—nationalism tied to military and economic self-interest unhindered by "idealistic" concerns like human rights—has led to mixed results.

Since the late 1930s the United States has fought three major wars and responded to a number of more limited military actions. The Reagan presidency thus far has avoided stumbling upon or leading the country into another major war. Unlike the Carter administration, however, there is no doubt about their fidelity to the prayer book offered by Amaranta Buendia's rejected lover:[54] The administration was prepared to employ military force without apology as it did in the invasion of Grenada and indirectly by financing and training the antigovernment contras in Nicaragua. Perhaps Grenada and Nicaragua will prove exceptions, limited engagements with no broader significance in anticipating what Reagan might do. Those of my generation, for whom the concept "peaceful planet" is an infrequent reality, can hope that the luck of the Irish will keep the United States out of another war. An unsentimental history of Ireland as a metaphor for American experience does not leave one optimistic; the subsequent fates of recent incumbents who sought and won election have been utterly dismal.[55] Dwight D. Eisenhower, at least on this one point, is beginning to look more impressive than many have conceded in the past.[56]

The area in which the Reagan administration proved most consistent—viewed from the perspective of what it promised in 1980—remains domestic policy, especially the economic and deregulatory package of 1981. Whether it has led to the promised consequences depends on how one weighs the recession of 1981-1982, the recovery underway in 1983-1984, the relative trade-offs of inflation and unemployment, and the relation of each of these to the administration's economic policies. Despite the increasing attention devoted to major questions of foreign policy, management of the economy is an issue which requires continuing White House involvement and upon which reelection strategy hinged, especially after supply-side rhetoric became politically indefensible. Maximizing the administration's commitment to free-market assumptions in a mixed economy suggests a return to pragmatic monetarism. It is difficult to imagine a post-World War II president, including Eisenhower, who has more consistently championed conservative values in matters economic, particularly if one disregards embarrassments like large federal deficits.

While Reagan's 1980 campaign steadfastly refused to be specific about actual figures in most of its projected economic package, one of the few areas where it departed from this strategy was on the question of deficits. In his September 1980 speech to the International Business

Council at Chicago, the president attached a "Fact Sheet" to the usual press release that promised the following if he was elected and subsequently implemented his economic package: deficits of $21 billion in FY 1981, $6 billion in FY 1982, and *surpluses* (that's right) of $23 billion in FY 1983, $62 billion in FY 1984, and $121 billion in 1985.[57] The actual figures, all deficits with no surpluses in sight, are $57.9 billion in FY 1981, $110 billion in FY 1982, and $195 billion in FY 1983.

Liberal Democrats have shown little concern with the adverse consequences of federal deficits over the years, so perhaps it is unfair to fault a conservative Republican for comparable behavior. The problem with Reagan's policies (other than those stemming from the political erosion among his own conservative and party constituents, many of whom clearly are dismayed) is that they are expanding both the actual and structural deficit. The latter is of far greater concern to economists of all schools except, apparently, supply-siders because it will increase the national debt and future interest obligations even when the economy is booming and approaching "full employment." This, in turn, will increase downward pressure on future investment and upward pressure on interest rates. To use the language of economics, these consequences are not reversible, as they usually are with actual deficits, because of cyclical fluctuations in economic activity.[58] Future generations will pay the costs of structural deficits, independent of whether the economy is sound or problematic.

The upbeat economic promises of the Reagan campaign in 1980 were (or should have been) demolished by the long recession, but many voters are well known for asking the old question, "What have you done for me lately?" And in the 1984 campaign, buoyed by the second-stage recovery, the president was once again upbeat in his promises about the future of the economy. Among those voters whose partisan and/or ideological sentiments are not firmly anchored—those who are most likely to waver between parties—the emphasis was on perceived economic outcomes, not promises about means. Of course, other issues and concerns also shape this group's voting behavior. The perception about economic performance is only one of several short-term influences on voting behavior in presidential elections.

Ironically, the administration's goal of reducing nondefense federal spending may well be achieved by another unintended consequence of their budgetary and tax policies. Virtually every economist writing on the subject has pointed to an important long-run consequence of large structural deficits: at some point in the future, Congress must either raise taxes and/or accelerate the contraction of the federal government's domestic activities. These pressures will grow after the 1984 election. Reagan's other broad goal, stimulating economic growth through a robust private sector, might simultaneously recede since unusually large future deficits create government demand for credit, which in turn absorbs private savings, keeps real interest rates high, and suppresses domestic investment, all of which slow the chance for sustained economic recovery. As Henry Aaron suggests:

> Whatever one may think of the pace of increase in expenditures on national defense; however one regards the significant reductions in nondefense spending; and whatever one's judgment on the size and form of the tax reductions fashioned by Congress in response to presidential leadership, these policies taken individually represent legitimate initiatives by a [conservative] president ... taken together, however, they are fiscally inconsistent. They have placed undue responsibility on monetary restraint as a means of lowering inflation. They have resulted in structural deficits that may abet recovery during its early stages but will place federal borrowing athwart the path to full economic recovery.[59]

In brief, the Reagan team maximized short-term goals and thereby reduced the long-term chances for achieving (some of) the ends of a conservative economic policy.[60] The effects of the administration's fiscal and monetary policy during 1981-1984 severely restrict the discretion of the next president. Publicly, Reagan has ignored this quandary. On the same day in January 1984 when he was promising a second term would mean "wringing out more waste and fraud in government, attacking the federal deficit, getting inflation and interest rates down further," his budget director, Stockman, was quoted in *Fortune* magazine:

> We have gone through a great testing process for three years ... now we have to figure out how to pay our bills ... some still think there are vast pockets of fraud, waste, and abuse out there. In fact, nearly every stone has been turned over.[61]

Almost all democratically elected politicians focus on achieving short-term goals at the expense of long-term planning. With the social agenda deferred into an indefinite future and the pressures of an election campaign in full swing, the promises of 1980 are fading in the deceptive optimism of that ancient campaign axiom: "Keep moving, keep firing, and never look back!" However attractive this axiom may be for campaigners, it is dysfunctional for presidential accountability.

Notes

1. Quoted in Jude Wanniski, "Will Reagan Be Thatcherized?" *Wall Street Journal*, Nov. 11, 1980.

2. Although administration officials never defined precisely what the "safety net" included, the following were mentioned frequently: Old-Age Survivors Insurance (OASI), which pays benefits to retired workers, their dependents, and survivors; the disability insurance program (DI), which distributes benefits to disabled workers and their dependents; Medicare (HI), which helps pay medical expenses of those 62 or over; perhaps Medicaid, a matching program assisting in the payment of medical expenses for those on state welfare (primarily disabled persons and AFDC recipients); and unemployment insurance. In fact, the administration proposed to alter some Social Security benefits (OASI) on May 12, 1981 (quickly rescinded after the Senate voted 96-0 to dissociate itself from the proposal); sought $5.5 billion reductions in 1982 current services outlays for Medicare and Medicaid during FY 1983, primarily by raising Medicare deductibles and altering Medicaid eligibility matching standards; and won congressional approval for raising the "state trigger" for unemployment, thus projecting a cut in FY 1983 outlays for unemployment insurance of $4.1 billion (their projections were wrong, despite making it harder for states to pay unemployed workers). The safety net, too, was vulnerable. On this, see *Setting National Priorities—The 1983 Budget,* ed. Joseph Pechman (Washington, D.C.: Brookings Institution, 1982) and *Setting the National Priorities—The 1984 Budget,* ed. Joseph Pechman (Washington, D.C: Brookings Institution, 1983).

3. Henry J. Aaron, "The Choices Ahead," in *Setting National Priorities—The 1984 Budget,* 203.

4. *Setting National Priorities—The 1983 Budget.*

5. White House Office of Public Affairs, "The Reagan Presidency—A Review of the First Two Years, 1981-1982," Jan. 20, 1983.

6. Ibid., 31.

7. Ibid., 45.

8. Urban Institute, *The Reagan Experiment,* ed. John L. Palmer and Isabel V. Sawhill (Baltimore: Urban Institute Press, 1982); Urban Institute, *The Reagan Record,* ed. John L. Palmer and Isabel V. Sawhill (New York: Ballinger Press, 1984).

9. Congressional Budget Office, "The Effects of Tax and Budget Reductions in 1981 for Households in Different Income Categories" (Washington, D.C.: Government Printing Office, February 1982).

10. Palmer and Sawhill, "Perspectives on the Reagan Experiment," in *The Reagan Experiment,* 21.

11. Quoted by Palmer and Sawhill in *The Reagan Experiment,* 26.

12. William Greider, *The Education of David Stockman and Other Americans* (New York: Dutton, 1981), 39.

13. "Federal Regulation," *Reagan for President,* Jan. 30, 1980.

14. "Environment," *Reagan for President,* Jan. 30, 1980.

15. James P. Pfiffner provides a good description of this process in "The Carter-Reagan Transition: Hitting the Ground Running," *Presidential Studies Quarterly* (Fall 1983): 623-646.

16. George C. Eads and Michael Fix, "Regulatory Policy," in *Reagan Experiment,* 146-147.

17. David Hoffman, " 'Revolution' Has Successes and Failures," *Washington Post,* Jan. 31, 1984, A7.

18. In fairness to prominent analysts associated with supply-side—Paul Craig Roberts, Arthur Laffer, Jude Wanniski, and others—it has been argued that

Reagan *was* "Thatcherized," that he reverted to classic monetary policy, failing to implement fully the theory of supply-side economics, and this explains why the recession persisted. Roberts criticizes his supply-side colleagues and his more conventional policy-making associates in the Reagan administration, particularly David Stockman, for abandoning the original and "real" credo in his *The Supply-Side Revolution: An Insider's Account of Policy Making in Washington* (Cambridge: Harvard University Press, 1984). I gladly leave the merits of his argument to other economists: Herbert Stein, *Presidential Economics: The Making of Economic Policy from Roosevelt to Reagan and Beyond* (New York: Simon & Schuster, 1984); and *Supply-Side Economics: A Critical Appraisal,* ed. Richard A. Fink (Frederick, Md.: University Press of America, 1984).

19. Greider, *The Education of David Stockman,* 58.
20. Pfiffner, "The Carter-Reagan Transition."
21. Rochelle L. Stanfield, "Reagan Courting Women, Minorities, But It May Be Too Late to Win Them," *National Journal,* May 28, 1983, 1118-1123.
22. White House Office of Public Affairs, "The Reagan Presidency," 37.
23. Stanfield, "Reagan Courting Women, Minorities."
24. Bill Keller and Nadine Cohadas, "Tactical Errors, Disunity Blunt New Right Social Legislation," *Congressional Quarterly Weekly Report,* Oct. 16, 1982, 2675-2678.
25. In addition to the scholarly studies already cited, see *President and Congress: Assessing Reagan's First Year,* ed. Norman J. Ornstein (Washington, D.C.: American Enterprise Institute, 1982); James P. Pfiffner, "The Reagan Budget Juggernaut: The Fiscal 1982 Budget Campaign" (Paper delivered at the 1982 annual meeting of the American Society for Public Administration); *The Reagan Presidency,* ed. Fred Greenstein (Baltimore: Johns Hopkins University Press, 1983); and the volumes of Urban Institute's Changing Domestic Priorities Project, particularly *The Reagan Record* and *The Reagan Presidency and the Governance of America,* ed. Lester M. Salamon and Michael Lund (Baltimore: Urban Institute Press, forthcoming).
26. David Broder, "The Reagan Script for '82—A Lot Harder," *Washington Post,* Jan. 3, 1981, C1 and C5.
27. Ibid., C5.
28. Dick Kirschten, "President Reagan After Two Years—Bold Actions But Uncertain Results," *National Journal,* Jan. 1, 1983, 4-14.
29. "Democrats Showed Renewed Strength in 1983," *Congressional Quarterly Weekly Report,* Dec. 31, 1983, 2781-2788.
30. Rochelle L. Stanfield, "Turning Back 61 Programs: A Radical Shift of Power," *National Journal,* Feb. 27, 1982, 369. The entire issue was devoted to an analysis of the administration's New Federalism programs.
31. Some "turn-backs" were later converted into block grant programs, with reduced federal support and numerous legislatively required guidelines.
32. Quoted in *National Journal,* Feb. 27, 1982, 357.
33. Linda Demkovich, "The Swap: Nobody Wins," *National Journal,* Feb. 27, 1982, 362.
34. *Time,* Aug. 15, 1983.
35. Williamson also was perceived as having "gone native" by some of his White House colleagues because he aggressively defended state and local interests against OMB in the FY 1983 intramural budgetary struggles. He was credited with saving revenue sharing for the cities and clearly was

184 Presidents & Promises

concerned about the negative political fallout of large budget cuts in state and local programs. For the political and policy aspects of this squabble, see Dick Kirschten, "New Intergovernmental Affairs Chief Charts a Less Abrasive Course," *National Journal*, Oct. 8, 1983, 2064-2067.

36. Quoted in Richard P. Nathan, *The Plot that Failed: Nixon and the Administrative Presidency* (New York: Wiley, 1975), 69.

37. More recently, see Bernard Rosen, "Effective Continuity of U.S. Government Operations in Jeopardy," *Public Administration Review* (September/October 1983): 383-393.

38. Pfiffner, "The Carter-Reagan Transition."

39. Pfiffner cites General Accounting Office studies that indicated the administration did not violate, during the transition, the "90-day rule" for the Senior Executive Service, which prevents senior managers from being arbitrarily transferred in their first 90 days. What happened after the transition and the "90-day rule" expired? Both the senior management of OPM and ambiguous provisions of the Civil Service Reform Act of 1978, which created the SES, were sharply politicized. Rosen, "Effective Continuity of U.S. Government Operations in Jeopardy," particularly, 390-391; and Chester A. Newland, "A Mid-Term Appraisal—The Reagan Presidency: Limited Government and Political Administration," *Public Administration Review* (January/February 1983): 1-22.

40. The quote and a brief report are from, "Trying to Make Amends—Reagan Extends a Clumsy Hand to Women, Blacks, and the Poor," *Time*, international edition, Aug. 15, 1983, 26-27.

41. Nadine Cohodas, "Voting Rights Extension Cleared for President Reagan," *Congressional Quarterly Weekly Report*, June 26, 1982, 1503-1504.

42. A critical summary is the National Wildlife Federation, *Marching Backwards: The Department of Interior under James G. Watt* (Washington, D.C.: National Wildlife Federation, 1982) and Steven Pearlman et al., *Presidential Candidates for 1984—Their Records and Positions on Energy and the Environment* (Washington, D.C.: League of Conservation Voters, 1984) 3-27. Scholarly accounts are provided in *Environmental Policy in the 1980s: Reagan's New Agenda*, ed. Norman J. Vig and Michael E. Kraft (Washington, D.C.: CQ Press, 1984) and Walter A. Rosenbaum, *Environmental Policy and Politics* (Washington, D.C.: CQ Press, 1985).

43. An in-depth study of why Reagan both succeeds and fails to persuade ordinary Americans, using his most impressive medium, television, is provided in Roberta Glaros and Bruce Miroff, "Watching Ronald Reagan: Viewers' Reactions to the President on Television," *Congress & the Presidency* (Spring, 1983): 25-47

44. James Fallows, who was Carter's chief speech writer until 1978, was the first to go public on this theme, doing it in a thoughtful and critical way, even if such a perspective is limited in assessing presidential performance. See "The Passionless Presidency," *Atlantic*, May 1979, 33-46. Some of the accounts that have followed are more arrogant and more self-serving: see Zbigniew Brzezinski, *Power and Principle: Memoirs of the National Security Adviser, 1977-81* (New York: Farrar, 1983).

45. Dale Tate,"Congress Clears $98.3 Billion Tax Increase," *Congressional Quarterly Weekly Report*, Aug. 21, 1982, 2035-2046.

46. T. R. Reid, "Reagan Lobbies on School Prayer," *Washington Post*, March 17, 1984, A11.

47. James L. Guth, "The Politics of the Christian Right," in *Interest Group Politics*, ed. Allan J. Cigler and Burdett A. Loomis (Washington, D.C.: CQ Press, 1983): 60-84.

48. A. James Reichley, "The Conservative Model of the Presidency" (Paper delivered at the 1981 annual meeting of the American Political Science Association):1.

49. I think it is more accurate to characterize the last goal as bipartisan. Carter, and perhaps some small component of the Kennedy administration, moved in other directions for a short period, reverting to traditional assumptions when the domestic and international environments challenged them. Accordingly, it is reasonable to assert that all presidents since Harry Truman have pursued "conservative" goals in foreign policy.

50. William W. Kaufman, "The Defense Budget," in *Setting National Priorities— The 1984 Budget*, 39-81.

51. Ibid.

52. I. M. Destler, "Reagan, Congress and Foreign Policy" (Paper delivered at the Conference on Presidential-Congressional Relations, American Enterprise Institute, Washington, D.C., Jan. 7, 1982).

53. Remarks of the late Senator Henry Jackson, D-Wash.

54. See the first and last page of Chapter 4.

55. I know the correlation is spurious, akin to those "amazing" examples of coincidence in the Lincoln and Kennedy assassinations, but it haunts me: of the four incumbents since Roosevelt who have been successful at the ballot box, three initiated, expanded, or intensified American wars (Eisenhower is the clear exception). The first, Truman, moved into Korea; the second, Johnson, expanded enormously our limited role in Vietnam; the third, Nixon, while reducing our combat role on the ground, greatly intensified the air war. Ford deserves more credit than he usually gets for having the courage not to resist when a Democratic Congress cut off aid to a thoroughly defeated South Vietnamese regime. There wasn't much American support left, and whether one attributes that to the policies of Nixon and Kissinger or to the inevitable result of 10 years of tragic fighting is a complex judgment. Of the other three incumbents who won election in the twentieth century, FDR was forced to confront Hitler in his third term; Wilson, like Johnson, chose clearly to move the country toward war, ultimately siding with the "allies" after a 1916 reelection campaign that promised peace; and Theodore Roosevelt spent a lot of time looking for someone to fight but, luckily, found no takers. Perhaps this outcome is no better than what one might predict randomly, using the flip-of-a-coin. Or, since FDR, perhaps incumbents have been unlucky ("war has many causes"). I am happy to leave the explanation of this pattern to the imagination of the reader.

56. Fred I. Greenstein, *The Hidden-Hand Presidency* (New York: Basic Books, 1982). In seeking to correct the caricature of Eisenhower as a bungling and largely ineffectual president, Greenstein may overestimate his political skill in using the "hidden hand"; in other words, avoiding public confrontation while pursuing private, backstage solutions. Only additional historical research can resolve this issue.

57. Reagan-Bush Committee, "Fact Sheet—Ronald Reagan's Strategy for Economic Growth and Stability in the 1980s," Sept. 9, 1980, Table 2.

58. Aaron, "The Choices Ahead," in *Setting National Priorities—The 1984 Budget*, 213-217. To most of us, the distinction between the "actual" and "structural"

deficits may seem unimportant. To economists, however, it is vital because structural deficits reflect government indebtedness that will not decline because of an upturn in the economy. Another Brookings scholar defines the structural deficit as a calculation "at a constant level of employment— usually near 'full' employment, but not a level associated with accelerating inflation. The . . . deficit that remains after the cyclical component has been removed is called the 'structural' or 'high employment' deficit." Pechman, *Setting National Priorities* (1984), 225.

59. Aaron, "The Choices Ahead," 223.
60. Their policies also have reduced the short-term probability of achieving "liberal" ends in government, at least of the New Deal/Great Society variety. Of the three Democratic candidates competing in the primaries after Illinois, only Jesse Jackson emphasized his support for large spending programs like National Health Insurance or a guaranteed national income plan modeled along the lines of Carter's 1977 initiative. Neither of these old-fashioned liberal programs was high on the projected policy agendas of former vice president Walter Mondale or Sen. Gary Hart. On spending for social/economic programs, the Reagan administration *and* the contraction of public support have shifted the public agenda to the right or, at least, seriously undermined the possibility of adopting liberal "breakthrough" initiatives in the near future.
61. The Reagan quote is from "Reagan and 3,500 Appointees Commemorate 1981 Inauguration," *Washington Post*, Jan. 21, 1984, A11; the Stockman quote is from "Reagan Said to Ignore Advisers in Addressing Budget Deficit," *Washington Post*, Jan. 21, 1984, A10.

From promise to performance: Kennedy to Reagan and beyond

7

If complexity doesn't beat you, paradox will.
—Tom Robbins

One straightforward conclusion emerges from this book: when presidential candidates make reasonably specific promises about future domestic policy, take those promises seriously! Most of the time.

If, on that proverbial social science "other hand," candidates claim they can actually achieve what they promise, discount their claims by whatever you know about the following: Congress; interest group power in Washington; "Cabinet government" and White House staff behavior; the executive branch and federal judiciary; state and local government; the Democratic or Republican party; a mixed but still market-based economy; the international economic and political system; unforeseen future events and crises; the candidates' demonstrated leadership ability in forging governing, not electoral, coalitions; and the next presidential election.

Presidents control what they initiate; other institutions control what presidents achieve. Presidents control *how* they initiate; others determine how to respond. The fundamental distortion of the "textbook" presidency is in uniting these different aspects of American political life into one measure of presidential performance. The New Deal, the New Frontier, the Great Society, and the Reagan Revolution are all merged in

187

a myth of presidential legend and celebration—or damnation—that undermines our capacity to assess the presidency realistically.

Presidential leadership *is* important. From Richard Neustadt to Paul Light, the evidence is incontrovertible.[1] The judicious mix of push and pull, the adroit calculation of resources and costs, the careful ordering of priorities, the selection of senior associates who are politically astute and substantively informed, and the capacity to articulate and sustain a unified vision of where the administration is going, and why, are essential to agenda building and accomplishment. "No amateurs!" declares Light. Amen.

Accordingly, agenda success and failure is affected, but not exclusively determined, by the president and the presidency. Policy responsibility, like political accountability, ought to be collective. In fact, the U.S. Constitution divides both responsibility and accountability, empowering Congress, the federal courts, and other institutions to act independently. The concept of "separate institutions, sharing power," Neustadt's justly famous description, is combined with an electoral system of different constituents and institutional incentives for Congress and the presidency, reinforcing distinctive patterns of accountability for the two institutions. Political leaders, voters, activists, journalists—everyone concerned with public policy—must continue, therefore, to seek appropriate ways of muddling through, knowing that a system of shared power rarely will provide simple answers to the problems of political responsibility and accountability.

After 200 years it should be clear that the most popular solution to this constitutional fact of life—a disciplined, responsible two-party system with its half-disguised preference for parliamentary government—is no closer to adoption today than it was when championed almost 100 years ago by Woodrow Wilson. What such systems maximize, at least in theory, is program coherence and collective accountability.[2] There are costs, large ones, in a diverse and pluralistic democracy of the sort the United States struggles to be, costs that are ignored by modern-day Wilsonians. If agenda formation and implementation lack ideological coherence and collective accountability in the United States, they encourage openness, flexibility, participation, responsiveness, and multiple "checks and balances." The premier example of a "responsible" party in the West, the British Labour party, is sinking in a morass of programmatic coherence and collective accountability.[3] Such behavior is distinctly un-American, as the authors of *The Federalist Papers*, among others, eloquently argued. Alternative conceptions of what is and is not feasible in the context of American institutions and practices seem far superior to the endless, quixotic pursuit of the British-style, Westminster model.

Agenda formation in campaigns: barriers and possibilities _____

Reflecting on the 1980 Democratic defeat, one of Jimmy Carter's senior and most liberal officials said: "I have a speech that I would like to give on every college campus in the country and I call it 'In Defense of Evasion!'" He continued:

> Presidents should never promise anything to anybody. I would like to see promises banned from presidential campaigns. Stu Eizenstat and I worked on him for weeks back in 1976, trying to persuade him not to be specific about promising to create a Department of Education. He wouldn't listen. So we got broadsided by Reagan for the "bureaucratic mess in Washington" because we created Cabinet-level departments like the Department of Education that mattered only to a few people at NEA [National Education Association]. The same is true for most of our other promises. All we got was a lot of grief from the press for being naive in making them, or interest groups who should have been our supporters but spent most of the time demagoguing us for not doing enough. The NEA, incidentally, is an exception. They were usually good and loyal friends. My general point is still right. *Campaign promises are poison.* [Emphasis added.]

These themes are echoed time and again by almost all senior White House and campaign staff, Democrat and Republican, liberal and conservative, old-timers and newcomers. Why? Because the single most important characteristic of American presidential coalitions is that they are alliances organized for the purpose of achieving or sustaining power. Where public policies enjoy a large, visible, and durable measure of majority support (Social Security, for example), any attempt to alter the existing mix of policies with highly specific alternatives will always be considered risky. Recall the fears articulated by a Carter staffer: "The issues can never help you but they sure can kill you!" So widespread is this fear that it is imperative to take it seriously.

It is "rational" for presidents and their operatives to be wary of "the issues," rational in the instrumental sense of how one gains and holds the presidency. It is also rational for groups who are part of the party coalition to honor this concern and be willing to compromise some of their policy goals if it helps candidates they support win and hold office. Compromise is rational for policy-oriented groups when they too can "calculate their best advantage over a protracted period . . . and see their best interests in light of the complexity of the political world in which they exist." [4] Political parties and policy factions share many of the same imperatives, a fact underappreciated in recent commentary.

Political parties and policy factions diverge when their perceptions about mutual gain begin to differ, and such disagreement is linked to the fundamental ways in which the groups differ. Factional leadership is concerned properly with advancing the goals, values, and interests of those for whom they speak. Party leadership, represented here by the presidential nominee, is concerned with aggregating, combining, and blending different factional elements to garner the most votes. Other functions are sometimes sacrificed by the imperative of winning elections. Austin Ranney puts it well: parties should be omelet makers, factions are the omelet's constituent elements.[5] "Watch out for those goddamn onions," wrote one of my students when encountering Ranney's recipe some years ago. Presidents and their campaign staffs are obsessed by the onion problem; factional leaders by the fear there will not be enough onions to give the omelet the right seasoning. Inevitably, therefore, group leaders and the president's staff will differ over the appropriate mix of issues in the campaign.

In the perfect world of simple economic models of electoral choice, these problems do not occur. Candidates adopt policies that reflect the preferences of minimal (or maximal) winning majorities.[6] Accountability and responsiveness are enhanced by anticipating what voters prefer. Elections either reward parties who succeed in anticipating what voters want or punish parties for failing to deliver. "Public opinion" theories, as Benjamin Page calls them, many of which have elaborate and elegant embellishment, help explain why so much campaign rhetoric is about broad goals, past performance, ambiguous future policy, and why campaign staffs would prefer to keep it that way.[7] It is rational for voters to save information costs, to ignore detailed policy information because it is too difficult to obtain and too complex to assess, to make choices on the basis of past presidential and party performance, and to get on with those problems of more immediate and direct concern in their lives. Presidents or candidates and their staffs, too, can focus on producing good policy ("peace and prosperity"), minimizing specific commitments that might interfere with their ability to do so, or at least do so in a way that meets simple majoritarian assumptions. They can devote most of their energy during campaigns to persuading voters that they have accomplished or will accomplish the broad ends that a majority prefers.

These "public opinion" models are consistent with either Burkean or delegate notions of representative democracy and are ingenious in simplifying a vast complexity while preserving the essentials of democratic control. Simultaneously, they help us understand why so much agenda building occurs *after* campaigns are over, providing a compelling justification for the risk-avoidance behavior of presidential candidates. Specific policy commitments that are not supported by majorities *are* potentially "poisonous"; indeed, they are irrational and undemocratic from the viewpoint of these models.

Public opinion theories fail, various commentators note, because the road to nomination differs from the road to election. Competing candidates offer different visions of the future and dissimilar versions of the past, along with specific policy promises that also differ, because organized, energetic, and "resource rich" factions within each party will not long support candidates who do otherwise. By resource rich I mean having access to the usual garden variety of money, expertise (political and policy), media, membership, and primary or caucus votes. Public opinion theories also fail because they ignore questions of leadership and elite manipulation (Nixon and Watergate in 1972), the mobilization of bias (class interests and cultural hegemony in majoritarian systems), the convictions of candidates themselves, and the ascendancy of private power over public interest.

Majority control is restricted by other factors, such as the geographical boundaries of the nation-state, even though presidents may advance policies that affect the fortunes and welfare of millions of people outside the United States. As Bernard S. Morris acidly observes, accountability for Johnson's and Nixon's leadership in Vietnam would have been treated differently had an older standard been operational: "Since [the] Geneva [Accord] and Nuremberg are in principle indifferent to the nationality of those who slaughter civilians, it is fortunate that the Viet Cong did not occupy Washington, D.C." [8] because the Viet Cong might have ordered the same fate for American officers as the Americans did for top-ranking Germans.

National boundaries that restrict elite accountability for wars, though questionable on moral grounds, are not likely to dissolve until the nation-state dissolves, or until nation-states are prepared to sacrifice part of their sovereignty in return for authentic collective security. Alternatively, when such sanctions have been imposed, as at Nuremberg, they have been carried out by victors who had the power, resolve, and support of widespread "world opinion" to implement them. The Viet Cong did not qualify on at least two out of three of these elements.

Public opinion models are deficient in a less global but equally important theoretical sense because they emphasize a mechanical, frequently ersatz vision of democracy that ignores the rich, complex *transactional and contextual nature* of democratic politics.[9] "Let's vote on it," an American way of life that confers what V. O. Key, in his gently skeptical way, called a "resplendent halo of legitimacy" on majority outcomes, underestimates the value of other decision processes. Voting is a necessary but not sufficient condition of democratic politics. Making decisions and reaching agreement through Quaker-style consensus, "synergy" (win-win, not win-lose), hierarchy (based on expertise), and concessions to passionate minorities are as essential to a viable democ-

racy as is majoritarianism. Anticipating majority preferences, responding
to majority wishes, and winning elections are dominant and valuable
influences on presidential coalitions. Other forces, what Page calls
"party cleavage," are influenced but not controlled by the need to win
majorities.

These countervailing tendencies are rooted in those older and
valuable contributions of pluralism: "extra-parliamentary" protest
politics, deliberation, bargaining, and mutual adjustment by those most
concerned and active in politics. Public opinion theories explain why
major policies, once enacted, are unlikely to be reversed. Civil rights
for blacks, other minorities, and women; income security programs for
the retired, unemployed, disabled, and disadvantaged; public enter-
prises as diverse as the Tennessee Valley Authority, the Communications Satellite Corporation, the Occupational Safety and Health Administration, and the national wilderness system all are afforded a measure
of protection from attempts to dismantle them because they enjoy
widespread majority support. They can be changed, and changed
dramatically, but they cannot be abolished. If these policies are now
protected by the centrist tendencies of presidential elections, it was not
always so.

Political risk and party programs

Policy factions have had to persuade or threaten presidential coalitions with high costs before candidates would take the risk of supporting policies that professional politicians feared might bring defeat at the
hands of a temporary electoral majority. The history of black protest and
the Democratic party, from FDR to Carter, and most recently in the
primary candidacy of Jesse Jackson, is ample testimony to the influence
of this movement in presidential politics. The goal of equal protection of
the law— once resisted bitterly and marked by two centuries of terror
and violence against black Americans—is now accepted and defended
by both parties. What is now urged—large government and private-
sector programs promoting greater economic opportunity and sustained
efforts at affirmative action—is resisted by most Republicans, championed (sometimes) by many Democrats. Jackson's primary bid was risky
for black Democrats and for progressives generally because, like all
multicandidate elections, it created an "Arrow problem." If one assumes
that most black voters prefer "A" to "B," and "B" to "C," then it is
possible that by voting their first choice (A) they will end up with their
third choice (C) as the nominee even though majorities of blacks
preferred "B" to "C." Short of abolishing primaries or introducing a

voting system that allocates second preferences, no guarantee against this distortion exists.

Democrats have worked since 1968 to restructure their nomination system, first increasing openness, participation, and social representation to correct the abuses of the old nomination process, then gradually reintroducing elements of peer review by government and party officials along with consensus-building alterations like a return to the "loop-hole" primary and "front loading" in the sequence of state primaries.[10] The 1984 election was the first since the early 1960s in which the number of primaries had declined, and the Hunt Commission's changes in other rules helped avert the potential distortions of an undiluted primary system. It is clear that neither front loading nor the reinstitution of loop-hole primaries permitted Democrats to identify an early winner more easily and unite behind that person.

The sharp and protracted struggle of Walter Mondale, Gary Hart, and Jackson made the platform-building process and other brokerage mechanisms at the 1984 national convention, particularly the rules change that seated a large number of public officials as "super delegates," essential in forging whatever unity Democrats reflected in the fall. Party cleavage theories predict that unity can be achieved only if the most important groups within the party coalition are satisfied, and promising these groups reasonably specific policy commitments is one important way of gaining their support and building party unity. It also serves to prevent the parties from becoming "Tweedledee and Tweedledum" across the board, so similar that it makes no difference who is in office.

Program differences between Democratic and Republican presidential candidates emerge on policies affecting blacks and other minorities, women, conservation and the environment, organized labor and those generally at the lower end of the income scale, teachers, older Americans with few resources, small farmers, students dependent on nonfamily financial support, consumers interested in greater protection from the "externalities" of the marketplace, and so forth. Of course, both parties also share basic values, some fundamental, like a preference for a market-based economy, and some less so, like the dance that is performed around nuclear power and energy (oil, natural gas) in general. "Look, sonnie," yelled a Texan at one of my acquaintances who was a Kennedy delegate in 1980, "Texas cattlemen and oilmen are Democrats too, by birth, breeding, and damn good horse sense, and don't you ever forget it!"

Campaign promises, therefore, are "poisonous" only when made to the wrong groups. Carter's staff assistant who damned promises was half right. He understood the differences—recall his comment about the loyalty of the National Education Association—but he exaggerated the negative consequences on the Carter presidency of creating the departments of Education and Energy. There are other reasons why the creation of these Cabinet-level departments may not have been good policy, but Ronald Reagan would have campaigned against "bloated bureaucracies" even if the Carter administration had shipped the entire federal apparatus down the Potomac River and moved back to Georgia. Running against Washington is a good "issue" for challengers, essential for Republicans who want to remain acceptable to the fold; it is riskier for Democrats who ought to know better and want to remain in office for longer than four years. If they challenge conventional Democratic assumptions about the utility of federal government programs, then it is imperative they frame a coherent strategy for decentralizing program responsibility that does not depend on a promise to "reduce ... the number of federal agencies to 200" and take the risk of attempting to make it work.[11]

The Hart campaign in the 1984 nomination struggle gained considerable political mileage over Mondale by accusing him of being a prisoner of "special interests," of promising these groups advantages that were not in the "public interest." Mondale's identification with organized labor and other organized Democratic constituencies was a constant target of Hart's primary rhetoric. From an agenda-building viewpoint, however, the AFL-CIO is a critical part of the Democratic coalition. Its policy claims must carry special weight in the party, whoever the presidential candidate is, because sustained AFL-CIO opposition to a Democrat, once in office, will undermine the president's authority and leadership in Congress and other institutions. Carter faced serious problems in governing because of early labor antipathy. The AFL-CIO's decision to endorse and back a Democratic candidate before the 1984 primaries may or may not have been a sensible political strategy. But any Democratic candidate who refuses to embrace *most* of labor's broad domestic agenda, whether or not a formal endorsement is sought or given, clearly is *not* acting sensibly. To reject labor's policy preferences is to risk losing one of the most important coalitional partners of the Democratic party—a risk, despite the rhetoric, that no Democratic nominee or president is likely to take.

The assertion that presidential candidates offer trivial choices to voters, merely echoes of the same monotonous symphony, is repeated so widely, believed so firmly, inculcated in the American political culture so deeply, that the counterevidence presented in this book may share the same fate as a rowboat trying to navigate the Atlantic. Political scientists who insist that "it does not pay to put much stock in the promises of candidates" and that "blueprints for the future are illusory"

convey a half-truth.[12] Presidential candidates do make promises, sometimes are successful in carrying them out, and groups within the fabric
of American society reap the rewards or pay the consequences. If the
reader still doubts this *other* half of presidential truth, ask anyone who
has been on the receiving end of President Reagan's promises to "reduce
case loads, costs, and error rates" in welfare programs, or to avoid the
"excessive" pursuit of environmentalism, and to "reexamine every
regulatory requirement," returning "to the states the primary responsibility for environmental regulation."

Comparing Democratic presidents

John F. Kennedy and Jimmy Carter, improbable as the comparison may
seem, shared many common features in their presidencies. Both attempted to redeem substantial parts of a moderately liberal domestic
agenda, and both met a resistant, frequently unwilling Congress. Some
of Kennedy's most important domestic initiatives were rejected by
Congress: Medicare, federal aid to primary, secondary, and advanced
education; the Youth Conservation Corps; an urban affairs department;
mass transit; a national wilderness preservation system; modest efforts at
civil rights legislation; and counterrecessionary measures like the tax
reduction bill. All were resisted by blocking factions in Congress. The
statistical performance data on Kennedy presented earlier reflects a
better record than he, in fact, achieved since it combines all legislation,
major and secondary, into one summary score.

Moreover, Carter's and Kennedy's basic attitudes and posture
toward Congress and its most important members were similar, though
not identical. Carter was sometimes aloof and formal, sometimes con-
temptuous and fearful, and this style inevitably was counterproductive.
By all accounts, Kennedy shared some of the same attitudes in dealing
with Congress, although his negative orientation was not as obvious or
consistent.[13] Kennedy, unlike Carter, had served in both the House and
the Senate, and certainly he had learned from this experience, but he
had never been a member of either institution's inner circle, a respected
workhorse, or a shrewd internal manipulator. His early and well-known
presidential ambitions while he was in the Senate, his disinclination to
master legislative policy and detail, his taste, indeed relish, for Washington's extracurricular social circuit placed him at odds with conventional
paths to political or legislative success. Kennedy's book, *Profiles in
Courage*, was a celebration of the Senate's most notable mavericks.
Kennedy, like Carter in the 1970s, was in important ways an outsider in
the Washington power structure of the 1950s.

Similarly, they arrived at the Democratic nomination via the then unlikely path of displacing or overwhelming the party establishment by judicious use of the primaries and mass media, particularly television. It seems certain, though not inevitable, that Hubert Humphrey, Lyndon Johnson, or Stuart Symington would have been the nominee of Democrats in 1960 had Kennedy not combined extraordinary skills at media exploitation and campaign electioneering in beating them. Whatever political deficiencies Carter and his team displayed in the White House, Hamilton Jordan and company were superb in mastering and utilizing the resources of the primary system. All this is well known.

Why, therefore, is Kennedy considered "above average" in his performance and Carter damned or dismissed? [14] If one excludes the mushrooming halo effect of the assassination and its aftermath and examines the records of the two presidents, one finds that Kennedy's policy record is not substantially better or worse than Carter's. Kennedy was able to move some of his campaign-relevant promises through the legislative process or to enact them by executive order, and his success in programs as diverse as the area redevelopment bill, minimum wage, housing, arms control, community health facilities, trade expansion, manpower development and assistance, and the Peace Corps reflected this pattern. In the context of the early 1960s and from the viewpoint of what Democrats had been gaining support for since the late 1940s, Kennedy's achievements were substantial but not exceptional. While I disagree with the revisionists, who treat the Kennedy presidency as all media showmanship or illusion, it is just as clear that popular perceptions of his achievements are greatly exaggerated. [15]

One important difference between Kennedy and Carter is hardly a secret: the relative political skills of their legislative liaison directors, Lawrence O'Brien and Frank Moore. Carter's Office of Congressional Relations, under Moore, has been pilloried so thoroughly that I can add little to these assessments. OCR changed dramatically after the first disastrous year of the Carter administration. The addition of William Cable for House affairs and the growing sophistication of Carter's Senate operation, buttressed by the "outside" advice of Walter Mondale, helped but did not overcome the negative perceptions about Carter and his team. The value of one of Kennedy's chief innovations—the establishment of an unusually competent liaison operation that for the first time in presidential history worked solely on legislative activities [16]—was negated by Carter's early mistake in appointing the wrong director. Perhaps Carter's behavior itself was the fundamental problem and Moore merely the lightning rod for congressional displeasure. Whichever interpretation is correct, Carter paid dearly for underestimating the perks and power of Congress. Democrats in the legislature, however, must share some of the responsibility for his program failures. After eight years of Nixon and Ford, congressional expectations of the president were excessive. But even a legislative horse trader as brilliant as Johnson would have had difficulty navigating the newly decentralized and factionalized institution that Congress had become.

Congress, it is frequently observed, helped create a "no-win presidency" during the Carter years. Congress, as an institution, was far different from the one that confronted Kennedy, Johnson, or Nixon. Because of the reforms of the late 1960s and early 1970s, Congress had grown not only more complex and decentralized but also more competitive with presidents for agenda control and more able to prevail over presidents.[17] The "good old days" of the 1950s and 1960s, it was said, when a few congressional barons—party leaders and committee chairmen—could negotiate directly for the institution with presidents were gone. This argument is accurate but too broadly drawn.

First, the "good old days" were few in number and far between; specifically, one-half of one Congress (1964, in the immediate aftermath of Kennedy's assassination), and one-half of the next (1965, when the 89th Congress broke a decade's log jam on the post-World War II Democratic agenda). Periods of remarkable congressional/presidential achievement like this have always been rare in American history. Witness the rapid demise of LBJ's authority after 1965, FDR's after 1937, and that of Woodrow Wilson after 1915. Second, the reforms of the 1970s centralized some processes in the House, mainly the Speaker's control over the Rules Committee and floor procedure and the majority party's control over committee appointments through the Steering and Policy Committee and Democratic Caucus.

Nelson Polsby observes that "it will not do to argue that the undeniably significant changes in the way Congress did business were at the root of difficulties that President Carter had in mobilizing congressional support for his proposals."[18] He notes further that Carter, a moderate, faced a Congress that "was controlled—overwhelmingly controlled—by middle-of-the-road veterans of the Democratic party."[19] Polsby attributes Carter's failures to his lack of political skill and, more generally, to the reformed nominating process that has excluded, or been boycotted by, leading members of Congress, permitting "antiparty amateurs" like Carter to gain the nomination.

Polsby, and others who focus on this explanation, ignore the fact that what constitutes the "middle-of-the-road," the fundamental nature of policy substance and hence policy cleavage, has changed considerably since the 1960s. He presents data, for example, showing that a "moderate" Democratic president should have had more than enough troops in the House to have gotten what he wanted through the legislative process in 1977-1978. He devotes considerable energy to chronicling the numerous errors of political commission and omission that plagued Carter and with which Carter plagued everyone else. Nowhere in his analysis does he discuss *any* of Carter's successes. Nor does he entertain the idea that "middle-of-the-roadism" may have changed considerably since he and other scholars first began to disentangle the complexities of congressional decision making, rescuing scholarly research from the "antilegislative" perspectives of an earlier generation.[20]

As was demonstrated in Chapter 5, Carter was most successful precisely in those policy areas where Democrats, moderates, and others still agree; he was least successful in areas where the classic liberal/moderate/conservative continuum does not clarify the basic thrust of Democratic factional disagreement. For example, the administration's most far-reaching environmental achievement, the final passage of the Alaska National Interest Lands Conservation Act, embraces diverse ecosystems totaling 110 million acres of national parks, wilderness areas, fish and wildlife refuges, wild rivers, and national monuments. It was a conservation measure that appealed to moderate and liberal Democrats, as well as some progressive Republicans, in an old-fashioned way (outside of Alaska, where it was opposed by the state's Republican and Democratic establishment).

The Sierra Club's indefatigable Alaska representative, along with other Washington-based conservation leaders in the Alaska Coalition, negotiated, pushed, argued, and reasoned with the Carter administration to keep the president and Interior Secretary Cecil Andrus committed to a comprehensive package. This had been a long legislative struggle, initiated by conservationists in 1971, but it was the Carter administration and its allies in Congress that took the risk and applied the muscle to see it through. For many environmentalists this bill was a compelling reason to applaud the administration's performance, and, like the National Education Association, the Alaska Coalition did not lose sight of the achievement during the outpouring of anti-Carter sentiment in 1980.

The administration also took considerable risks in championing the policy preferences of the Democratic party's most liberal faction on some issues for which it still has not been forgiven by others in the party. The White House reversed the original position of its two senior black officials in the Justice Department and thereby saved whatever is left of affirmative action after *Bakke*. The administration's efforts to find and appoint women and minorities to important positions were sometimes ridiculed by both right and left factions among Democrats. Eleanor Smeal and NOW, quite simply, were misguided in their harsh denunciations of Carter even if one can understand their mistake in terms of group theory and the long pent-up frustrations of women in American life. Carter's human rights policies, applied in a hit-and-miss fashion around the globe, could never satisfy those who valued consistency or those who ridiculed the possibility of any morally guided American foreign policy that champions values other than "realism," "power politics," and "nationalism," narrowly defined. Finally, the administration's most important legislative victory in foreign policy, the campaign for the Panama Canal Treaty, has been ignored by those who condemn Carter's political operation as incompetent and bankrupt.

Carter's policy achievements, measured against the art of the possible in a growing gulf of *policy and institutional fragmentation among Democrats,* were as substantial as Kennedy's. I trust this assertion will not be misconstrued, although I suspect many will dismiss it as a Carter apologia. Kennedy possessed advantages absent in Carter. His cosmopolitan charm, wit, grace, sense of irony, and his talent for articulating a coherent vision of presidential and political grandeur were exceptional. That vision, as many since have conceded, was flawed, containing within it an arrogance about American power, capability, and values. Subsequent events in Vietnam, Latin America, and Africa demonstrated how unjustified and naive that arrogance was. The Kennedy aura lingers because he affected, and affected deeply, many Americans in a fashion that Carter did not and could not. Arguably, Kennedy also was a better politician.

Many of Carter's failures, when compared with Kennedy's, were "failures" of style, but judgments about style are idiosyncratic, matters of personal taste, carrying with them a large amount of the observer's personal and historical baggage. So, the more important test stems from process (political) management in the broadest sense and circumstance. Presidents can affect process management. Paul Light's suggestions (establishing a better sense of presidential priorities, moving it or losing it, and so forth)[21] ought to be basic reading for any group within a primary's throw of the White House, no matter how much "deliberation and peer review" is reintroduced into the nomination system. Certainly Carter and his team could have done far better—it needs repeating, far better—than they did.

Of greater importance to Carter's rate of success was historical "circumstance." I am skeptical that the circumstances most often cited— the increasing complexity of congressional structure and policy making or the "reformed" nomination system—are as central here as others have made them. Both of these institutional factors, noted earlier, were important; they were not fundamental.

The policy areas in which the Carter administration foundered—energy, a guaranteed income, national health insurance, management of the economy so that unemployment *and* inflation are controllable, appropriate goals and means for American policy so that Soviet power is neither minimized nor exaggerated—are precisely the areas in which the Democratic party has been struggling since 1968. Policy, Theodore Lowi reminded us some years ago, frequently shapes process.[22] *Carter failed where the majority party fails.* The inability of Democrats to evolve a coherent, post-New Deal political vision and gain party consensus around its central elements the same way they did during the 1950s and 1960s, for what became the Great Society, doomed the Carter presidency just as surely as the administration's political mistakes. The logic of this interpretation is strengthened by considering briefly the major successes of another Democrat during the period, Lyndon B. Johnson.

Of Johnson's consummate legislative genius, there can be no doubt. More than any president since FDR, he understood, used, and manipulated the political process to get what he wanted. The personal distortions of Johnson's character also are well documented. He was, as one observer puts it, "devious, driven, crude, ambitious, indefatigable, manipulative, selfish, shrewd, and unidealistic and all of these to extremes." [23] Johnson came to the presidency through the assassination of Kennedy, enjoyed a temporarily swollen Democratic majority in Congress after his successful 1964 campaign, and presided over one of the most remarkable outpourings of legislation since the New Deal.

Some of that outpouring—the creation of the Office of Economic Opportunity, for example—clearly was shaped by what he and his staff contributed, their extraordinary political and policy leadership skills. Most, however, was a result of the long, steady buildup in the agenda of the post-1940s Democratic party; it was pushed forward by outside forces like the civil rights movement and the Kennedy assassination, shaped by the planning councils of the Kennedy administration, and given widespread support by a temporarily united Democratic party in Congress.[24] To this mix, one should add the critical support of a few Republicans, like Everett Dirksen in the Senate and William McCulloch, ranking Republican on the House Judiciary Committee, who provided key levers for passing and legitimating the civil rights bills. Since we can never know whether another Democratic president would have been equally successful, it is impossible to calculate accurately what proportion is attributable to the "Johnson factor," and what proportion to all the favorable circumstances surrounding the dynamics of legislative achievement in 1964 and 1965. Neither Carter nor Kennedy, however, enjoyed what Johnson momentarily possessed: a structural responsiveness in the policy-making system that was ripe for effective presidential leadership in helping forge agenda break-throughs.

The negative aftereffects of Great Society programs have received considerable attention in recent years. The rhetoric of Johnson's promises about the Great Society was inflated far beyond what these programs could actually accomplish. The magnitude of his rhetorical commitments—to wipe out poverty, unemployment, slums—was unmatched by actual program support or performance. In addition, his exceptionally high record of follow-through in domestic affairs was eclipsed by the most important foreign policy promise he made and failed to keep. The reversal of what he promised, or seemed to promise, about potential American intervention in Vietnam during the 1964 campaign poisoned the American political process for at least a decade. The aftershocks, some small, some large, remain well into the 1980s.

Comparing Republican presidents

Cyclical theories of agenda formation emphasize the pendulum character of American politics, as periods of activist innovation alternate with periods of conservative consolidation. Writes James L. Sundquist:

> Because the governing party stands either left or right of center, it finds itself in a state of permanent disequilibrium with the electorate. It is either moving too fast and doing too much—the pitfall of the Democrats—or moving too slowly and doing too little, the bane of the Republicans.[25]

This accurately describes the cleavages of the period Sundquist studied, 1952-1968, but such rhythm is applied less appropriately to the behavior of two Republican presidents after 1968, Richard M. Nixon and Ronald Reagan.

The Reagan administration has served in one important respect to consolidate policies advanced and adopted in prior Democratic presidencies. Those who suspected he would seek to abolish the major pillars of the New Deal were wrong. Such Draconian measures were neither proposed nor sought by Reagan and certainly not by Nixon.

But both Republicans emphasized the need for a fundamental shift in the scope and management of major federal programs. These shifts in direction can have harsh consequences. Nixon gutted the Office of Economic Opportunity by transferring its major programs elsewhere in the federal government, reducing and impounding program appropriations, and appointing as its director an individual fiercely hostile to it and all it stood for. The Reagan team slashed social/economic program budgets, attempted to abolish agencies like the Legal Services Corporation, sought to halt affirmative action, changed the makeup of the U.S. Commission on Civil Rights, and eliminated the Community Services Administration.

Within the constraints of broad public support for an activist federal government, a consensus conservatives ignore in their more extreme rhetoric, Republican presidents can challenge, alter, and reshape specific federal programs. Since constitutional power is shared with Congress, however, efforts to dismantle existing programs confront formidable barriers. Congress, long damned as an institution of excessive restraint, has also proved enormously resourceful in defending against attacks by Nixon and Reagan many of the programs originally proposed by the Democrats.

The Nixon and Reagan presidencies were more than reflections of an essentially passive, Eisenhower-like vision of government's role. Both were activist, and, because of this thrust, are not accurately described in terms of a pendulum, activist-conservative theory of policy making. Their activism, particularly in the use of the administrative presidency, *did* seek to enhance the "private sector" as the preeminent center of power in one area, economic policy. Thus it might be said they were activist in support of an ideology favoring a more passive role for government on economic matters. This judgment requires proper contextual balance: a more passive role in the 1980s is inevitably more activist than what was considered "normal" 20 years earlier, even by Democrats such as Kennedy. Sundquist is correct in suggesting that the pendulum in this regard has been one of "fits and starts but the direction of its movement is constant." [26] Moreover, the Nixon and Reagan presidencies differed, and these differences are just as important as the similarities of their administrations.

Nixon's presidency

"Nixon," suggests one observer, "was an individual of conservative instincts, not conservative principles." [27] No other explanation is as compelling in helping one understand so spectacular a deviation from his campaign promises as the imposition of mandatory national wage/price controls in 1971. Nixon overrode all the usual Republican "free enterprise" rhetoric in forcing the creation of a government-controlled system of wage and price standards in the third year of his administration. Reelection was a goal to which the Nixon administration subordinated *every* principle, economic and otherwise, as everyone learned after the 1972 election. The Watergate scandal represented the most extreme violation of the promise Americans take for granted in their presidents, and both his administration and the Republican party paid a high price for the transgressions of the president and his responsible senior staff.

Nixon v. United States is more than a constitutional case involving executive privilege; it symbolizes with great irony the failure of the presidential selection process. Of course, the lack of principle also aided this Republican in taking some great risks in foreign policy. The opening to mainland China and a mixed strategy of détente with the Soviet Union are examples. The Nixon administration's détente policy was "mixed" precisely because it involved "playing the China card" as an anti-Soviet gambit. Nixon and his national security adviser, Henry A. Kissinger, usually are applauded for these initiatives, except among disgruntled Republicans, but there was another part to their lack of foreign policy "principle." The secret bombings of Cambodia and Laos, the destabilization of Chile, and the savage, postelection bombing of Hanoi in 1972 were of concern to leaders in both political parties, no matter where they placed themselves on an ideological continuum.

Nixon, like Reagan, followed through on a substantial number of his promises about domestic policy, although his administration failed to take any action on a far larger proportion than any other studied here. He broke the most important promise presidents make, involving the oath of office. This "unindicted co-conspirator" came closer than any president to spending his retirement years in federal prison. The fact that he avoided impeachment and prison, instead spending most of his recent years writing on leadership (!) from a position of comparative prosperity, is testimony to the generosity and/or naiveté of his successor. Others allege, but have been unable to prove, baser motives in the decision that led Gerald Ford to grant a pardon.[28] Whatever the Nixon administration accomplished in other areas of policy, its main "success" was to contribute to a deepening erosion of public confidence in the integrity of the presidency and the electoral process that selects leaders for it.

Accountability was enforced, crudely and dramatically, through the Supreme Court's decision and the impeachment hearings, but cynics continue to dismiss Nixon's forced resignation as insufficient evidence that "the system works." One suspects that these cynics require an American version of the guillotine and the televised use of it to challenge their skepticism. Nixon paid a price that no other president has paid, as did many of his senior staff under harsher circumstances. For Nixon, the political punishment roughly fits the political crime. This conclusion requires a degree of charity. Moralists and some of his former staff, who went to prison and were understandably bitter that their boss did not, remain unconvinced.

Reagan's presidency

The Reagan presidency, while pursuing many of the same goals sought by Nixon, diverges in obvious respects. The president himself is by all accounts an engaging individual, open and charming,[29] confident in his environment and in his self-esteem, not driven by the haunting fear of failure and the potential loss of self-control that characterized Nixon. Indeed, one concern is that he is not "driven" by anything.[30] The White House staff structure, although moving toward more hierarchy in early 1984, is considerably less rigid than Nixon's, more consultative in its decision-making processes, verging on a "board of directors" model, reflecting in this sense Reagan's strengths and weaknesses.

More important from the viewpoint of this study, the Reagan team's conservative "principles," while not inflexible, are more pronounced than they were in the Nixon White House.[31] The intensity with which the administration pursued its economic and deregulatory package, presaged in general outlines during the 1980 campaign, was remarkable. The early push produced a series of legislative victories unmatched since Johnson's first year. Yet conservative discontent with the administration increased—partly because of excessive expectations, partly because of the nature of group leadership, and partly because Reagan's social agenda, intensely important to New Right conservatives, was defeated in Congress. In addition, the administration deferred action on many initiatives, and these "deferrals" seemed like abandonment to prominent New Right figures. As was suggested earlier, the Reagan presidency is best characterized by high and focused early achievement, but sporadic effort in the attempts to redeem what he promised in 1980. The administration naturally emphasized its achievements; the New Right and other conservative critics its sporadic effort. Reagan's achievements require additional clarification.

The campaign promises of the president in 1980 were few in number, compared with those of his predecessors, but he promised far-reaching consequences if his programs were adopted. Should the rhetoric of supply-side economics be ignored as typical of campaign sloganeering, requiring control over so many variables that no candidate can be held accountable when the predicted results go awry? I think not. First, Reagan was reasonably specific about the means he intended to use in rescuing the economy, linking these specific initiatives to a series of economic outcomes that, of course, proved wildly unrealistic. Second, important aspects of the economic recovery under way in 1984 contradicted the predictions made by the president and his campaign advisers in 1980. The most obvious discrepancies involved the harsh recession of 1981-1982, the size of the deficit, the relative importance of consumer demand, and the increasing (not decreasing) ratio of federal expenditures to gross national product. In 1980, for example, federal expenditures constituted 21 percent of the gross national product; in 1984, despite the cutbacks in domestic programs, federal expenditures were 24 percent of GNP. Since supply-side was used intentionally by Reagan strategists to circumvent the harsh political realities of what had occurred during economic downturns in the past (high unemployment, low industrial output, extensive business bankruptcy), holding them accountable for the inadequacy of their supply-side "blue-mirrors" seems essential.

The Economic Recovery Tax Act of 1981 (ERTA) failed to alter the severe recession of 1981-1982, and there is little evidence that any similar supply-side strategy will do any better in curbing the harsh effects of future economic downturns. ERTA and the administration's budget cuts did what they promised about "counterproductive programs" and taxes: they reduced the income, in services and cash, of families earning $10,000 or less and increased dramatically the real income of families earning $80,000 and more. ERTA's across-the-board reduction also provided a modest decrease, averaging an estimated 4 percent, in the tax rates of the broad middle class—if its members were fortunate enough to be employed with some stability during the period. The paradox of the Reagan administration's performance was that it sought to redeem a significant part of its campaign promises about economic strategy and in doing so reduced its capacity to deliver on all the promised consequences.

Midterm elections provide a very rough check on an incumbent president's broad performance. These contests also reflect various local, state, and congressional incumbency factors, requiring that observers avoid overinterpretation of national forces.[32] The deficiency of midterm elections as presidential accountability devices is obvious— they are congressional. Presidents can remain "flexible," altering course in ways that reflect a different mix in the second part of their terms.

The Reagan administration, needing an improved economy, followed that strategy precisely. Since voters focus on outcomes more easily than means, the recovery was defended as a delayed consequence of White House economic policies. "We need more time" is a perennial defense of all presidents seeking a second term. For voters to believe in Reagan means that they must ignore the state of the economy during the first two years of his presidency, as well as the contradictory nature of his promises, and gamble that he and the Republicans, rather than Mondale and the Democrats, would better sustain "peace and prosperity" in the future.

Assessments of presidential performance among many voters are so powerfully affected by short-term factors, like the economic upswing of late 1983 and 1984, that incumbents seeking reelection in a year of economic prosperity can push a personalized version of retrospective accountability to the extreme, emphasizing an upbeat version of the present and *recent* past, ignoring with impunity past mistakes, policy reversals, and specific future commitments. Accordingly, the Reagan campaign declined to produce in 1984 anything like the policy statements it developed in 1980, ambiguous as the 1980 versions were. The 1984 campaign stressed the president's "Mr. Feel Good" image and programmatically meaningless bromides, obscuring more than it did in 1980 the conservative agenda to which it was still committed. "If you want to know where the administration will be heading," said one RNC staffer, "read the [FY 1985] budget!"

This is back-channel communication with a vengeance, so far "back" in the back channel that even those with sufficient interest and knowledge will have difficulty using it. As was pointed out earlier, the in-party always has an agenda, implied in its budget decisions and in those unfulfilled promises and new platform planks that are supported by the administration. These items are the most specific hints that one will find of what constitutes a projected second-term policy menu. In circumstances like this, it is up to the opposition—the candidate, party, and organized factions—to develop, publicize, and exploit the incumbent's budget and other choices, obscure to the voters as they are, as indicative of the administration's future policy commitments. If the opposition fails in this role, either because of poor research and articulation or because of an inability to get the message across, policy accountability is undermined in presidential elections in which incumbents are seeking a second term.

Presidential elections and presidential accountability

Presidential discretion is an inevitable part of governing. Redeeming the promises of the past campaign assumes that domestic and international problems remain stable—a false assumption. Presidents must be willing to change, to be flexible about some of their promises in light of new problems, different priorities, faltering policies. The question is: how much flexibility is possible and necessary before it becomes wholesale abandonment of earlier promises? Carter was unsuccessful in defending the political rationale behind his reversals on economic and defense policy, reinforcing the willingness of Ted Kennedy and a largely progressive faction in the Democratic party to challenge him in the primaries. Johnson failed for the same reason on Vietnam. Reagan avoided primary competition in 1984, but doubts about the the economy challenged his claims that the administration's economic policies have produced the intended consequences.

Other aspects of presidential discretion also challenge theories of electoral accountability that seek to hold presidents responsible for what they promise as candidates. Understanding the flexible range of presidential response once in office, moving on a continuum from drafting legislation to committing the full weight of presidential resources behind a program's adoption, requires that quantitative assessments are balanced by intensive case studies. Factions outside of the administration inevitably apply standards to presidential effort that differ from those inside the White House. Opponents, naturally, use yet another group of standards for assessing presidential effort. Accordingly, presidential fulfillment depends on the personal and political, that is to say, a subjective assessment by leaders of outside groups, and their judgments in turn depend on how they respond to the demands of leading their own organizations. The "art of ambiguity" applies just as much to governing as it does to campaigning.

Presidents frequently are judged on performance in high policy— governmental management of the economy and major foreign policy initiatives—providing a yardstick that establishes priorities, and this ordering principle is sufficient for the demands of simple economic models of retrospective accountability. More complex models face more complex problems.

Imposing a hierarchy of preferences on the larger bundle of issues that candidates and presidents must deal with is impossible. Environmentalists, right-to-lifers, pro-Israel groups, civil libertarians, anticrime advocates, feminists, civil rights workers, monetarists, one-worlders, stockholders, welfare recipients, coastal developers, restaurateurs, right-to-work forces, the AFL-CIO, hunters, birders, anti-gun controllers, decentralists, bikers, and civil servants—all have policy preferences that reach the president's agenda and are reflected in party platforms and presidential campaigns. Assuming that each of these groups has its own priorities and also a stake in some of the other areas, how might the groups assess presidential fulfillment?

The historical answer of political science is that the major political parties provide the only feasible institution for simplifying and aggregating choices among policy bundles. "Third forces" like Common Cause can simplify and aggregate some of these concerns for those predisposed to share their values, but they do not run candidates. Yet. The mass media sometimes claim to "speak for the public" on a large variety of issues, but Walter Cronkite apparently preferred Martha's Vineyard to John B. Anderson, declining to stand as Anderson's vice presidential candidate, and an overwhelming majority of American citizens preferred a Republican or Democrat to Anderson. The organizational vitality of the major parties, despite their well-known deficiencies, is essential to presidential accountability.

Since elections and parties *influence but do not determine policy*, responsibility, accountability, and responsiveness cannot be restricted to the electoral process. Authentic pluralism, mixing electoral inducements and rewards with active and sophisticated group lobbying and direct action in the governing process, is compatible with modern democratic theory and modern democratic reality. The biases of pluralism are substantial, but then so are its advantages. Being American, I suffer from a weakness for amelioration. A good place to find some suggestions for improving the American political system is in the recent work of one of pluralism's most able contemporary analysts, Robert A. Dahl.[33]

Fundamental alternatives to improving what has evolved would require changes far beyond what the existing party, electoral, and nomination process can sustain. Political change that proceeds organically and incrementally, flexible in its ability to correct unanticipated consequences, is usually spurned by purists and ideologues as morally and politically counterfeit. But it need not be. An incremental decision-making process need not lead to incremental outcomes, nor reflect uniformly the values of groups who believe in incremental change. Political change has been achieved in some areas because of the actions of groups who sought more than the art of the possible deemed reasonable and who were willing to take the risks and pay the costs of seeking it. The diverse coalition that led to the tremendous advances in civil rights of the 1960s and 1970s is a clear example of a mix in the goals and strategies of different groups, some radical and confrontational, others prudent and risk-avoidant.

Campaign issue papers and party platforms are imperfect but useful guides to critical aspects of future presidential policy. Most voters ignore them. Activists and opinion leaders ignore them at their own peril; indeed the accountability of presidents for important promises about policy depends on the role and energy of those most active in the political system, as well as those whose participation is restricted to voting.

What kind of "role" and how much "energy" are questions for which there are no obvious answers. For the major parties, campaigns *must* be oriented to winning the presidency, and this requires a strategy of appealing to at least a minimal winning majority. Otherwise the accountability that stems from competing in elections is "academic"—in the worst sense of that sometimes honorable term. Group leaders who insist on imposing maximum demands on party platforms or who repudiate candidates or incumbent presidents because they are unwilling to accede to those demands undercut their own capacity to influence presidential decision making.

Factional leaders whose primary interest is public policy have a clear stake in promoting a candidate and a party with whom they are in *general* agreement, despite disappointment about specific aspects of the candidate's platform. Party leaders whose primary interest is in winning elections have a clear stake in promoting the policy fortunes of a faction with whom *they* are in general agreement, despite disappointment about specific aspects of the faction's "unreasonableness" or "bullheadedness." So far as candidates and faction leaders are unable to accept responsibility for assisting each other in meeting their distinctive goals, agenda building and accountability will be weakened. The reasons should be apparent: factional leaders will be tempted to push for promises or policies that are too specific and/or too controversial, thus damaging the candidate's electoral credibility; candidates will be tempted to evade and hedge on policy commitments that are not already supported by a huge majority of the population, thus disregarding the faction's essential and legitimate policy objectives. Either way, agenda building and policy accountability are diminished.

Some critics of American elections speculate about the abundance of "promiscuously promising politicians," suggesting the "real" problem is that candidates made *too* many promises that confound their ability to function as "intelligent statesmen in a complex world." Every analyst has a favorite example of presidential promiscuity, and every platform chair of the past 25 years has begun his or her term proclaiming, "this year, we will avoid a laundry-list platform." It should be clear why such sentiments are confounded by political reality: what is seen as a laundry list by one person is regarded as absolutely essential policy by another. One person's laundry list is another's essential clothing, one person's promiscuity is another's normal behavior. Presidents need flexibility just as they need supporters who are "well-clothed." Presidents can use the platform-building process and their own issue staffs to provide more specific policy information without, as a recent participant put it, "trying to write detailed promises that resemble the 1986 budget." Indeed, most of the specific and reasonably detailed promises uncovered in this study leave considerable room for presidential flexibility. Any attempt to revert to the older style of platform writing—for example, stressing only thematic messages that lack the detail of post-1968 versions—will further undermine the policy relevance of presidential elections. Detailed campaign promises are still the exception in presidential politics.

Arguing that candidates should stick to thematic presentations, ignoring the utility of having more detail about what they might do, when, how, and with what cost, is an open invitation to increasing the amount of voter confusion already evident in American elections.[34] Voter misperception, projection, and ignorance are encouraged by the vagueness of campaign promises.

The goal of those party leaders, organizational activists, and journalists who believe that platforms and candidate policy commitments are essential in judging presidential aspirants and their performance in office is to convey this policy-relevant information in such a way that voters can use it. Otherwise, elections will always verge on being exercises in "hiring and firing" one's leaders, leaving presidential accountability to political elites, the manipulative capabilities of modern advertising, and crude retrospective judgments.

The future of presidential agendas: another 'end of ideology'?

Ronald Reagan and Walter Mondale differed in important ways on many of the problems facing the United States in the 1980s. The fact that the Reagan presidency, the most conservative in decades, was unable to achieve all that it promised dismayed many conservatives and cheered many moderates and liberals. This failure, plus Carter's inability to carry through on many of his most ambitious proposals despite enjoying a Democratic Congress, has led some observers to assert, once again, that the United States is entering a period of agenda convergence, that "breakthrough" policy is being replaced by a "rationalizing" politics that corrects, modifies, extends, regulates, reorganizes, disengages, but does not alter fundamentally what has been established.[35]

Government, the argument continues, has grown so enormous that past breakthroughs, once achieved, create a new politics of essentially technocratic error correction in an environment where groups disagree less over ends than they do over means. This analysis has much to commend it: properly managing what the federal government now does is a considerably more complex enterprise than it was in 1960, at the dawn of the Kennedy administration.

Passion, vision, and the moral commitment that infuses a more ideological (breakthrough) politics is being replaced, Lawrence Brown argues, by an outlook of prudence, skepticism, technical analysis, and careful experimentation. "The end of ideology," an old social science vision, is resurfacing now in more sophisticated fashion, in part because of the blocked aspirations of Ronald Reagan, one of the most ideological presidents of this century. Despite the conservative rhetoric and achievements of the Reagan administration, it has not seriously changed the contours of the Positive State. This, Brown suggests, means that fundamental changes in the role of government, liberal or conservative, are unlikely to emerge in the future.

Some of the major themes in Gary Hart's primary campaign clearly were an attempt to reflect this viewpoint in the context of nomination politics, a context that is considerably less orderly, and hence less neatly classifiable, than Brown's scholarly treatise. Hart's neoliberalism—a term he steadfastly and understandably refused to use—seems well suited, however, to building *one* type of post-New Deal Democratic agenda that is consistent with a rationalizing rather than a breakthrough politics. Independent of Hart's political future or that of any other presidential candidate like him, many of the assumptions underlying the newer end-of-ideology argument are plausible.

The civil rights revolution, it is noted, has institutionalized the principle of equal opportunity in voting, access to public facilities, housing, education, and employment. Realizing the full benefits of this legal equality will take much longer, as numerous activists have lamented. The campaign and appeal of Jesse Jackson were dramatic examples of how and why the Second Reconstruction is far from complete. At the same time, his candidacy symbolized the political achievement that blacks have made since the mid-1960s. Other minorities low in resources, most notably Hispanics, also are far from equitably sharing the abundance of the United States. Nevertheless, policy debate now centers on how to achieve a just distribution, not whether it should be accomplished.[36]

The Positive State, begun in earnest in the New Deal and growing during the 1960s and 1970s, is a stable part of all administrations, including those of conservative Republicans. Women have won new forms of legal equality and appear to be winning (some!) other forms as well, as their revolution is said to be entering a "Second Stage."[37] Environmental "extremism" appears to be more of a virtue and less of a vice than Reagan and his team initially believed. The struggle between environmentalists and multiple-users is likely to continue for as long as there is any environment worth using and protecting, but in a rationalizing rather than breakthrough way. Finally, government management of the economy is not going to revert to Eisenhower-like homilies about "free enterprise" no matter what the rhetoric of candidates might suggest.

Where are future breakthroughs in domestic policy likely to emerge? Brown suggests that national health insurance and/or a national guaranteed income might provide agenda items similar in scope

to Medicare or federal aid to education, but he doubts that future
government will, or should, adopt these policies in the same manner
used for earlier breakthrough agendas. His answer, summarized, is that
domestic breakthroughs are through:

> Rationalizing policies may be here to stay . . . the pre-eminent political
> fact of the present is that the ideologies that gave order, confidence,
> and vision to political thought . . . New Deal liberalism, socialism, and
> conservatism, both libertarian and Burkean . . . have faltered badly,
> transparently unable to offer consistently defensible, comprehensive
> answers to public problems. A new reasonableness, based on acknowl-
> edged ambivalence and with due regard for complexity . . . could be the
> reward. The problem lies in communicating these points. Politics
> driven by the lack of convictions (in playwright Tom Stoppard's words)
> have no power to stir men's souls or elevate their visions . . . a good
> thing or bad, depending on one's point of view.[38]

His argument dovetails perfectly with *some* aspects of the Democratic 1984 primary campaign. Neither Mondale nor Hart championed
large, federally sponsored breakthrough items like national health
insurance or a guaranteed national income as top priorities in their
projected agendas. After examining the provisional budget proposals of
leading Democratic candidates, one reporter noted that the

> numbers reveal an additional surprise: only Jackson appears to have
> ambitious plans for new government spending. . . . The largest domes-
> tic spending increases [other than Jackson's] are those proposed by
> Mondale . . . and they would total only $30 billion in fiscal 1989, when
> by all accounts, the federal budget will exceed $1 trillion.[39]

One explanation for this is apparent. The sizable deficits created
during the Reagan administration made the 1984 presidential election
one of the "most budget-focused campaigns in history"—at least for
Democrats! Republicans can be excused for deriding this claim, made by
a Democratic campaign official, since the Democrats' preoccupation with
large deficits coincided with the election of a Republican president.
Nevertheless, the long-run consequences of Reagan's economic and
budgetary policies severely reduce the discretion of any future president
from either major party. In this sense, Reagan certainly succeeded in
shifting the agenda to the right. Because there is still room for party and
candidate differences about *how* to divide a modestly growing federal
pie, and, because equally important differences of philosophy are
concerned with social, life-style, and foreign policy questions, to argue
that the entire agenda has shifted to the right is to overstate the
importance of budgetary constraint. Moreover, the long-term commitment of Democratic party platforms to some form of national health
insurance suggests they cannot simply abandon it, even if they hedge

and fudge on the question of how and when they will seek to implement their commitment.

So perhaps Brown and others who share his opinions are correct. The older ideologies so clearly reflected in the agenda-building process of presidential campaigns since the New Deal may be faltering, unable, as he writes, to provide defensible and comprehensive answers to public problems. Does it follow, therefore, that advanced industrial democracies are moving toward a benign, prudent, political technocracy, free of the passion and vision that "stirs people's souls" ? I am skeptical.

Future crises and/or catastrophes—nuclear or other wars and energy scarcity are the most obvious—could so reorganize politics that concepts like "rationalizing" and "breakthrough" would lose all meaning. Brown understands this. What his analysis lacks is an appreciation of breakthrough currents that might be percolating outside the political debate that has informed the industrial revolution and its consequences; in other words, outside New Deal liberalism, socialism, and conservatism *and* outside the ideology of a technocratic if benign form of social engineering. Nor, intentionally, does he deal with foreign policy, although he hints that a "warfare state" might have consequences different from the "welfare state" he describes.

Two frequently mentioned alternatives to Brown's scenario focus on a reinvigorated class politics, stemming from future scarcity and distributive problems, or the fundamental paradigm shift embraced by those concerned with Transformational or New Age politics. Neo-Marxists and liberals have emphasized the possibilities inherent in the first alternative, "Third Wave" humanists the possibilities of the second. Transformational politics is less well identified in political science than the neo-Marxist arguments, although good general statements are available.[40] New Agers differ from neo-Marxists, regular liberals or conservatives, and from those advocating the inevitability of a political technocracy because they seek to create a politics that fuses left *and* right, vision *and* skepticism, passion *and* rationality, evolution *and* revolution, the local *and* the global, individual choice *and* social responsibility, the secular *and* the spiritual—in a process that radically alters the structure of modern society. A central failure of the end-of-ideology debate, both old and new, is that it poses the choices as exclusive alternatives: either we move toward habits of skepticism, rigorous policy analysis, undogmatic error correction *or* toward a muscular, passionate, visionary politics. Certainly, there are other alternatives.

Long before there was "New Deal liberalism, socialism and conservatism," visions of the Good Life moved people to political action in passionate ways. I suspect that long after contemporary ideologies are relegated to their appropriate historical niches, people will find new visions, new passions, new outlooks that "stir their souls"—and their minds and bodies. Brown drifts toward the same error that derailed Daniel Bell, S. M. Lipset, and his other end-of-ideology forebears. The sources of a rejuvenated breakthrough politics cannot be fully anticipated in the present for the same reason social scientists writing in the late 1950s did not foresee what was coming in the 1960s and 1970s: the future is open-ended, always subject to multiple scenarios, never reducible to a single line of projected development. One scholar concluded of the older debate, "we may wait as long for the 'end of ideology' as the positivists have waited for the end of religion." [41]

Presidents and presidential candidates do not wait. Like all elected officials, their "long-run" futures are 30 minutes from the present. Their agendas are immediate and concrete, anchored in the present, even as their presidencies and the next election depend on their ability to anticipate the (near) future. Occasionally, they gallop off in wildly unanticipated directions, 180 degrees contrary to what voters and others might reasonably expect. More often, they seek to redeem most of the specific promises about policy that they make in their campaigns. Converting their intentions and effort into policy achievement, however, is a formidable challenge. Over the past 24 years, Nixon, Carter, and Reagan failed more often than they succeeded on this second measure of performance, and Kennedy barely reached the 50 percent mark. Only Johnson succeeded handsomely in converting pledges into programs. His principal reversal, Vietnam, is a stark reminder of the costs of presidential flexibility.

Whether the patterns of presidential success and failure examined in this book are judged favorably or negatively depends on the individual's political values and on one's assessment of the U.S. Constitution. By constitutional design and political custom, presidents share responsibility with Congress, the executive branch, and the federal courts for what ultimately becomes public law. Predicting what presidents will support in their legislative and executive agendas and what they will abandon or defer is hazardous. It seems useful, therefore, to recall the wisdom of a principled Republican, one of those much maligned 1964 supporters of Barry Goldwater:

> My friends kept telling me that Goldwater is trigger-happy, would shoot from the hip, turn over everything to the generals.
> If I voted for him, they warned me, America will go to war!
> Well, I stuck to my principles, voted for Goldwater, and, by God, they were right: we went to war!

Notes

1. Richard E. Neustadt's updated classic, *Presidential Power: The Politics of Leadership from FDR to Carter* (New York: Wiley, 1979) and Paul Light's fine study of presidential agenda building, *The President's Agenda* (Baltimore: Johns Hopkins University Press, 1982) are essential reading for everyone concerned with these issues.

2. There has always been more slippage than admirers concede between how the British system *ought* to function and how it in fact operates. See Anthony Birch, *The British System of Government*, 4th ed. (London: Allen & Unwin, 1980).

3. The 1983 election further weakened the British Labour party. It is unclear whether their new leadership team, headed by a younger and apparently more pragmatic group, will succeed in rebuilding the party's fortunes.

4. Nelson Polsby, *Consequences of Party Reform* (New York: Oxford University Press, 1983), 65.

5. Austin Ranney, "Are Political Parties Necessary?" (Paper delivered at the 1976 annual meeting of the Midwest Political Science Association).

6. The different implications of minimal versus maximal strategies are addressed in Joseph Schlesinger, "The Primary Goals of Political Parties: A Clarification of Positive Theory," *American Political Science Review* 65 (1975): 840-849.

7. Benjamin Page, *Choices and Echoes in Presidential Elections* (Chicago: University of Chicago Press, 1978).

8. Bernard S. Morris, "Accountability in U.S. Foreign Policy: An Exploratory Essay" (Paper delivered at the 1979 Congress of the International Political Science Association), 1.

9. A good elaboration of this orientation will be found in Ralph M. Goldman, *Behavioral Perspectives on American Politics* (Homewood, Ill.: Dorsey Press, 1973).

10. The activities of the Hunt Commission and other 1984 rules changes are reviewed by Rhodes Cook, "1984 Democratic Party Rules Seek to Cure Past Problems But Could Create New Ones," *Congressional Quarterly Weekly Report*, Aug. 6, 1983, 1609-1614.

11. The reorganization task forces of the Carter administration sought extensive changes in program management and implementation, much of which was lost in continuing battles with congressional committees, bureaucratic agencies, and affected interest groups. Some of the administration's proposals would have centralized management functions, others would have decentralized them. For an early assessment of Carter's transition and management initiatives, see Bruce Adams and Kathryn Kavanagh, *Promise and Performance: Carter Builds a New Administration* (Lexington, Mass.: Lexington Books, 1979). A thoughtful overview of presidential management in domestic policy is undertaken by Lester M. Salamon, "The Presidency and Domestic Policy Formation," in *The Illusion of Presidential Government*, ed. Hugh Heclo and Lester M. Salamon (Boulder: Westview Press, 1981), 177-203.

12. The quotes are from Gary R. Orren ,"The Changing Style of American Party Politics," in *The Future of American Political Parties*, ed. Joel L. Fleishman (Englewood Cliffs, N.J.: Prentice-Hall, 1982), 4-42.

13. James L. Sundquist, *Politics and Policy: The Eisenhower, Kennedy, and Johnson Years* (Washington, D.C.: Brookings Institution, 1968).
14. Summary "ranking games" of this sort are as inevitable as they are superficial. For a review of different polls on presidential "greatness," see Robert E. DiClerico and Eric Uslaner, *Few Are Chosen: Problems in Presidential Selection* (New York: McGraw-Hill, 1984), 186-189. On public opinion and the presidency more generally: George Edwards III, *The Public Presidency* (New York: St. Martin's Press, 1983).
15. John Hart is critical of both those who underestimate and overestimate Kennedy's achievements in his "Assessing Presidential Leadership," *Political Studies* (December 1980): 567-578.
16. John Hart, *The Presidential Establishment* (Forthcoming).
17. Among the many, James L. Sundquist, *Decline and Resurgence of Congress* (Washington, D.C.: Brookings Institution, 1981).
18. Polsby, *Consequences of Party Reform*, 113.
19. Ibid., 105.
20. Polsby borrows a serviceable classification scheme from the late Rep. Clem Miller, whose eloquent "Letters of a Congressman" (published as *Member of the House* in 1962) helped many people better understand Congress from the perspective of a thoughtful insider. Regrettably, Polsby does not examine the content of those bills on which Democratic factions were in agreement or disagreement, nor does he examine Carter's different rates of success in the House and Senate.
21. Light, *The President's Agenda.*
22. Theodore Lowi, *The End of Liberalism* (New York: Norton, 1969).
23. The observation of Nelson W. Polsby in his review of *The Years of Lyndon Johnson,* by Robert Caro, *Congress & The Presidency* (Autumn 1983): 256-258.
24. Sundquist, *Politics and Policy,* and Jeff Fishel, *Party and Opposition* (New York: McKay, 1973), chapters 6 and 7.
25. Sundquist, *Politics and Policy,* 501.
26. Ibid., 502.
27. Personal communication from Bruce Miroff.
28. Seymour M. Hersh seeks to unravel the threads of the Nixon pardon decision, suggesting, but not proving to my satisfaction, that it was a quid pro quo to appoint Ford as president, in his "The Pardon—Nixon, Ford, Haig, and the Transfer of Power," *Atlantic,* August 1983, 55-80.
29. Contrarily, Reagan's frequent misstatements and factual distortions, along with a seeming indifference to being corrected, drove many White House reporters up the wall. Said one: "He may be charming but he's also, consistently, a goddamn liar!" So extensive was the president's "factual gap" that by 1983, one of Washington's best selling coffee table books was *There He Goes Again: Ronald Reagan's Reign of Error,* Mark Green and Gail MacColl (New York: Pantheon, 1983).
30. Stories about Reagan's abbreviated work schedule and ignorance about important details circulated throughout Washington from his first year on. They are difficult to assess because it is clear that for a person in his seventies, Reagan carries on an energetic schedule, and the obsessively long (15-hour plus) daily schedules of some presidents has not improved the quality of their leadership. The partisan bias is obvious but the quote is worth repeating because it summarizes—with Democrat Thomas P. "Tip" O'Neill's usual zest—four years of complaints: "He only works three to three

and a half hours a day. He doesn't read his briefing papers. He lacks the knowledge that he should [have], on every sphere, whether it's the domestic or international ... he lacks competence as far as having done his homework, and as far as knowing what this government is all about, and what world affairs are all about." Quote from an interview with the Speaker by James Reston, *New York Times*, Nov. 3, 1983.

31. John Kessel, "The Structures of the Reagan White House" (Paper delivered at the 1983 annual meeting of the American Political Science Association).

32. Edwards, *The Public Presidency*, 24-35; and Thomas Mann, *Unsafe at Any Margin: Interpreting Congressional Elections* (Washington, D.C.: American Enterprise Institute, 1978).

33. Robert A. Dahl, *Dilemmas of Pluralist Democracy* (New Haven: Yale University Press, 1982).

34. Page makes a similar argument in *Choice and Echoes in Presidential Elections*. For some examples of voter confusion in 1980, see the Conclusion of Chapter 5.

35. Lawrence D. Brown, *New Policies, New Politics: Government's Response to Government's Growth* (Washington, D.C.: Brookings Institution, 1983).

36. This is tricky. I can recall similar arguments being made when I was a college student in the late 1950s, *before* the Second Reconstruction could be said to have had any effects.

37. The title and theme of Betty Friedan's book, *The Second Stage* (New York: Simon & Schuster, 1981).

38. Brown, *New Policies, New Politics*, 67.

39. Timothy B. Clark, "Promises, Promises—The Presidential Candidates and Their New Budget Plans," *National Journal*, March 10, 1984, 452.

40. See James Dator, "A Vision of a Transformational Society," *Visions of Desirable Societies*, ed. Eleanora Masini and Johan Galtung (New York: Pergamon, 1982); Mark Satin, *New Age Politics* (New York: Delta, 1978); Willis Harman, *An Incomplete Guide to the Future* (New York: Norton, 1979); Paul Hawken, James Ogilvy, and Peter Schwartz, *Seven Tomorrows* (New York: Bantam, 1983); Walter Anderson, ed. *Rethinking Liberalism* (New York: Avon, 1983); and Corinne McLaughlin and Gordon Davidson, *The Spirit of Community* (Forthcoming, 1985).

41. Clifford Geertz, as quoted in Joseph LaPalombara, "Decline of Ideology: A Dissent and Interpretation," *American Political Science Review* (March 1966): 342.

Index